£1·50

Len Hutton Remembered

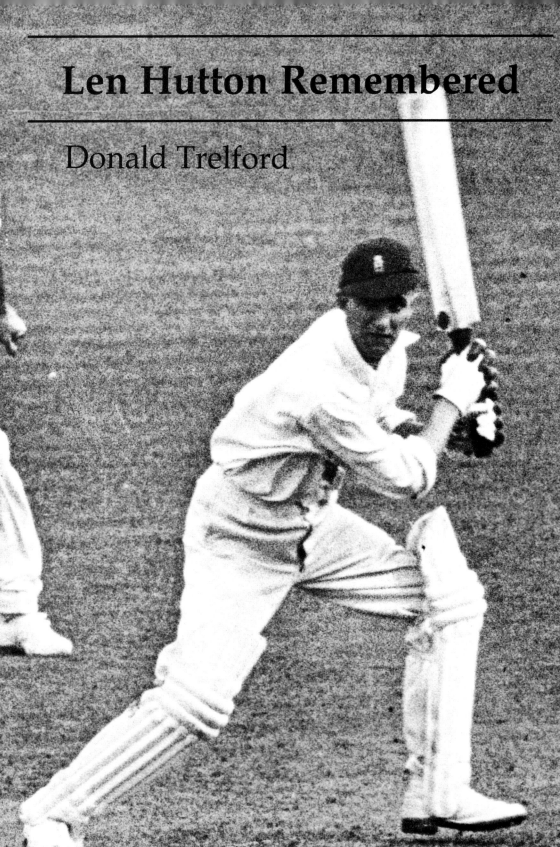

Len Hutton Remembered

Donald Trelford

H. F. & G. Witherby Ltd

First published in Great Britain 1992
by H. F. & G. Witherby Ltd
14 Henrietta Street, London WC2E 8QJ

A catalogue record for this book is available
from the British Library

ISBN 0 85493 213 5

Researched by Simon Davie

Picture Acknowledgements

pp 2–3, 12, 36, 46, 51, 56, 70, 71, 77, 87, 93, 107, 113, 127, 147,
149, 163, 169, 171, 182, 187, 189, 193, 199, 210, 222: The Hulton
Picture Company; p 14: Jane Bown; pp 63, 207: Ronald Burnet;
p 127: Solo Syndication & Literary Agency Ltd

Overleaf. Record-breaker: the historic moment when Hutton
cut Fleetwood-Smith to the boundary to pass Bradman's
score of 334 against Australia at the Oval on 23 August,
1938. He went on to 364, and set a record for the highest
individual innings in Test cricket – acording to R. E. S.
Wyatt, it was 'one of the most astonishing feats of
endurance and prolonged concentration ever known in
the history of the game.'

Designed by Peter Guy

Photoset in Great Britain by
Rowland Phototypesetting Ltd, Bury St Edmunds, Suffolk
Printed and bound by Butler and Tanner Ltd,
Frome, Somerset

Len and Dorothy Hutton at their wedding near Scarborough in September 1939, two weeks after the outbreak of war. Her brother, Frank Dennis, played for Yorkshire.

Contents

Acknowledgements

I should first like to put on record my gratitude to the Davie family, father and son, without whose invaluable help and encouragement this book could not have been written. Simon Davie conducted the bulk of the interviews, especially those involving travel to distant parts of the country that a busy newspaper editor could not be expected to reach. He also checked all the cricketing records and statistics with a painstaking attention to detail which a Yorkshire opening batsman of the old school would have been hard-pressed to match.

His father, Michael, who recruited Len Hutton to write on *The Observer* in the 1960s, was the source of many of the anecdotes recounted here, and also took time off in Australia to talk to the old-timers whose salty recollections appear in Part Four.

I am profoundly grateful to the many great cricketers who gave up time so readily to recall their experiences with Hutton, both on and off the field, and whose first-hand recollections give this book any lasting historic value it may be thought to possess. Their contributions took the form of taped interviews, which were then edited down, mainly to avoid repetition. I have taken care not to unbalance or misrepresent their views in this process, which is sometimes difficult to avoid. I hope they will feel that I've succeeded; if not, I'm sorry.

Any student of Hutton owes a debt to Gerald Howat's biography, *Len Hutton*, published by Heinemann, and to *Fifty Years in Cricket*, which Hutton wrote with Alex Bannister. Richard Hutton's account of life with father in Part Five first appeared as the foreword to *Fifty Years in Cricket*, and is reprinted here by kind permission of the publisher, Stanley Paul. Like every cricket writer, I have found myself quoting from *Cardus in the Covers* (Souvenir Press). My special thanks to Alan Ross, *The Observer*'s former cricket correspondent, for permission to reproduce his poem, 'Watching Benaud Bowl'. It is a pleasure to acknowledge the quotation from *Innings of a Lifetime* (Collins) by Ralph Barker, since it was his enthusiasm for RAF cricket 35 years ago which ensured that I spent rather more of my National Service on the ground than in the air.

Keith H. Moss, Chairman of Pudsey St Lawrence Cricket Club, gave much willing help, not least by providing access to a scrapbook of Hutton memorabilia kept lovingly for many decades by Malcolm R. Healey. This was a treasure trove. Thanks also to J. Featherstone, editor of *The White Rose*, the quarterly magazine of Yorkshire County Cricket Club.

More valuable material, on which I have drawn freely, was discovered in the archives of *The Observer*, for whom Hutton wrote on cricket for nearly 30 years. I gratefully acknowledge quotations from the columns he wrote for the *News of the World* and the *Evening News* in the 1950s. I have used transcripts of BBC interviews about Hutton by Bowes, Leyland and Yardley in 1955 and of the 'Maestro' interview I did with him for television in 1988. Acknowledgements are also due for quotations from the *Daily Express* and *Leeds Mercury* on his historic innings of 364 in 1938, from *The Times* on the death of George Hirst in 1954 and the *Independent on Sunday*'s fine obituaries by Alan Ross and Mike Brearley on Hutton's death in 1990. I am grateful to Geoffrey Copinger for permission to reproduce his statistical summary of Hutton's career record, prepared originally for *Wisden Cricketers' Almanac*.

As we were going to press, the launch was announced of the Sir Leonard Hutton Foundation Appeal, which aims to raise £364,000 to help young cricketers in Yorkshire. I feel sure that anyone who enjoys this book will want to join me in a contribution to the Fund – £364 a head seems an appropriate sum!

The original idea for this work came from David Burnett, who had urged me to write a book on sport ever since we left Cambridge together more than 30 years ago. I'm only sorry that I took so long about it that he had left Gollancz before it was completed.

Thanks finally to Michael Walker for picture research and, as ever, to my secretary Barbara Rieck for her unfailing patience through countless revisions.

With Hedley Verity, who nursed him through his epic innings in 1938
– 'I loved that man', said Hutton.

Hutton on Top of the World

*Extract from the BBC Radio commentary by Howard Marshall
of the moment at the Oval on 23 August 1938
when Len Hutton broke the world record for the highest innings
ever played in a Test match*

707 for 5; Hutton 332, and all our hearts are with this young York-shireman at this moment. Here's Fleetwood-Smith bowling to him. He bowls, Hutton hits him, drives him, but he won't take a single; it's gone to mid-off, deepish mid-off, no run. Well, it's a great day this for Hutton, and what I admire so much is the character which enables him to carry on like this. Fleetwood-Smith bowls to him. Hutton late cuts this but Hardstaff sends him back as he trots up for a run to third man. Hardstaff quite rightly says: 'No you don't, it's not worth taking a risk just now.' Well, this morning Hutton's gone from 300 to 332 in an hour and a quarter. He's been in for twelve and a quarter hours. It just hardly bears thinking of the amount of strain that that's involved.

Here's Fleetwood-Smith to Hutton, Hutton right back and tries to turn it round the corner, doesn't quite get hold of it and drops it down. Quite all right, perfectly safe, but no run. Barnett, the wicket-keeper, is round there to pick it up. Hutton's total: 332. It sounds like the total of a whole side. The England total: 707 for 5. And the gas-ometer sinking lower and lower and here comes Fleetwood-Smith running up to bowl. He bowls and Hutton gets a short one. Hutton forces it past silly mid-off, where Bradman's fielding; yes, it is Brad-man himself crouching at silly mid-off. It's difficult to see in this brilliant sunlight with the big peaks of their caps which throw dark shadows over their faces.

Now here's Fleetwood-Smith in again to Hutton. Hutton hits him. Oh, beautiful stroke, there's the record! Well, that was the most lovely stroke, a late-cut, off Fleetwood-Smith's leg-break, which absolutely flashed to the boundary for four runs to give Hutton a record, beating Bradman's record made at Leeds in 1930 of 334, beating that record with the highest score ever made by an individual in Test matches between England and Australia, and equalling Hammond's record in Test matches of any kind, made at Auckland in 1933.

They're singing. Terrific reception. The whole crowd's standing up and cheering, all round the ground. Thousands of them all standing up. Bradman's rushed over to shake Hutton by the hand. The whole Australian team have congratulated him and now everybody's cheer-ing. It really is a wonderful scene this; here in this brilliant sunshine they won't stop cheering. And they're having drinks now, a dignified gentleman in a tailcoat has come out and brought them drinks which, my word, are richly deserved. Most of us are feeling pretty well bereft of speech by the excitement and tension of this morning and we do all so very, very warmly congratulate young Hutton. And we're sure that in Pudsey they're listening and that they're extraordinarily proud of this young man, who's come to such great things from that town.

. . . And now, Fleetwood-Smith beginning to bowl to Hutton again, here he comes, he bowls and Hutton just pushes it forward. There you are, this is the remarkable thing about Hutton, he's more like an Australian batsman, in a sense, than an English one because he doesn't give in when he's past a point; the 100, 200 or 300, or a record. He doesn't take liberties and go mad and bang about, he just keeps steadily on.

Here's Fleetwood-Smith again. Ahhh, there we are, there's another record, round the corner and it's going for four down here. I don't think Hassett can possibly cut it off, no, well that's gone for four. And that is the record; it's the highest score ever made by an individual in any kind of Test match. He's beaten Bradman's record in England v Australia Tests, he's beaten Hammond's record in all kinds of Test matches. And there we are: Hutton is on top of the world.

Members rise to Hutton as he leaves the field at the Oval during his marathon innings of 364 in 1938.

PART ONE

A Complicated Genius

Donald Trelford

'The twinkle from those wide-apart blue eyes' – a portrait by Jane Bown.

THIS BOOK IS A LABOUR OF LOVE – NOT JUST FOR ME AND my collaborators, Michael and Simon Davie (who, frankly, did most of the work), but also for the many friends and former playing colleagues of Sir Leonard Hutton who gave up time to frame the recollections gathered here. They have paid him the supreme tribute owed to a great man of thinking hard and pulling no punches about him.

Len Hutton aroused remarkably strong feelings for a man who rarely showed emotion himself. For some reason people felt challenged to explain why they felt as they did about him – a process assisted, I think, by the fact that he had recently died. As Bishop David Sheppard pointed out at the memorial service in York Minster – in an address reproduced at the end of this book – Len's fame was of a kind that even people who had never met him felt 'they had a personal involvement with him'.

When it became known that I was putting this memoir together, I received letters from complete strangers who said they had never met Len Hutton but desperately wanted to say what he meant to them. One came from a retired policeman in Ontario who introduced himself thus: 'Let me state at once that I am nobody of importance whatsoever. However, I would consider it an honour to contribute a few words in sincere respect, even adulation, in memory of a man I was never even introduced to. My early years were *ruled* by this great man, whom I idolised. I followed his career as only an English schoolboy could. When batting, I *was* Hutton. Who wasn't?' Who indeed?

Thousands of similar fans could doubtless be found all over the world. I have included the reminiscences of one self-confessed 'Hutton worshipper' to represent them all. Michael Rines, now a marketing consultant, got closer than most fans as a dressing-room attendant at the Scarborough Cricket Festival in the late-1940s. From that vantage point, cleaning the players' boots and pads and fetching their 'often copious amounts of beer', he enjoyed a privileged glimpse into the private demeanour of his idol – 'I brushed my hair like his, I carried my left arm slightly bent in the Hutton manner. I even learned to write his autograph – and I can do it still, without having to think about it'. He also caught sight of less attractive features of the Yorkshire dressing-room. When he grew up, Mr Rines fulfilled every fan's Walter Mitty dream by playing with his hero in a country house fixture.

Roy Hattersley belongs to a generation brought up to believe that 'one baby boy in five sprang into the world fully armed with bats and pads ready to play cricket for Yorkshire and England'. He remembers playing for Sheffield City Grammar School in the villages of the West Riding in the years immediately after the Second World War: 'I touched the peak of my cap between every ball in the way that Len Hutton touched his – not realising that even in England's opening batsman it was a sign of nerves not professionalism.' I quote later from Hattersley's book, *Goodbye to Yorkshire* (Pan Books), to explain the moral milieu in which Hutton grew up. Had it not been for the

General Election, Hattersley would have contributed to this book himself; it was something he badly wanted to do.

So did Harold Pinter, the playwright, who eagerly promised to write an introduction, then withdrew the offer when I declined to publish a strongly worded poem he had submitted to *The Observer* about the Gulf War. Mandrake in the *Sunday Telegraph* commented on this episode, recalling that Pinter had once told an interviewer: 'Cricket is the greatest thing that God ever created on earth . . . certainly greater than sex, although sex isn't too bad either. Everyone knows which comes first when it is a question of cricket or sex. All discriminating people recognise that.' Mandrake added: 'It seems that one thing beats both: the wounded pride of a rejected poet.'

I am grateful to Mr Pinter, nevertheless, for alerting me to Tim Bleach's touching poem on Hutton's death in *Wisden Cricket Monthly*. The reference to his 'strokes of gliding feather and quiet reserve' appealed particularly to him. Pinter, I am told, once wrote a poem on Hutton himself and distributed it among his literary friends. It went like this:

> I saw Hutton in his prime.
> Another time.
> Another time . . .

Puzzled by the lack of reaction from his friends, Pinter challenged a cricket-loving fellow playwright, Simon Gray: 'What do you think of my poem?'

After a pause Gray replied: 'I'm afraid I haven't finished it yet.'

True or not, Len would have loved that story, which matched his own laconic wit. He might even have liked the poem itself, though he would never have let on.

Pinter wrote more eloquently of Hutton in an essay for *The Cricketers' Companion* (Eyre Methuen): 'He was never dull . . . His play was sculptured. His forward defensive stroke was a complete statement. The handle of his bat seemed electric. Always, for me, a sense of his vulnerability, an uncommon sensibility. He never just went through the motions; nothing was glibly arrived at. He was never, for me, as some have defined him, simply a master technician.'

He had some other surprising disciples. I remember being astonished at Lord Goodman's 75th birthday party in University College, Oxford, where he was Master, to hear the great man – someone who had been loaded with virtually every honour available in British public life – declare that if he could have been someone else, 'I would like to have been Len Hutton.' When John Major first met him at Lord's, introduced by Jeffrey Archer, he was completely overawed by the experience. Later Archer said to Major's son, James: 'Did your father ever tell you he met Len Hutton?' 'Daily,' replied the young Major.

Part of the explanation for Hutton's universal appeal relates to the circumstances of his world record innings of 364 against Australia at the Oval in 1938, which made him a national hero. Not only did it come on the brink of the Second World War, at a time of national gloom and recession, when the country was desperately arming for battles it hoped would never take place, but the endurance of this apparently frail young Englishman, just after his twenty-second birthday – at the crease from Saturday to Tuesday for a total of 13 hours and 17 minutes, the longest innings on record – captured the public imagination.

On the morning he went out to bat at 300 not out, needing 35 runs to beat Bradman's record, Movietone News intoned: 'The Empire holds its breath.' In its editorial that day the *Daily Express* ignored Hitler and Chamberlain and the gathering clouds of war:

> The thoughts of millions throughout the Empire centre on Hutton, steadily batting at the Oval. For the third day he stands before the wicket as his score mounts to within reach of the Test record of 334 runs set up by the great Don Bradman in 1930.
>
> Can Hutton do it? The strain on his nerves and body is terrific. He is only 22, slim, almost frail in appearance. He shows no sign of weariness, so his appearance is no guide to his stamina. In all the great crowd at the Oval he is the only one showing no excitement. His nerves are good.
>
> In the offices, clerks and managers share the interest and excitement, and in the factories, too, master and man follow Hutton's grand stand.
>
> Already England has put up her highest total, and still Hutton is batting with astonishing skill. The Yorkshiremen in the crowd talk of 'Yorkshire grit'. The excitement soars until at last Hutton breaks the record, and cheers hold up the game. England finds her Bradman.

The innings seemed to symbolise the tenacious spirit of the underdog, the boy on the burning deck, the bulldog breed incarnate. He became a household name, part of the national myth, like Sir Francis Drake. The words 'Len Hutton' became synonymous with cricket in the minds of British servicemen during the six years of war. His name was as much a part of my war-time childhood as spam and ration books. Yorkshiremen of his time, and many other Englishmen besides, could tell you exactly where they were when Hutton beat Bradman's record, just as a later generation knew where they were when President Kennedy was shot. Later, as England's first professional captain, he touched the nation's hearts again by recovering the Ashes for the Queen in Coronation Year – a feat that linked him to other great British sporting heroes of 1953, Stanley Matthews and Gordon Richards, both also knighted, and to the men who planted the Union Jack on Everest.

I recently discovered in the files an aspect of that famous innings which may not be widely known – I certainly hadn't remembered it. Hutton had evidently just returned from a seven-week absence from the game through injury, a broken finger inflicted in a county match by the bowling of Bill Edrich. (Although Len was generally thought of as injury-prone, certainly by himself, this was the only fracture he sustained at the crease throughout his long career – apart, that is, from his famous broken nose, which he suffered at the age of sixteen in the Yorkshire Second XI when Bill Farrimond, the Lancashire wicket-keeper, hit him accidentally between the eyes while throwing the ball back to the bowler.)

Len later came to believe that the broken finger played an important part in his 364. 'First, the seven-week absence gave me a good rest from the everyday round of cricket in a hard season and increased my zest for the game when I went back to it. Second, after I had been batting an hour or so at the Oval, the same finger became swollen and began to ache. To avoid more discomfort than was necessary, I cut open my glove where it protected the finger, and in making my strokes I concentrated on using my left hand a good deal more than my right. Now, throughout my career I have sat down quietly after each innings to analyse the cause of my dismissal in an attempt to guard against repeating the error, and frequently I have been certain that I lost my wicket through too much right hand. Here was a case where circumstances compelled me to make the absolute minimum use of my right, and partly as a result, I restrained myself from playing careless or unorthodox strokes.'

It is hard now to recapture the scale of national – and indeed international – publicity that innings attracted in a pre-television, pre-pop star age. It was front-page news throughout the Commonwealth. One headline sang: 'World-Beater Hutton – London Catches the Fever'. In the *Manchester Guardian* Neville Cardus heard a wider roar of celebration: 'As the ground became resonant with the cheering, the thought occurred to me that it was being heard far and wide all over the Empire. People walking down Collins Street in Melbourne would hear it and it would roar and echo in Candy, Calcutta, Allahabad and Penang; they would hear it in the Cocos Islands and join in, and on liners patiently going their ways on the Seven Seas they would hear it too and drink Hutton's health.'

Pudsey, where the bells were pealed 364 times in the parish church, suddenly found itself a focus of world-wide media interest. Film cameras poked their way into the austere privacy of the Hutton family's terrace house at Fulneck, a hillside village to the south of Pudsey, sloping down to a stream in the valley below. The *Leeds Mercury* reported the scene with bated breath: 'At six tonight a Universal film unit arrived at Fulneck, Pudsey, and Mr and Mrs Hutton and their son Reg became, for the evening, film stars. You have to imagine a working-class home in which a film camera has never been seen and a middle-aged mother, tired but very proud, having to be cajoled into being filmed.'

Greetings telegrams arrived at the Oval at the rate of more than one a minute. When one sack arrived in the dressing-room it was so big that Bill Bowes joked: 'It might have held three or four sets of my flannels.' But there was no message from the family. Asked about this, his father replied in Pudsey: 'Nay, Len knows what we're thinking. We don't have to go sending telegrams.'

The *Leeds Mercury* crowed over its local hero: 'The spirit of Drake lives among us. We can win our game and still have time to defeat the Spanish Armada or whatever has taken its place today.' An Australian businessman gave Hutton a gift of £1,000 to match the sum he had given to Bradman eight years before. The *Yorkshire Post* opened a shilling fund in Hutton's name. Billy Butlin sent a Rolls-Royce to take him to Skegness to judge a beauty contest. Len told Dorothy, to whom he was about to become engaged: 'I'm being talked about more than Mrs Simpson.' He said later: 'I was famous overnight and I wondered what had hit me.'

Hutton came to regret the fact that one single innings had dominated his life in this way. 'I sometimes wonder', he wrote on the fiftieth anniversary in 1988, 'if it was not the second worst happening of my career to become a record-breaking national celebrity at an age when I had just qualified to vote.' He admitted to being 'vulnerable to pressures and private misgivings', of 'being overwhelmed by the suddenness of fame and worried about its penalties'.

Like other sporting and musical prodigies, Hutton had had to miss out on many of the normal pleasures of boyhood and youth, sacrificing them for the lonely hours refining his craft. He said once: 'Almost all of my boyhood was spent with older men'. When I asked him how he had celebrated his twenty-first birthday, he replied: 'In an opening partnership of 315 with Herbert Sutcliffe for Yorkshire. I remember Herbert was furious when I got out.'

The first 'worst happening' of his career, of course, was the appalling double fracture of his arm, just above the left wrist, while on commando training for the Dieppe raid in 1941. It happened when the mat slipped under him as he did a fly-spring in the gym. He returned to cricket two and a half years later, after several bone-graft operations, with the left arm – the guiding hand for a right-handed batsman – more than two inches shorter than before. The left arm was never again as strong as the right; it was thinner, with wasted muscles, as one could tell just by watching him use a knife and fork, let alone a cricket bat. No wonder it ached after a long innings. There were times when he and his doctors thought he would never play again. J. R. Burnet, the former Yorkshire captain, who played with him in league cricket when he was recuperating towards the end of the war, says it seemed inconceivable then that he could ever return to cricket at county or international level.

In the pages that follow we learn from his contemporaries just what limitations that injury imposed on his batting – no hooking, a schoolboy's bat, a restricted flow in stroke-making. Neville Cardus noted after the war: 'All his hits leave an impression of power not entirely expended . . . The sadness is that physical disability struck his career in its prime.' There are photographs showing him driving with the right hand alone when the pain was too much. His Yorkshire and England captain after the war, N. W. D. Yardley, said: 'Had it not been for the war and the unfortunate injury to his arm, no record would have been beyond his grasp.' Len told me himself in a television interview in 1988: 'I knew I wasn't the player that I could have become had there been no war.'

This needs to be seen in context. The record shows that his post-war

Sergeant Hutton (*left*) at the Army School of Physical Training, where he broke his wrist in the gym and was left with one arm three inches shorter than the other.

batting average of 58 was ten runs higher than in the 1930s. But he scored 36 centuries in the five years before the war compared with 93 in the 15 years afterwards. The figures themselves tell only part of the story. They cannot show how many runs he would have scored – or how he would have scored them – had he not suffered the fracture at all.

It wasn't just the injury, of course, that interrupted his career. The war deprived him of six seasons at his peak – from the ages of 23 to 29, nearly a third of his professional span. Bradman, in the equivalent period of his life, scored 17 of his 29 Test centuries, including two over 300 and eight over 200 – which is some measure of the potential loss to Hutton and to cricket caused by the war. There were other flowering English batsmen, of course, notably Compton, Edrich and Hardstaff, who also lost vital years in the war – and Compton was to suffer a serious injury to his knee, albeit in peace-time.

Len never betrayed any bitterness about the double deprivation he suffered, but once I thought I detected a faint sense of longing. It was over lunch at the Garrick Club, where a member had accosted him on the stairs and reminded him of a great innings he had seen Len play in South Africa in 1939. 'Ah yes, 1939', he said wistfully as we sat down. 'Everybody remembers 1938, but I was actually better in 1939. I was nearly as good as Bradman. After the war, of course, I was a different man. I'll never know how good I might have become in those lost years. I might not have got any better at all. The trouble is, you see, I'll never know.'

Two Yorkshire contemporaries support the view that Hutton reached a peak in 1939. J. M. Kilburn, the cricket writer, says: 'It was absolute joy to see him at that time. You got little thrills down your back.' J. R. Burnet says: 'He tore attacks apart in 1939'. A contemporary report from South Africa suggests that Hutton in 1939 had just developed the confidence to break out of his austere batting style: 'Those who had the opportunity of seeing one of the most delightful stroke-players yet to have visited South Africa will look back with pleasant memories on the hours spent watching Hutton, the slightly built hero from Yorkshire. Free from the watchful eye of selectors and his own crowd, Len Hutton took toll of the bowling whenever he went to the wicket with a feeling of abandon.' That 'feeling of abandon' was only rarely noted in Hutton's batting after the war. One famous exception – recalled by a number of witnesses here because it was so out of character – was a flamboyant 37 he scored in 24 minutes at Sydney in 1946 before hitting his own wicket off the last ball before lunch.

In his last pre-war Test match – against the West Indies at the Oval in August 1939, facing Constantine and Martindale – he scored 165 not out. What puzzled him about Constantine, he said, was not just that he bowled with his shirtsleeves buttoned up, but that he had a habit of glancing up at the ball in his hand at the moment of delivery – which shows how closely Hutton was watching. According to *Wisden*, 'he never neglected a scoring chance and his off-driving off the back foot was superb'. Then, with the war only days away, he played in the last county match at Hove, scoring another century, while Hedley Verity took 7 wickets for 9 runs in 36 balls to win the match for Yorkshire.

Gerald Howat's description of that valedictory game, a benefit for Jim Parks, and of the gloomy journey by coach back to Yorkshire, was read out by Richard Hutton at his father's memorial service. It captures the poignancy of that historic time:

> Close of play at Hove, at half past two on Friday 1 September 1939, had a disquieting and sombre sense of finality about it. In Europe, German troops were marching through Poland and German aeroplanes bombing Warsaw and Cracow. Members and friends crowded into the picture-lined Long Room to say goodbye to the Sussex and Yorkshire players.
>
> Hutton was not the only one who wondered if he would ever play cricket again. He felt very serious and he looked very pale. Presently the Yorkshire party boarded a charabanc. They included Sutcliffe, who a few days earlier had made his 50,000th run for Yorkshire and had stood down in this last game, and who would play no more for Yorkshire; Verity, who would die of wounds received when leading his men on a July night in Sicily four years later; and Bowes, who would languish for three years in a POW camp.
>
> So these men, united in the bond of cricket and friendship, each nursing his own fears for the future of themselves and their families, set off from Hove for home. As they approached London

they were met by car-loads of people hastily leaving the city, usually with children being taken to some place of safety. They spent a short night at Leicester, not even bothering to unpack their overnight kit. Next morning they travelled northwards through blacked-out towns, along with holiday-makers anxious to be back in their own homes when (no longer *if*) war broke out. By mid-day they were home themselves.

This side had won the championship for the fifth time in seven seasons, and was said to be the strongest, most efficient and the best example of what an XI can be. The averages for 1939, the last season this side played together, have a certain symbolism: Hutton, the successful pupil, top; Sutcliffe, his teacher, second; Leyland, Barber and Mitchell – the rocks on which so many Yorkshire innings were built – third, fourth and fifth; Yardley, the future captain, sixth; Sellers, the current captain and without a peer at county level, seventh; and Turner, dependable, perhaps undervalued, eighth. First and second in the bowling averages were Bowes and Verity.

Together with Wood, the wicket-keeper, Robinson and Smailes, these were the men who dropped off the charabanc, one by one, as it drove through Yorkshire on the morning of Saturday, 2 September 1939. When it reached City Square, Leeds, it was empty and one of the finest county teams of all time was no more.

There are various views expressed in this book about the difference between the pre- and post-war Hutton. Some players failed to detect any difference in his style. There are also some skilled and closely observed analyses of his batting, his stance, his footwork and, above all perhaps, his unyielding concentration, from people who played with or against him. What comes through them all, however, despite the emphasis on character and technique, is a sense of majestic beauty. For people like me, as for Roy Hattersley and Harold Pinter, Len Hutton's stylishness became a schoolboy ideal in the immediate post-war years. For us, as for C. L. R. James, he represented 'dignity and elegance', a quintessential Englishness at its finest. R. C. Robertson-Glasgow wrote: 'There are no mannerisms, no tricks, no showmanship. He gives proof before your eyes that orthodoxy can also be genius.'

For Cardus, he was the supreme embodiment of the classical style, in a tradition that ran through Hammond and Sutcliffe to Hobbs. 'He plays so close to the ball, so much over it, that he has acquired a sort of student's slope of the shoulders; at the sight of a fizzing off-break, he is arched like a cat . . . A strength that is generated effortlessly from the physical dynamo, through nerve and muscle, so that we might almost persuade ourselves that the current of his energy, his life-force, is running electrically down the bat's handle into the blade.'

Edmund Blunden, the poet, saw something similar when he watched Hutton at the Oval in 1938: 'The batsman's body and his bat were as truly one as love itself.' In *Cricket Country* he describes 'this immensely patient and serious yet charming innings – thirteen hours of temptation repelled' – as 'the most remarkable example of character

Yorkshire in khaki.
Left to right:
Captain Verity,
Sergeant-Major
Smailes, Captain
Sutcliffe, Sergeant
Leyland and
Sergeant-Instructor
Hutton.

shown in a cricket performance. I believe that this patch of ground had witnessed, two centuries earlier, the fortitude of some political prisoners, sentenced to a public execution. But I should not easily credit that a greater nervous strain could be put upon a modern man than what a Test between England and Australia, at the later date, imposed.' If that was the level of strain among the winners, what about the *losers*? No wonder Bill O'Reilly, who bowled till his fingers were raw, later described it as 'Gethsemane at the Oval' and said he could 'think of 364 reasons' for not shaking Hutton's hand.

Denis Compton, the debonair, swashbuckling Southerner, was often contrasted with Len the dour Northerner – the Cavalier versus the Roundhead – but Compton himself feels the contrast was unfair to Hutton's natural grace at the wicket. E. W. Swanton was essentially a Compton man, having once batted with Denis for Middlesex Second XI (few people know that). Michael Rines recalls the fun Hutton had with 'Jim' once in a friendly game, obliging the portly and perspiring doyen of cricket writers to puff and pant his way to the boundary. Swanton saw the 364 in 1938 and remembers following a weary Hutton up the ladder to the BBC hut to be interviewed by Howard Marshall. His flannels were stained brown from the marl on the Oval wicket.

For all his marathon scoring feats, however, Len Hutton's main appeal lay in the *way* he made his runs. People still argue whether his cover-drive or his on-drive was the more sublime. An *Observer* profile, written in 1951 on his appointment as England's first professional captain and bearing the imprint of R. C. Robertson-Glasgow, said: 'To admire Len Hutton for the *quantity* of his runs is like praising Milton for the length of "Paradise Lost" or Schubert for the number of his songs. In Hutton's batting there are poetry and rhythm which no critic can translate into words. It has been said that some go to see Hutton make runs, while others go to glory in the perfection of his style. The former are seldom disappointed; the latter almost never.'

Whenever I read Alan Ross's poem 'Watching Benaud Bowl' – one of the few good poems about cricket among hundreds of bad ones – I think of Len Hutton as the batsman described, his feet twinkling down the pitch to meet the ball's embrace:

> Leg-spinners pose problems much like love,
> Requiring commitment, the taking of a chance.
> Half-way deludes; the bold advance.
>
> Right back, there's time to watch
> Developments, though maybe too late.
> It's not spectacular, but can conciliate.
>
> Instinctively romantics move towards,
> Preventing complexities by their embrace,
> Batsman and lover embarked as overlords.

Ross, a former *Observer* cricket correspondent, wrote when Hutton died in September 1990: 'There was about him always a wonderful stillness, an absence of hurry. The least theatrical of men, he nevertheless commanded attention in the way that a great actor does. You could not take your eyes off him, the slightly splay-footed, thoughtful walk, the nervous tuggings of the cap peak, the fastidiousness of manner and line that marked his deportment and stroke-play as it does that of a dancer.'

The dancing analogy would have appealed to Hutton, for he had something of an obsession about feet. He once told me: 'Bradman had us running all over the field for the whole of a day. Afterwards, on an impulse, I went into the dressing-room and looked at his boots. Do you know, his feet were the same size as Fred Astaire's!' He used to propound the theory – how seriously I never knew – that the reason why players like Viv Richards and Colin Cowdrey, for all their talents, were not finally as prolific as Bradman was that they had big flat feet, which prevented them getting quite to the pitch of every ball and keeping it on the ground. Likewise, he thought Sunil Gavaskar's tiny feet were the source of his genius.

Len's own feet were 'moving all the time', as one former player puts it here. Another, Fred Trueman, says: 'He was so quick on his feet, like a ballet dancer.' Bob Appleyard, the former Yorkshire and England bowler, recalls walking behind Len down to a golf tee: 'I suddenly got this feeling that his feet weren't touching the ground.'

Hutton also had an obsession about hands, as a result of his wartime injury, which forced him to think deeply about the role of the hands in all forms of stroke-play. I can still remember a day playing golf with him about 15 years ago. He played straight and tidy golf, unlike mine, and was immaculate with his short game, but he was plainly handicapped for length by his bad arm and used only a three-quarter swing. As I sprayed the ball all over the Royal Wimbledon course that day (and sometimes beyond it onto the Common), I could hear that gentle Yorkshire voice of admonition in my ear: 'It's all in the hands, Donald.' He explained how great stroke-players like Graveney and Cowdrey had a superb touch with the irons. He dissented strongly from the view propounded by pundits like Henry Longhurst that the secret of golf lay in the legs: 'It's all in the hands, Donald.'

Because of the problem with his arm, Hutton used bats weighing between 2lb 2oz and 2lb 5oz, compared with the three-pounders wielded today by Gooch and Botham. These astounded him. He once wrote: 'Before yesterday's play I picked up Botham's bat after his spell in the nets. It was like picking up a railway sleeper.' Hutton's relative lack of physical strength, compared with Hammond or Compton, denied him his full run-scoring potential. Even Swanton admitted in Compton's 'annus mirabilis', 1947, when he scored 3,816 runs: 'If Len Hutton had been blessed with Compton's physical strength and vigour this summer he might have made 4,000'. Compton, always generous to Hutton, would not demur.

Sir Leonard on the golf course – he got down to a handicap of 3 despite the problem with his injured arm.

Len's former county team-mates have been more revealing than they know about the curious atmosphere and tensions in the Yorkshire dressing-room in the period before and after the war. Hutton clearly revered the great pre-war father figures who taught him so much – Sutcliffe, Hirst, Rhodes, Leyland, Verity, Mitchell. He makes a good point about the value of having the skipper accommodated in a separate dressing-room, so that the rest of the team could talk openly about his tactics, thereby passing on the game's folk wisdom to eager young ears.

Herbert Sutcliffe was the strongest influence on the young Hutton, who said he looked up to him as a lad 'with the reverence that a pious Roman Catholic has for the Pope'. Sutcliffe had played cricket with Len's father for Pudsey St Lawrence Cricket Club in his teens and later came to live at Pudsey 'a seven-iron shot from our house'. He was a source of great encouragement to Len, describing him, before he was 18, as 'a marvel, the discovery of a generation'. He was perhaps the main reason why it seemed natural for Len also to become an opening batsman. When Sutcliffe died in 1978, Hutton paid warm tribute to his example both as a player and as a man. He was 'the finest hooker of the short-pitched ball I have seen and the quickest between the wickets . . . He led me through those early days of doubt and indecision. I thank you, Herbert. May God bless you.'

Sutcliffe was his idol, but his coach was George Hirst. The type of man Hirst was, and the example he gave the young Hutton, may be gauged from the tribute paid to him in a leading article in *The Times* when he died in 1954: 'He brought to everything he did a courage, an integrity, a vigour and a tenacity that meant no game in which he took part was decided until the last ball had been bowled and the last stroke made.' It was Hirst above all, reinforced by Bill Bowes, Maurice Leyland and Emmott Robinson in the nets, who instilled Yorkshire grit into the young hopeful from Pudsey. In later life, reflecting on a 'spineless' England team that had given up the ghost without a fight, Len recalled that formative period in his life: 'I was brought up to believe you can always win. Never let the possibility of your opponents doing so worry you one bit. Victories come to the side which works the harder.' When he was 12, he had heard a spectator say to Wilfred Rhodes that Yorkshire might be about to lose. He often quoted Rhodes's curt reply, 'We *won't* lose,' and adopted it as his personal philosophy.

Bill Bowes recalled seeing Hutton for the first time at the Headingley Winter Shed: 'It was the winter of 1933. One morning I got a postcard from George Hirst: "Can you come to the nets on Thursday? Urgent. George." I went, and George greeted me: "I'm glad you've come. I've got a youngster here and I can tell him nowt. I wondered if your bit of extra speed might show up a mistake or two, it's no good him coming if there's nowt I can tell him." Of course, that youngster was Len Hutton, then 16. George was quite right in his assumption that speed might show up a fault. Playing beautifully whenever the ball was on the off stump, young Hutton over-positioned when the ball was anywhere near the leg stump. George spent a lot of time with him and at the end of that particular afternoon young Hutton had tears in his eyes when he came out of the net. He thought he had failed. A few kindly words from George made Hutton determined to master his weakness rather than feel sorry about his failings. That was Yorkshire's method, and it was the type of school Hutton was reared in.'

Maurice Leyland had a similar recollection: 'There were two nets in the Winter Shed. George Hirst was the coach and it was virtually impossible for one man to look after two nets, so what George used to do was to ask one or two of the first-teamers if they'd look after the other net for him. He came to me one day and he said: "There's a boy going into that net, Maurice, I wish you'd help him if you can.

Just watch him.'' He had three bowlers at him for about a quarter of an hour. Well, for a quarter of an hour Len batted beautifully against them and I never said a word to him. His technique, to my mind, was pretty right perfect, just a little bit short of strength. When he came out of the net George said: ''What do you think to him, Maurice?'' I said: ''Well, I couldn't tell him anything''. He replied: ''I'm glad you've said that because I couldn't either''.'

There was something almost monastic about the initiation Hirst gave him at the Winter Shed. Words of praise were few and far between. Hutton recalled one occasion when Hirst 'put a kindly hand on my shoulder and said ''Well done''. Simple words to lift my heart'. The moment he knew he was out of the ordinary was when Hirst said to him on the tram home after an early practice session: 'Whatever you do, don't get like that Victor Trumper', by which he meant that Hutton should avoid becoming obsessively superstitious like Trumper, who wore the same threadbare batting trousers throughout his career. (Len's only superstition was to put his left pad on first, as Hobbs had done before him.) To the young Hutton, then only 15, to be bracketed with the great Trumper at all sent him into a daze all the way home.

As some of our witnesses show in this book, Len was no more forthcoming with praise himself. In fact, as David Sheppard recalls, the team that retained the Ashes in 1955 presented him with a commemorative silver salver inscribed with the words 'Are you all right?' to record the closest their skipper ever got to fulsome encouragement.

When he got into the Yorkshire side, Len received most encouragement himself from Hedley Verity, the great left-arm spinner, who nursed him through his epic innings at the Oval in 1938, just as others were to nurse him through other Test match marathons in later years, most notably in Jamaica in 1954, when his double century in searing heat saved the series. Hutton later recalled Verity's role at the Oval:

The ever kindly and wise Verity made it his duty to stay with me during every lunch and tea break while I nibbled at a sandwich and sipped tea. We both knew that the most likely way I could lose my wicket was by sheer fatigue, or by a lapse of concentration causing a careless stroke. Hedley sat by my side like a faithful ally to make sure my thoughts did not wander, and that I concentrated and disciplined myself as never before. His quiet, natural dignity was an immense source of strength to me throughout those long hours. Even on the Sunday, the rest day, he slipped me off to Bognor Regis for a few relaxing hours by the sea and to have lunch with Dr Swain, a real Yorkshire cricket enthusiast. And what did we do after lunch? We played beach cricket.

Hutton wrote nothing more moving than his description of the pilgrimage to Verity's grave when the ship carrying his 1954 team to Australia docked in Italy:

Captain Hedley Verity, of the Green Howards, lies in the military cemetery at Caserta, Italy. The liner *Orsova* had docked in the Bay of Naples under a warm September sun. The Sicilian skies must have been as blue when Hedley was mortally wounded leading an attack in a cornfield on that fatal day in 1943. He died from his wounds in a POW camp. We stood in a respectful line in front of the headstone. There was Bill Bowes, who had heard of the death of his old friend and constant companion while a POW himself, Bob Appleyard, Johnny Wardle, Abe Waddington, representing an older generation of Yorkshire stalwarts, Bill Edrich and Alec Bedser. I placed a spray of white roses, held together by a Yorkshire County Cricket Club tie, around the simple stone cross. No words were spoken, for there are times when words can be gross intruders into intensely private thoughts. If I had spoken I would have said: 'I loved that man.'

Wilfred Rhodes, who had played in W. G. Grace's last Test in 1899, had just retired when Len first got into the Yorkshire team, but his legend survived. On one occasion, when Rhodes must have been well over sixty, he bowled to Len in his braces in the nets at Sheffield, folding his jacket neatly on the grass. Hutton's description says much about the technique of both the master bowler and the master batsman:

> The old man in the braces began to bowl with a classic, effortless and unforgotten rhythm, but after a few deliveries some of the misplaced confidence of youth took hold of me. Was this really the bowling that had captured 4,187 wickets? It seemed easy enough; slow, a long time in the air; surely I would have time to go down the pitch and hit him on the full toss. True to the textbook, I duly advanced with eyes unwaveringly on the ball, head still and with my footwork precise and balanced. But, to my surprise, I could not get far enough, and I realised the ball was arriving at a different speed from the action indicated by the arm. So I altered my tactics to stay back and cut and pull. I was still obliged to go forward. The lesson I learned was that the truly great spinners drag the batsman forward. With Rhodes the ball was never there when you arrived. A God-given talent of arc and flight sparingly bestowed.

In his later life Len recalled the man he regarded as the supreme symbol of pre-war Yorkshire cricket: 'If ever I had been unsure about the right and wrong approach to cricket, I could not have found a better model in the Yorkshire side in which I graduated than Arthur "Ticker" Mitchell. I was struck by his unfailing honesty. He never claimed a catch he hadn't taken and never waited for the umpire's decision when he knew he was out.'

Another powerful force in Yorkshire cricket at the time he began was Emmott Robinson, who had got Bradman out for a single at Bradford Park Avenue in 1930, the first time Len saw the great man bat. (A few days later, in the Headingley Test, the young schoolboy sat entranced as Bradman scored 309 in a day and went on to make the record 334 which Hutton, then just 14, was to beat eight years later. Len was so inspired by Bradman's innings that he went home and practised until it was dark.) Robinson, who was one of the umpires at Trent Bridge when Hutton and Compton both scored centuries in their first Test innings against Australia in 1938, was once described by Cardus as 'a grizzled, squat, bandy-legged Yorkshireman, all sagging and loose at the braces in private life, but on duty for Yorkshire he was liable at any minute to gather and concentrate his energy into sudden and vehement leaps and charges and scuffles'. He once bowled a batsman at Fenner's with a ball that pitched on the leg stump and whipped away his off-bail. 'That was a beauty', said the Cambridge man politely. 'Aye, it were', said Emmott, 'and it were wasted on thee.'

Bill Bowes was the prime example of the 'thinking' bowler, a category in which Len later included Lindwall, Trueman and even Botham, whom he described as 'the first rock 'n' roll cricketer'. Because he was thoughtful himself, he admired a cricketing brain in others. 'One of the first things I look for in any young cricketer', he wrote, 'is this: is he *thinking*? That is why so many reach a certain age and go no further.'

Evidence of what Hutton himself was thinking on the field of play came in this recollection of his, while walking out to bat one morning with another player. 'More to make conversation than anything else, I said to him: "Tell me, what are you thinking right now?" "Well, er . . .," he said, in some embarrassment, "nothing in particular." "Do you know what I'm thinking?" I continued. "I'm wondering if the dew has disappeared from the grass yet and whether it was the greenness in the turf or the heavy atmosphere last night that helped the bowlers to move the ball. I'm wondering whether, because the wind has changed, the bowlers will change ends, and whether it will be safer to play back or forward. I'll know better when I've looked at the pitch."' This must be the only recorded instance of Hutton saying anything other than 'good luck' to his partner while walking to the wicket.

People have often drawn a parallel between the batting of Hutton and Geoffrey Boycott, but the comparison is not a valid one. They were both Yorkshiremen, of course, and both openers, and both had immense powers of concentration, a textbook correctness and an inbuilt reluctance to give up their wicket. But players who saw them both are incensed by any suggestion that the likeness went beyond that. Boycott never saw Hutton bat until after he retired, but still admired his footwork. Hutton's view of Boycott in his prime may be worth repeating: 'In some ways Boycott is like Bradman – both come from small places and both are run-hungry. The big difference is that every ball bowled to Bradman was a delivery to be scored from. Boycott plays an attacking stroke at the last moment, when he is pretty certain that there is no fear of losing his wicket: action is an afterthought with him. Bradman hit the ball like a horse, with no thought or feeling for the bowler or the ball. Boycott hurts no one. He might bore, but he does not hurt.' The difference between Boycott and Hutton, however, was not one of power, but of elegance, beauty, class.

Hutton's complex relationship with the post-war Yorkshire players and Committee can be read between the lines in their various recollections here. I have deliberately left them to speak in their own, sometimes highly flavoured language, even where they appear to contradict each other over the same events, in the hope that the truth, whatever it is, will not be lost through compression or distortion. The politics of Yorkshire cricket make the old Kremlin look positively open and benign. I'm sorry that Ray Illingworth, who followed in Hutton's footsteps from Pudsey to the England captaincy, was unavailable when we prepared this book. His insight into the Yorkshire scene would have been invaluable. I can only quote his words on Hutton's death: 'He was the best player I have ever played with or against. He was brilliant, but a very quiet man who kept himself to himself and was never boastful. On the field his bat did all the talking.'

There are some intriguing insights here into the daily routine of the professional cricketer and into the English class system as it operated between the wars. Not only did Hutton have to change in a separate dressing-room from an amateur – on some grounds, including Lord's, in a separate pavilion – but he had to walk to the wicket through a different gate, even when the pair were batting together. Fred Trueman says some of the pre-war amateurs were 'downright rude, bad-mannered people' with whom a pro like Len would have had to watch his tongue and his step. No wonder it was such an ordeal for Hutton to be England's first professional captain, elevated to a lofty social status that would have been unthinkable when he started playing. Even then, after he had been lionised all over the world and become the most famous living Yorkshireman, the county still refused to make him captain.

Some interesting questions about the timing of Hutton's retirement are raised, but not convincingly answered: would he have continued in the game for several more years, even though he was plainly tired, if he had been given the captaincy of Yorkshire? Did he quit early out of pique as much as ill-health? What role did Norman Yardley play in all this? J. M. Kilburn, the historian of Yorkshire cricket, whose recollections of Hutton are published here, says 'he left cricket with a feeling of relief rather than regret. He had completed an exhausting journey'. Others think he could have been tempted back, at least at county level, for a few more years.

An outside observer has to wonder what significance, if any, can be read into the fact that he came to spend nearly 30 years, more than half his adult life, at Kingston-upon-Thames in leafy Surrey, away from his beloved Yorkshire and his and Dorothy's family friends. Was he nursing a deep wound he would never talk about? He was certainly capable of bottling up hurt feelings. It was only many years afterwards that he admitted to the personal anguish he had suffered in 1948 when he was dropped for the Old Trafford Test against Australia after failing against Lindwall and Miller, or in 1950, when Denis Compton was chosen ahead of him as vice-captain in Australia. Others have more practical explanations for his migration to the stock-broker belt: there was more money in the South, it was better for the children, and the climate was warmer for his lumbago.

As for his attitude to Yorkshire, he admitted to me two years before
he died: 'The older I get, I feel the roots pulling a little stronger.' He
was proud to be invited to become President of Yorkshire County
Cricket Club, but he didn't live long enough to heal the angry div-
isions he found there. Sadly, the hassle and the travel may have
contributed to his death. Had he been summoned north earlier, when
he was stronger, who knows what he might have achieved?

There is some wry and mostly good-humoured dressing-room
banter here about Len's legendary tight-fistedness, especially over
sharing cigarettes or buying his round, and about his subtle and
less-than-subtle tactics, both as an opener (getting to the other end
when the ball was flying) and as a captain (he was the first to slow
up the over rate deliberately). He also had his favourites – notably
May and Bailey, because they shared his dedication to winning – and
players he took against, sometimes for odd reasons, such as Graveney
('never trust anybody with a ruddy complexion'), Reg Simpson ('a
back-foot player' who enjoyed sunbathing among the fans, both
anathema to Hutton) or Gower ('he finds the game too easy').

At the risk of being over-protective of Hutton, who had his failings
like the rest of us, I feel a need to enter a defence on his behalf against
some of the barbed comments about his behaviour. There are many
accounts here, for example, of Len the loner, staying on his own in
the evenings rather than drinking with the lads or going out on the
town. As with the stories of how 'careful' he was with money or
drinks or cigarettes, these doubtless improved with the telling. When
a leader is reclusive, as many leaders have to be, his followers feed
on scraps of gossip about him, some of which may be untrue or
exaggerated. As Shakespeare put it: 'What great ones do the lesser
will always prattle of'.

After all, there were sound practical reasons for working in his
room at night, such as dealing with his voluminous correspondence,
about which he was always conscientious, without the aid in those
days of managers, agents or secretaries. By the time he became captain, he was a good deal older than many of the team and had different interests. After being with the same crowd all day, who could
blame him for wanting to enjoy his own company or a bit of peace
and quiet? He also had a highly responsible approach to the job. As
for buying drinks, he was offered more than he could cope with by
people who lionised him, and he felt obliged to accept their hospitality whether it was welcome or not.

Hutton's cricket writing deserves a book of its own. But I've quoted
some extracts here where they are revealing about the man himself.
Hutton's tribute to Sir Donald Bradman, penned for his eightieth
birthday in 1988, is reprinted at the back of the book. Bradman said
of Len in the same year: 'I salute him as one of the great craftsmen
of all time, whose skill and style were the envy of us all.'

Len's first article appeared in the *Pudsey and Stanningley News* of 9
May 1941, signed 'Sergeant Len Hutton'. While recovering from his
broken arm, he saw a Pudsey St Lawrence league match against
Lightcliffe in which his brother George appeared. The austere report

concludes with a flourish: 'For the few Pudsey people who followed the fortunes of their team their journey was, indeed, worthwhile. Not only did they see a grand victory but they spent several serene hours – broken at intervals by a demonstration of our efficiency in the air from Spitfires on manoeuvres.'

Towards the end of his career he wrote a column for the *News of the World* (which in those days often carried cricket on the front page) and then, after his retirement, for the London *Evening News*. Some of these articles were 'ghosted', according to the union rules of the time, by the author Leslie Thomas, who told me he soon realised that Len had no need of a 'ghost'. From 1963 until shortly before his death he wrote a regular commentary in *The Observer*.

He was brought on to the paper by Michael Davie, the cricket-loving deputy editor, and nursed by the late Clifford Makins, a sports editor who relished his writers' eccentricities almost as much as his own. One of Len's early articles began: 'I used to play this game a bit.' A sub-editor, with the insensitivity of his breed, had crossed this phrase out, but it was lovingly restored by Makins, who brought it to me for approval.

As a writer, Len liked someone to bowl to him, putting the questions, and didn't much mind if they were slow lobs or bouncers. This was usually done, as I recall, by Davie or Tony Pawson (the former Oxford and Kent player whom Len recalled as one of the fastest runners between the wickets he had ever seen) until Scyld Berry took over the bowling. At first he used to dictate his comments for someone else to write down and shape into an article. Then one day he said cryptically to Michael Davie in the press box: 'You've got an advantage over me. When I was playing, you see, I used to have a bat to hold.' Davie realised that this was Len's way of asking for a pen with which to write down his own comments.

I met Len when I was called upon to arbitrate on his contract, which I did over a round of golf. We had a good-natured relationship which became warmer towards the end after I had interviewed him for the 'Maestro' series on BBC Television. We mostly talked cricket or golf and once played snooker, at which he was very sharp (in Australia in 1954 he had challenged the world billiards champion, Walter Lindrum, to a game, but never got a shot). I was thrilled to attend his seventieth birthday party at Lord's and witnessed his special affection there for his old antagonist Keith Miller – who, he once said, was the man he'd most want in his side. (Another was Cyril Washbrook, his favourite opening partner.)

He sometimes surprised me with an unexpected telephone call that seemed to be motivated purely by goodwill. On one occasion, when I was engaged in a public dispute, he rang up to say: 'I've only got one word of advice: keep your eye on the ball!' When I attracted some unwelcome personal publicity, he rang up out of the blue to say: 'Are you all right?' That was all, but it was enough, as it had been enough for the younger players in his England sides. He had a great gift, certainly in later life, for making everyone feel they were his special friend. He rang shortly before his death to apologise for missing me at Lord's: he went on to praise Gooch's 333 ('I always thought he was the modern player most likely to challenge my record') and the promising young Indian star, Tendulkar. He would have approved of the choice of Tendulkar as Yorkshire's first overseas player.

He was amused when 'Tiny' Rowland, the head of Lonrho, bought my paper. They had met on the *Durban Castle* taking the MCC team out to South Africa in 1948. Hutton later bought shares in his company. He recalled 'a remarkably handsome blond giant' who had placed wagers on the deck quoits and the team's other shipboard games. Rowland had given Hutton a gold watch in exchange for one of his bats. Len recalled this one day and added wryly: 'Do you see him? Will you tell him the watch has run out?'

Many of Hutton's *Observer* pieces were, of necessity, running comments on a particular Saturday's play, some of it unmemorable. But I've sifted through them all to pick out general comments on the game and judgements on players that seemed worth preserving, or random asides that capture his idiosyncratic wit. Phrases like this, on a leg glance by Tom Graveney, deserved a better fate than being lost for ever in a newspaper library: 'This fine shot was played as a man would flick the ash off his cigar after a good dinner.' Or this on the portly Cowdrey's temperamental reluctance to hammer the bowling: 'Perhaps a little less lunch, or a little less breakfast, would do the trick.' (We learn how Hutton, as captain in Australia, once sent out the twelfth man with two bananas for Cowdrey just before lunch because he thought he was playing as if he must be feeling peckish.)

Because of his own austere apprenticeship, Hutton's judgement of a batsman always took account of the man's background. He once wrote of Cowdrey, for example, a player whose talents he recognised early but whose inability to live up to his full potential always baffled him: 'I sometimes wonder how good this wonderful Kent batsman would have been had he been born in the back streets of Leeds or Sheffield.' Of Gavaskar he wrote: 'Bombay is a far cry from Pudsey, but I see a lot of myself in Gavaskar's early years.'

David Gower caused him – and, indeed, the rest of us from time to time – the most exasperation. He couldn't understand how a man of such natural brilliance should fail to exploit his God-given qualities: 'David Gower's so talented he makes the game look easy, too easy. For me it was always very hard . . . The price he pays for that languid fluency is a firm-footedness that often defeats him.'

His descriptions of players were sometimes like those of a quirky theatre critic, especially about West Indians: 'He may be descended from cane-cutters and slaves, but this Richards bats like a millionaire, as if he owned six sugar plantations'; 'Constantine's limbs appeared boneless'; 'Sobers and Kanhai play Calypso shots'; 'Walcott is such a giant of a man his bat looks like a toy, a father playing on the beach with his children. But when he hits the ball, it's like a punch from Joe Louis.'

In real life Len Hutton had an eccentric turn of phrase that was often even funnier when you thought about what he'd said. His friends treasured these 'Lenisms'. Usually delivered deadpan with an unblinking stare from those wide apart blue eyes, followed by a slow crease of a smile, they could be devastating. Take this one, for instance, repeated to me by Ted Dexter. Asked what he thought of a once fashionable England player, Len replied carefully, wrinkling what Russell Davies called his 'knob of garlic' nose: 'Well, he lacks something at the highest level, some quality . . . there's a word I'm seeking . . . it'll come to me in a minute . . .' Then, with a twinkle and a flattening of vowels: 'I've got it. *Ability* . . . that's what he lacks . . . that's the word I'm looking for.'

I went over to him at the last MCC dinner he attended at Lord's and found him surrounded by Essex supporters, who were demanding that Len should give a public stamp of approval to their favourite Essex man. 'You've got to accept, Len', one of them finally pleaded, 'that he knows a great deal about the game.' Len saw me approaching and winked. 'The thing is in this life', he declared, 'you can know a great deal about something and still be wrong.' His hearers were as perplexed as most of us were at such cryptic remarks. As Mike Brearley put it, 'often what emerged was both oracular and deflating'.

There are two stories about his sons, possibly apocryphal. When someone told him that John had appeared in *Wisden*, credited with some cricketing feat, Len is said to have replied: 'Well, it just goes to show – you never know what your kids get up to.' When his other son, Richard, was on the verge of being capped, an interviewer asked Len if he thought he was a Test player. 'No,' was Len's reported reply, 'but I expect he'll play for England.' Richard did, in fact, get five caps in 1971, scoring two fifties, one of them as a makeshift opener. Richard's thoughts on 'Life with Father' are reproduced later in the book.

David Sheppard, now Bishop of Liverpool, who made a century opening partnership with Hutton for England in 1952, once surprised me by saying that the clue to Len's complex and elusive character was to be found in the Protestant movements of Bohemia. He was referring to his upbringing in the Moravian community at Fulneck, near Pudsey, Leeds. This sect, which had inspired John Wesley, was founded by Count Zindendorf when he came over from Czechoslovakia in the 1730s. It provided an austere upbringing – 'strict but caring', as Hutton later described it. The Huttons had been part of the Fulneck community since the end of the eighteenth century, and the house in which Len was brought up dated from that time.

He was the youngest of five children. His father, Henry (who once scored a fifty watched by the infant Len and was also a bowler), and his three brothers all played for Pudsey St Lawrence Cricket Club. Len joined them in the first XI at the age of 14. His grandmother's brother, Seth Milner, had been a fine cricketer in money matches in the 1880s. There was a cricket ground at the Huttons' back door in Fulneck. Even the local vicar was cricket-mad. Len was given a cricket bat for his second birthday. 'I took to this game', he once said, 'as naturally as a Sherpa to the mountains.' He also showed an early talent for soccer, though his career was abruptly shortened when he cut a knee and his doting aunts, solicitous of his cricketing future, threw his boots on the fire.

His father had taken over the family building business, but this fell on hard times in the First World War and had to be sold just before Len was born on 23 June 1916. The family had to move. Is it fanciful to suppose that Len's reputation for being 'careful' over money had its origins in these early childhood memories?

There is an early photograph of Len himself in an apron and Fair Isle pullover working at a lathe in the Fulneck handicraft centre. It was probably then that he learned to relish the feel of a cricket bat. He kept his first one under his pillow to touch fondly in the night. Even when he was over seventy, at Alf Gover's cricket school, I watched him pick up some new bats and feel their texture lovingly, like a baby with a blanket.

Fulneck would have instilled in him a stern sense of duty and social obligation that he carried into his cricket, qualities developed further in the austere rituals of the Winter Shed at Headingley. His legendary powers of concentration at the crease – he once had severe toothache before and after an innings but 'forgot' it out in the middle – were akin to a carpenter's absorption in his craft. Tom Graveney described Hutton's absorption: 'Len wasn't on this earth when he batted. He was in a trance. During an interval he would just sit down and drink his tea and look into space while someone else unbuckled his pads'.

'Yorkshire', wrote Roy Hattersley, 'is an idea not a place. Yorkshire represented a set of particular values – the compulsive desire to compete and the obsessive need to win, a certainty in the righteousness of every favoured cause and truculent scepticism about other people's convictions, an absolute faith in the eventual triumph of industry and the ultimate victory of thrift, the unrestrained aggression that gets men knocked down and the determined pride that makes them stand up again, the belief in the importance of self-improvement and the propriety of self-confidence, a weakness for mock piety and false sentiment and – above all else – a strong suspicion that the tender virtues are not really virtues at all.'

If Yorkshire provided the temperamental foundation for Hutton's career, the bitter bodyline controversy of 1932–33 provided the background. As C. L. R. James said of his innings in 1938: 'Bodyline may have vanished. Its temper remained.' That same temper was still evident in the five post-war series he played against Australia, even 20 years on. The aggression of Lindwall and Miller were the Aussies' answer to Larwood, just as (for Hutton) Tyson was Larwood reborn. When the student Tyson rapped Hutton on the pad in a friendly match at Redcar in 1950 – a year when he was the world's best and few balls beat his bat – he afterwards found a bruise on his leg that reminded him of playing Larwood in the 1930s, and his immediate response was to write off to Lord's about this promising new fast bowler. 'I remembered that bruise a few years later', he said wryly, 'when we chose the squad to go to Australia.'

Len aged 15 in Fulneck handicraft centre. He had a craftsman's feel for the wood of a cricket bat.

Above right. On Blackpool sands at the age of eight. His grip on the bat, doubtless taught by his father and older brothers, never changed.

Brothers Edmund, George, Reggie and Len Hutton in 1938. All played for Pudsey St Lawrence Cricket Club.

HUTTON FOOTSTEPS TO FAME

A tribute by Yorkshire for his benefit year in 1948. *Top left*, Hutton at three; *centre*, scoring a century for England; *top right*, as a boy with his hero Herbert Sutcliffe; *bottom left*, walking out with his favourite opening partner, Cyril Washbrook; *bottom right*, the scoreboard at the Oval in 1938 showing Hutton's record score at the moment he was out.

Jardine, the England captain on the bodyline tour, wrote to Hutton frequently in Australia in 1954–55, comparing their respective tasks. Len told me that an important part of his thinking on that tour was that he should retain the Ashes 'without leaving a smell'. It was as if his whole Test career had been dominated by a need to beat the Australians at their own game on their own turf and lay the ghost of bodyline bowling for ever. He embodied and recreated the spirit of pre-war Yorkshire cricket in order to achieve it. He was obsessed by the men from Down Under: 'Losing is foreign to their nature. They may appreciate the birds and flowers over here, but their real delight is beating England at Lord's . . . Australians have made me fight for every run I have ever made. It is a hard game against them. The grounds are hard, the ball is hard, the men are hard: you need to be harder than they are to beat them.'

He was, and he did – but only after some macho head-to-head confrontations, not least when Bradman himself came in to field at short mid-off when Hutton approached his record at the Oval in 1938, staring intimidatingly into his eyes as every ball was bowled. At Sydney in 1946, on the first tour after the war, Hutton took strike against the Aussies' new fast bowler, Ray Lindwall, whom Sutcliffe had already seen and warned him about. Two overs were fairly routine stuff. 'Then it happened. The second ball of his third over reared from the pitch as though the devil had taken possession of it. Imagine putting the index finger of your right hand under a sledgehammer swung by a blacksmith. That was how my finger felt as it was flattened into the bat handle, paralysing the whole of my right arm for about thirty seconds. I glanced down the wicket at Lindwall and the look he returned startled me. The glint in his eyes was a message I could not mistake – "I've a lot more where that one came from".' And of course he had – for another decade.

Although Hutton, along with the other England batsmen, was regarded as a failure in 1948 against the pace of Lindwall and Miller – so much so that he was dropped for the first time in his career – he finished the series with an average of 42, scoring four fifties in eight innings. By the tour of 1950–51, after Bradman's retirement, he was undisputed as the greatest batsman in the world, as he showed the Australians on a rain-affected pitch at Brisbane. The *Sydney Morning Herald*, quoting the Australian team, described it as 'glorious'. Even though England lost and he scored only 62 not out – 300 runs less than his record – it was widely regarded as the greatest Test innings he ever played. 'This was Hutton's Test', said the *Herald*. 'He dominated the cricket, the complete batsman. His mastery of the bowling and of the wicket had the spectators enthralled. He seemed always to be in position for every type of ball. His courage, control and mastery of technique combined to make it an unforgettable fighting effort, stamped with the class of the batting champion'. Another writer said: 'As he returned to the pavilion unconquered, he looked as if he could have won the match off his own bat if there had only been a cap and a pair of pads at the other end'. Later, on the same tour in Adelaide, it was again 'Len Hutton versus Australia' as he carried his bat for 156 and lifted the team to such an extent that they went on to Melbourne to win their first Test against Australia since the Oval triumph of 1938.

Melbourne was not his favourite ground, holding hidden terrors. 'To walk into the harsh Melbourne sunlight from the shadowy dark of the dressing-room', he once wrote, 'and find yourself facing the largest crowd you have seen at a cricket match is like entering a gladiatorial ring, and loud though the applause for you may be, you cannot escape the conviction that secretly all the thumbs are pointing downwards. And when the ball hits your pads as you play at and miss your first ball, the appeals are like the roar of the lions.' Len had a special feel for some cricket grounds, especially his favourite, Old Trafford, and the Oval, where he had so many successes. 'Old Trafford', he wrote, 'looked as always like a Savile Row suit . . . It was the sort of wicket I would have liked to roll up and carry around in my bag.' But Lord's he never liked: 'Its magic to me is that of a witch doctor . . . it was like going into a mortuary.'

In later years he felt that the preparation of pitches had made for duller cricket. He played, of course, in the days of uncovered pitches and only Jack Hobbs could challenge him as the best player of all time on all kinds of wicket. He also believed that the new leg-before-wicket rule, introduced in 1935, had put batsmen at a disadvantage, especially in England, penalising back-foot play and restricting the brilliant stroke-making which had brought in the crowds between the wars. 'Cricket used to be a gentleman's game', he said towards the end, 'but no longer. It is now a cruel, hard, tough form of public entertainment.' How unlike, how very unlike – I couldn't help thinking when I read that – those halcyon days of Larwood, Lindwall and Tyson . . .

A year after his death, I went to Pudsey for the opening of the Sir Leonard Hutton memorial gates. Len once said: 'Many of the most blissful hours of my life were spent with Pudsey St Lawrence.' The ground was edged by gritty stone buildings with a housing estate behind, though green fields were not far away. It was a damp and bitterly cold day, with the wind sweeping across the ground and penetrating the defences of a soft southern overcoat. The club scoreboard was set at 770 for 6, with Len's 364 marked at the moment he had been out at the Oval 53 years before. I was reminded that that was the point at which Arthur Wood, the Yorkshire wicket-keeper, had gone in for his first Test innings. As he went down the steps he glanced at the scoreboard and joked: 'I'm always at my best in a crisis.'

Virtually everyone huddled together in the Pudsey tent had some personal connection with Len. Old men claimed to remember the first time they had seen him bat as a teenager. Sir Lawrence Byford, the former Inspector of Constabulary who had succeeded him as President of Yorkshire CCC, vividly recalled the thrill of being taken to see him play before the war in baggy white flannels and short back-and-sides. (Not only that, but he remembered the exact date – 22 May, 1937 – and Hutton's score, 104, made for the North versus

Fifty years on: Pudsey St Lawrence Cricket Club marks the anniversary of Hutton's record innings by showing the England score when he was out in 1938.

the South against the bowling of Kenneth Farnes. Sir Lawrence keeps a picture of Hutton in his office and admits to consulting the oracle whenever in doubt about Yorkshire's needs: 'What should I do now, Len?'.) The vicar called Hutton 'a true son of Pudsey'. Others recalled that in later life he would try to slip unnoticed into a seat at Pudsey St Lawrence on the Sunday of a Headingley Test match. Plaques and photographs in the pavilion commemorated his world record, with an original stump and bail, and a picture of him meeting the Queen. It was a bleak shrine that day.

The Hutton family were there in force, including his sister Florence and his four grandchildren, sons of Richard and John. Len told me before he died that he had enjoyed watching the boys play cricket more than going to Test matches, perhaps because he regretted not seeing enough of his own boys when he was in his prime. There is something appealing about the idea of Len Hutton, who had faced the bowling of Wilfred Rhodes, who in turn had played with W. G. Grace in 1899, knocking a ball about with little boys in a Surrey garden

90 years later. It says something about the enduring nature of cricket. It thrills me to think that I, too, once tossed up a few tweakers to the old master, who serenely disdained to destroy them.

Seeing Lady Hutton formally opening the Pudsey memorial gates, I was reminded of an observation by Trevor Bailey that both Hutton and Bradman had exceptional wives and that this had played a big part in their success. But, as I sensed strongly in that cold tent in Pudsey, Hutton attracted an affection, a warmth of personal feeling denied to the Don, who has been more admired than liked (partly perhaps, as Len once found on a visit to Adelaide, because he 'liked the sound of his own voice'). I am still baffled by the end of that profile of Hutton which appeared in *The Observer* in 1951. Although it paid fine tribute to his play, it was cool about his personality – 'He is the greatest living batsman and, behind this, he is the greatest living batsman' – and concluded that, like Milton, he was not 'very lovable', if only because he didn't much care whether he was loved or not. As I said when he died aged seventy-four: 'I think he did care, though he needn't have worried about it.'

Former players have suggested that the Len I met in his later years was different from the hard taskmaster they knew. He had mellowed, lost some of the shyness that came across then as rudeness or North Country cussedness. Like many shy people, he could strike strangers as coldly aloof. I've been told stories which reflect well and badly on him – occasions when he appeared to behave churlishly or with the barest courtesy, others where he performed, according to one correspondent, 'a noble act of considerable kindness and benevolence'.

To be England's first professional captain at that time would have been a social ordeal for anyone; for a self-enclosed man like Len, more sensitive by nature than his situation encouraged or allowed, it must have been a private hell. When he left Alec Bedser out of the team at Melbourne on the last day of 1954, allowing him to learn his fate from the team-sheet on the dressing-room door, I'm sure it was partly because he shrank from seeing the old warrior hurt. But it wouldn't have seemed like that at the time, especially to Bedser himself, who still bears a grudge to this day. Asking Alec to inspect the pitch with him before the day's play must have seemed a cruel twist of the knife. To be fair to Len, he had been unwell himself that morning, waking up white-faced and shivering, and had to be cajoled by George Duckworth, Bill Edrich and Godfrey Evans to leave his hotel room and go to the ground.

The worries of captaincy added to the strains on his body, which was never robust at the best of times. He also carried the English batting on his shoulders; after Washbrook he lacked a regular, reliable opening partner to share the burden. 'Hutton out, side out', was a cricket saying of the post-war years. As N. W. D. Yardley said at the time: 'The England batting has been so rocky since the war that nearly always Hutton's had to get his nut down and stay there, just to try and stop the rot. Nobody can deny he's done that time and time again.' This was the beginning of the accumulation of pressures, both mental and physical, that led to his retirement within a year.

When Colin Cowdrey's father died during the same Australian tour, Len could hardly cope. Ralph Barker described the scene in the team's Perth hotel: 'That evening Cowdrey went down for a drink and a meal. Either beforehand or during dinner, most of the players shook him by the hand and expressed their sympathy. Len Hutton didn't come near him. It was not until they were having coffee in the lounge, and it was getting on for bedtime, that he appeared at Cowdrey's table. Cowdrey immediately realised why he hadn't seen him before. Hutton came up to him shaking his head from side to side, biting his lip and unable to speak. After two agonised expulsions of breath that spoke volumes, he wrung Cowdrey's hand before turning his back. He was too upset to articulate.'

He found it hard, even as captain, to offer more than token encouragement to young Oxbridge graduates like May and Sheppard, despite the fact that they hung on his every word, just as in his own youth he had revered giants like Sutcliffe and Rhodes. In a curious way they stood in awe of each other, a paradigm of Disraeli's 'two nations'. Trueman thinks the habitual silence was instilled into him in the Yorkshire dressing-room of his youth, where, he once said: 'Had I been ordered to walk on broken glass, I would have instantly obeyed.' When he said anything at all, he seemed to be speaking in riddles, never quite finishing a sentence, then saying 'See what I mean?' (which, of course, nobody did).

May remembers making his Test debut while still an undergraduate and batting for hours with Len, who surprised him by staying virtually silent while each of them compiled a century (it was May's first in Tests and Hutton's 100th). Sheppard had the same silent walk to the wicket while opening with him as a youngster, but in later years he recalls a more friendly reaction. 'I was batting for Sussex and Len was captaining Yorkshire in the field that day. I was having trouble getting Johnny Wardle away through the covers, playing him as an orthodox left-arm spinner. After a few overs of this, Len came over to me and said: "Didn't they teach thee anything at that Cambridge – everybody knows Wardle doesn't spin the ball. Hit him back where it came from". Next over I tried this, playing Wardle through the leg-side. The ball went for four and Len – the fielding captain and a Yorkshireman, too, remember – stood nodding his head in approval.'

Denis Compton was one of the few people to whom Len ever spoke between overs, and that was only once. When Lindwall and Miller were giving them the treatment in 1953, Len summoned him to the middle of the pitch for a word. 'What's he going to say?' thought Denis. 'I can think of easier ways of earning a living than this, can't you?' said Len, and returned to his blockhole.

No wonder people found him hard to make out. He was a bit of a mystery to himself at times and enjoyed people's bafflement about him. Trevor Bailey's verdict was succinct: 'Beautiful batsman, difficult man'. For E. W. Swanton, he passed two searching tests: 'Would you choose to take him as a model for any young cricketer? And would he have been great in any era?' For Compton, who played with him before and after the war, the key word was 'balance', one of the classical virtues: 'He was the most beautifully balanced player I ever saw, never ruffled, never without dignity – it was the same in his life, I reckon.' One of the few aphorisms attributed to Hutton is this one: 'The science of life is making money; the art of life is a sense of humour'.

There was a kind of moral quality in the way he played and the way he approached the game. Once, when he saw an old photograph of Ponsford playing an immaculate forward defensive stroke, he suddenly enthused: 'Look at that. Now *that's* what I call a straight bat. That's what the left elbow's *for*. Show 'em the maker's name. A straight bat isn't just a symbol of moral rectitude, you know, it's as we say in Yorkshire, a more *businesslike* way to play.'

Like Pinter, Alan Ross saw Hutton as a vulnerable figure: 'The impression he left was of economy, of timing, of being effortlessly in the right place. He never seemed to sweat or flap, remaining the same sallow, even pale figure, frail almost, vulnerable. It was perhaps Leonard Hutton's vulnerability, the sense of his playing a heroic part in a drama of tragic dimensions, one in which he alone had to keep superior forces at bay, that set him apart and made him interesting.'

Was Len Hutton finally a contented man? Mike Brearley, the former England captain and a professional psychoanalyst, wrote when Hutton died: 'I suspect that behind the engaging surface was an unease, even a sadness.' In my own dealings with Len I sometimes detected the same thing, but I put it down to a wistfulness about what might have been – if the war hadn't interrupted his career in his prime, if he hadn't damaged his arm, if he hadn't had to bear the full brunt of the Australian attack in the immediate post-war years, if Yorkshire had behaved better towards him . . . above all, a sense that he didn't know, and would never know, whether he had reached the peak of his talents.

But my impression was that he looked at that reality with the same straight gaze he applied to the bowling of Lindwall and Miller. Beyond that I sensed an enviable serenity, the wry fulfilment of a Conradic hero who had been severely tested by life and had finally come through, though he wished perhaps that he could have found a way to talk about these things more openly. A phrase by J. M. Kilburn in these recollections caught my eye: 'Hutton's is a very romantic story, but Leonard wasn't a romantic.' He said to me in our TV interview two years before he died: 'It's nice to be remembered for the 364 and so on, but really and truly I would like to be remembered for the sort of person I am, rather than for what I've done.'

Archbishop Runcie is an authoritative, if unlikely witness to the fact that Len will indeed be so remembered. He wrote in a letter of condolence to Lady Hutton: 'When you have idolised anyone in youth, it's sometimes a disappointment to meet him in later life. Of nobody was this less true than Len. Someone so modest, so free from cant or pretentiousness, was an inspiration. He seemed to me to have the highest standards for character as he did for the game of which he was such a master. Of course he was the first to admit that he was a sinner like the rest of us, but aiming for the best and knowing his faults and being such a natural delight as a human being.'

That Len Hutton should have obliged such serious people to think so hard about him – both as a man and as a player – is, I hope, some justification for this book. In producing it I have been conscious of something Mike Brearley also felt in writing about him – an anxiety about intruding and thereby hurting or embarrassing him. It is a mark of the unusual spell he cast that such considerations should still have force beyond the grave.

Len once offered these cryptic words of advice to Tony Greig about leading an England team on tour: 'Don't say too much.' He might have said the same to some of us who remember him in this collection. But I hope not. Unlike most cricketers, Len Hutton deserves to be remembered for rather more than cricket.

PART TWO

In the England Dressing Room

Harold Larwood

R. E. S. Wyatt

C. H. Palmer

Cyril Washbrook

Denis Compton

Godfrey Evans

Alec Bedser

Trevor Bailey

Colin Cowdrey

Peter May

Brian Statham

Roy Tattersall

Tom Graveney

Frank Tyson

Peter Loader

The all-star England team that regained the Ashes in 1953. *Back row, left to right*: Bailey, May, Graveney, Laker, Lock, Wardle (12th man), Trueman. *Front row*: Edrich, Bedser, Hutton (captain), Compton, Evans.

Harold Larwood

Born 1904. Nottinghamshire: 1924–38. 21 Test matches: 1926–33. His model action and run-up made him, some say, the fastest bowler ever. Hutton described his action as 'lethal poetry'. Not only was he fast, but he had control and accuracy. His last series was the 'Body-line' tour to Australia in 1932/33, during which even Bradman was unsettled by his pace and lift. He took 100 wickets in a season 8 times and was top of the national averages in five seasons. He was a quiet man, short for a fast bowler, and worked as a miner in his youth. He emigrated to Australia in 1950.

I played against him only twice. I bowled him out for five in 1935 and for four in 1936. I know he was a good player. We could do with him now, and one or two more like him. Ah, he was a good player. He had everything. He was a Yorkshireman. He was here with his wife and came to my house; I've got a photograph of them sitting on the settee.

It's always good to have a Yorkshireman in a side. In my second Test I played with Wilfred Rhodes; I was twenty-one and he was forty-eight; that was in 1926. The previous four Tests had been drawn and the last one at the Oval was to be played to a finish. The experts said Larwood was too young and Rhodes was too old. But he wasn't too old and put up a useful show and we won the game and the Ashes. That's Yorkshire; they're fighters.

This team now, there's no fight in them. Hutton was a fighter. I bowled him out and that was the last I seen of him on the field. I used to like these new young lads. I liked the idea of Compton and Edrich, but by Gee they finished me. They gave me some hammer. I'll never forget it. They were good. Hutton was good too. Ta ta.

R. E. S. Wyatt

Born 1901. Warwickshire (Captain 1930–37) and Worcestershire (Captain 1949–50): 1923–51. 40 Test matches: 1927–37 (Captain in 16 Tests 1930–35). A versatile batsman who filled every position from 1 to 8 for England, Bob Wyatt was also a swing bowler and off-spinner. He was a great thinker and strategist and displaced the popular Percy Chapman to lead England in the last Test against Australia in 1930. He was Jardine's vice-captain to Australia in 1932/33 and took over from him in 1934, but was ill for the first Test. He was an England selector from 1949–53, and chairman in 1950, when Hutton was made England captain.

Len Hutton had tremendous concentration and that record innings he played at the Oval in 1938 was mainly concentration. Although he was a fine player, it was a very easy wicket and he wasn't the only one to make runs on it. But if Hutton hadn't that tremendous concentration, he probably wouldn't have gone on for so long. He didn't score particularly quickly, but he gave absolutely nothing away. He played magnificently, of course, but although it was his greatest score I wouldn't say that 364 was his greatest innings, not by a long way.

He was a very intelligent thinker, a bit cautious in his attitude, but by no means without a sense of humour. He had that rather attractive smile. He didn't always finish his sentence. He would finish with a smile, and sometimes it was a bit difficult to know what he was thinking.

I usually agreed with him and, funnily enough, he usually agreed with me, especially on the changes in the laws of cricket over the years. I had a letter from him the day before he died. He'd been in the box we were running at Lord's and he wrote a very charming letter saying how much he'd enjoyed being there.

I was mainly responsible for Len Hutton being made captain of England. I didn't find it a difficult decision. I saw no reason, especially in those days, why a professional shouldn't be captain, provided he was fitted to do the job. There was nobody, in my opinion, who would be better. One knew there were certain things he understood about the game, simply by talking to him about technique and about various players, and about the bowling he had at his command. You knew he wasn't going to let you down.

Len made a very good captain, apart from the fact that he was a bit on the cautious side. His attitude was not to give anything away, not to take any risks. From a tactical point of view, and for appreciating the weakness of the opposition, he was very good.

One of the reasons for his success on sticky wickets was that his technique was so good, and the more difficult the wicket the better your technique has to be. His technique came from watching others and thinking about it. He had a good example in Herbert Sutcliffe, who played some fine innings on turning wickets. All good players on turning wickets are good back players. You hear such nonsense these days. People say: 'He's going well, he's got on the front foot.' What that means goodness only knows, but I hear it on television and I read about it. A really good player on all wickets is every bit as good on his back foot as his front, or probably even better. Playing on the back foot is essential on a turning wicket. Forward and back, they're complementary one to the other. All the really good players on turning wickets are good back players, like Hutton.

I don't think the majority of players really know what flight is. People think it's just a variation of trajectory and pace, but it's more than that. Clarrie Grimmett, for instance, had a peculiar flight, quite regardless of whether the ball pitched up or pitched short. Owing to the spin of the ball, it took a curious flight in the air. Jack White, the Somerset left-hander who was so successful in Australia in 1928–29, always made the ball dip. That, coupled with the fact that he varied his trajectory and pace, made him difficult, and it was the same with Grimmett and O'Reilly. You don't really hear much about flight these days. You hear so-and-so gives the ball air, a very good thing to do, but it's not flight. I know Hutton would agree with what I'm saying. I've discussed it many times with him.

Personally, I would have sent Hutton to Australia in 1936, when I went myself. I should have sent Compton too, even though they were both barely twenty years old. They were class and that is what you've got to look for in Test cricket. If he'd been Australian, they'd have sent him over here.

I was influenced before I ever saw Len by Herbert Sutcliffe, who'd gone in with him on several occasions. So when I saw him first I was looking at something I already knew was pretty good, but I saw it straight away.

Hutton's play depended very largely on his temperament. He had a lot of strokes, but he was a cautious player and a cautious captain. He appreciated the honour of being captain of England. He had an ideal temperament. But I wouldn't call him a great captain because he was too cautious. A great captain also has to be a lucky captain.

My recollection of him as a batsman is mainly his off-drives. 'Quick on your feet' is really a misnomer. People who get the reputation of being quick on their feet are people who judge the length of the ball sooner; they have more time in which to play their stroke. That would apply to Hutton. It is attained largely by keeping the head absolutely motionless. If you are taking a photograph you hold the camera still: when you're batting you should hold your head still in order to judge the length. All the really great batsmen I can remember, their heads were motionless. Take Don Bradman, for instance, Jack Hobbs, Herbert Sutcliffe, Patsy Hendren, Len Hutton, their eyes were on the level and their head was absolutely motionless.

One of the most important things in batting is knowing where the ball is going to pitch. Hutton was one of the lucky ones in that respect. When you know where it's going to pitch, you decide whether you're going to play back or forward.

I can't imagine Len Hutton being anything other than gentle, determined but gentle. In his early days I can imagine him being rather shy, but in the latter part of his life he was at home in any company. He was a great character, I got a lot of pleasure out of talking to him. He was rather evasive at times if you asked him a question – he'd have made a good politician.

C. H. Palmer

Born 1919. Worcestershire and Leicestershire (Captain 1950–57): 1938–59. 1 Test match: 1953/54. Charles Palmer, an all-rounder, toured South Africa in 1948/49, and the West Indies in 1953/54 as player/manager under Hutton's captaincy. Palmer, Ames, Allen, Robins, Yardley and the chairman, Altham, formed the selection committee that appointed Hutton captain for the 1954/55 tour to Australia. He was President of the MCC in 1978–79.

Hutton was a fairly distant figure for me before the war. He and Compton were a bit older and already established England players. After the war I first toured with him to South Africa in 1948–49, with George Mann as captain. The two genuinely great players on that tour were Compton and Hutton, and they were a great contrast. The difference between them was that when Len Hutton played one of his perfect cover drives there was a sort of divine inevitability about it and everything was right in the world. You sat back in your chair and felt comfortable and complacent, whereas with Denis Compton you sat on the edge of your seat and thought: 'How the hell did he do that shot?'

When batting with Hutton one felt a bit of a student, batting in the company of a caring professor of batting technique. He was always very proud of his professionalism and his professional skills. Batting with Compton was more of an explosive experience. I remember batting with Denis, for example, when he got 300 runs in three hours and one minute in South Africa – I always said he was never on time. The main difference between his innings and mine was a mere matter of 300 runs! In South Africa I also saw Hutton and Washbrook put on that wonderful opening partnership of 359.

In 1953–54 I was player/manager when Len went to the West Indies as the first professional captain. This inevitably had some effect on him, but there never could have been a more single-minded, conscientious and brave captain of great integrity. I remember well in

Sportsman of the Year,
1953, after winning
back the Ashes as
England's first
professional captain.

British Guiana, when we experienced the bottle-throwing episode, it really was an explosive situation. We didn't really know whether it was politically inspired or whether somebody had had too much rum. The officials in British Guiana were also highly perturbed and went on the field and suggested that Len took the side off. He said: 'No. I'm going to battle through this. We might get some more wickets before the close.' In fact, the riot squad was moved in the next day.

I wonder how he would have coped with the modern limited-overs game. He had genius and was bound to have succeeded. I don't think his would be the swashbuckling approach. It would be a very calculated assessment of risk: what was, and what was not, possible given the bowling, fielding, and general wicket conditions. It takes me back to an innings he played in Barbados on the 1953–54 tour. He wasn't feeling very well and placed himself down the order. The scoring had been slow. He unleashed the most astonishing stream of beautiful strokes, some of which appeared risky. But I think he'd calculated that, in the circumstances, if a certain bowler bowled him a certain ball he could do a, b, or c with it, and he chose the one which would be most effective. It really was a magnificent innings with beautiful strokes, some of which he would have hidden under a bushel in a Test match. But of course, as an opener for England, he had this tremendous ability to play according to the circumstances. That was the difference between him and Compton. As an opener for England, he'd got a great responsibility, particularly when he was facing Miller and Lindwall, he had to blunt them before the others came in.

When I was captain of Leicestershire, and Len was in form on a good wicket against us, I recalled what George Geary said when asked how he bowled to Bradman, when Bradman was getting his 334 on a good wicket at Leeds in 1930. Old George said: 'I just kept on bowling and bowling, waiting for the bugger to faint.' You just wait for them to make a mistake. You couldn't spot a particular weakness through which he repeatedly got out.

That tour to the West Indies in 1954 was a difficult one. We went out there into a fairly volatile atmosphere. The West Indies wanted their independence, and they looked at the England team in a fairly critical way because England was the mother country. I think Len and I worked in great harmony. He helped me and I helped him on an explosive tour.

I think Len felt his isolation as a new captain. He was not a party-goer in any great way and there were one or two people that were. Off the field I think we were perfectly happy to fraternise with the opposition, but didn't particularly want to fraternise on the field. He was a shrewd captain. I think that tour took a lot out of him. I think he was drained; everybody was. I'm sure being captain placed a great strain upon him. He was never a chap of very robust physique and I'm sure it would have taken a lot out of him; pressures were pretty high both on and off the field.

His 200 in Jamaica was a tremendous test of character and technique. Len knew that we should have lost the series had we not won that match. We could halve the series with that win and I think he knew damn well that unless he got a good score we couldn't do it.

He was serious-minded with a professional approach. But he had a very dry sense of humour and sometimes we were very amused by what he said. It was the way he said it rather than what he said. There was nothing slapstick about him.

Cyril Washbrook had the same serious-minded approach. When you're opening the innings and you've got Lindwall, Miller and others at you, it's no laughing matter. Way down the order it might be a different matter – you can fling the bat at the ball, like Godfrey Evans. Hutton and Washbrook ran beautifully between the wickets; they were extremely good judges of a run. It was something that tripped off the tongue: Hutton and Washbrook.

Cyril Washbrook

Born 1914. Lancashire (Captain 1954–59): 1933–59. 37 Test matches: 1937–56. Hutton's favourite opening partner. They opened the England innings 50 times together and achieved eight century opening stands, including 359 against South Africa in 1948/49, a world record in Tests. No opening partnership could face a sterner test than they did facing Lindwall and Miller in 1946/47, 1948 and 1950/51. Recalled to the England team in 1956, aged 41, he scored a famous 98 against the Australians. He is now President of Lancashire CCC.

I first played with Len in a Lancashire and Yorkshire Second XI match. It was his first match for Yorkshire seconds and my first match for Lancashire seconds. The amazing thing is that I scored 202 not out and he scored 0. That was just coincidence, but that was the first time I knew him. His ability became apparent to me a little later on.

We had a very good understanding. In all the years we played together there was only one run-out, so we had a pretty good understanding between the wickets. The one blot on our record was in Cape Town on the first tour of South Africa after the war, in 1948–49. Len was run out after we'd put on 88. There was a slight misunderstanding, not a very serious one; I'm not saying that it was the fault of either of us. We were going for a short single and it so happened that somebody picked the ball up and hit the stumps. I can't remember whose call it was, but I can remember that that was the only time that we were involved in a run-out, which is fairly good considering that we opened for a number of years. If there was a run there we took it.

We had confidence in each other's ability, which is very important when you're opening the innings. We didn't do anything crazy. We didn't talk much during the innings. We settled down into a good partnership because I think we had respect for each other and we generally coped. A couple of times we failed, like everybody does. Runs we made, we made them together, without any jealousy or anything of that sort. He was a very fine opening partner, my best opening partner. I would say that Len was the easiest batsman to be with in the middle.

He always faced the first ball of the innings. I don't know why he liked to, perhaps he was used to doing it for Yorkshire. I didn't mind him doing that at all. We did it automatically and he liked it that way, and I didn't mind.

The first time we got together was in the Test against New Zealand in 1937. That was my first Test match, at the Oval, and Len had been in the side prior to that. I didn't open the innings with him then. I went in at number three. He was almost established, having already scored a Test century. He opened with Charlie Barnett from Gloucestershire.

We really came together after the war on the first tour to Australia in 1946–47. The Australians had a very, very good side and we had been languishing, playing very little serious cricket during the war. I think they played a fair amount more and of course two great fast bowlers had arrived: Lindwall and Miller.

I think the 1948 Australian side that came over here was the greatest touring side that I ever played against. Many people think it was the greatest side of all. They took an awful lot of beating. We had a fairly rough time against Lindwall and Miller, they were great bowlers. We did our best to cope with it and we appreciated that they were the two best in the world. There's no doubt about that. That includes the West Indies when they had their fast bowlers. They had Ramadhin and Valentine too, but they weren't going to hurt you if they hit you. For two quick bowlers playing together, bowling consistently, there couldn't have been a better pair. If you survived and did reasonably well, you'd done a good job, that's my opinion.

They were very good to play against because if you played well they didn't mind saying so. I remember one occasion in Adelaide; we were playing in a Test match and Len and I had opened the innings and Lindwall and Miller, naturally, were opening the bowling. After about thirty to forty minutes, after they'd really let it go, they were given a rest. I always remember that we met in the middle of the wicket and Len said: 'I'll tell tha what it is,' in his Yorkshire accent. 'These people use Tommy guns and we use water pistols.' I said, 'I think you're right too.'

During the war he was in the army and I was in the R.A.F. The services used to play each other but I can't remember playing against him. I don't know if he was invalided out after he damaged his arm. He was left, of course, with one arm shorter than the other, which was to some extent a handicap, but you wouldn't think so when you saw him batting.

He didn't hook much after the war and I've no doubt that it was due, probably entirely, to the fact that one arm was shorter than the other. I used to hook quite a lot and get criticised if I holed out at long-leg or something like that. But if you're fond of the shot and you play it well you always think: 'Well, here's four runs coming up.' He was a magnificent player off his front foot, through the covers and on the onside. He was a very fine timer of the ball without any real effort.

He was a very quiet and reserved man and spent a lot of time on his own, even on tours. He was with you absolutely one hundred per cent during the day, but in the evening he very often seemed to disappear to his own room or to find a bit of quietness somewhere. Len always had a very quiet approach to doing anything and after the end of the day he was somewhat of a loner. He didn't mix much after the end of the day. He was there to play cricket and nothing else; that was his purpose. You had to go to certain functions but he did as little of that as possible. He didn't volunteer to go to those sorts of things. He was a very good tourist; he didn't find fault with junior players but if they wanted help they would have to go to him and he would help them. He never imposed himself on anyone. If they played a bad shot he never went to them and told them it was a foolish thing to do.

We didn't discuss technique much, we had confidence in each other. We played our own particular game and that is probably why it was a success, or a great reason why it was a success. We didn't give each other advice or anything like that. We used just to say: 'Well played, you've done a jolly good job,' and that was it. He never criticised me and I never criticised him.

I don't think he was ever very concerned about records. I remember we were playing in a Test match in Johannesburg against South Africa around Christmas 1948. We were both not out at tea-time and as we walked down to go in to bat after tea some young fellow said: 'You want 24 to beat the record.' Len turned to me and said: 'What's that record, do you know?' I said: 'I don't know.' He said, 'Well, we'd better try and get them and see what it is before we do anything silly.' But I don't think he was ever too record-conscious. We beat the world record on that occasion, 359, which is still a record opening partnership for England. Poor Denis Compton had to sit with his pads on all day.

Len always played according to the ball that was delivered to him. He didn't sacrifice his wicket and I don't think he expected anybody else to either. I can't remember where I was when he scored his 364. He was capable of playing a long innings; he had the stamina to do it. He didn't look very strong physically, but he had great powers of concentration and that is the secret of it all. The more you can concentrate, the better you become. When you let that go, you are in danger of getting out, of doing something stupid, but he didn't. I can't remember any occasion on which we played together when he did something stupid and got himself out. I don't honestly remember one single occasion when he did that. You can concentrate like that when you're young, though you are very tired after concentrating so much and running so much, especially in hot climates.

All the team was very pleased to go to Australia in 1946 and we were made very, very welcome. It was a reaction after the war. We were made very welcome wherever we went and on every occasion. They were so pleased to start international cricket again. I think our side was probably a bit older than theirs because there hadn't been any county cricket during the war, but there had been some cricket in Australia.

Len played a marvellous innings at Sydney in the second Test. He played the most magnificent shots for 37 in 24 minutes, absolutely marvellous. I couldn't honestly tell you why he played like that. He was playing shots at the balls that were bowled to him and they were magnificent. They were some of the best 37 runs that I've ever seen

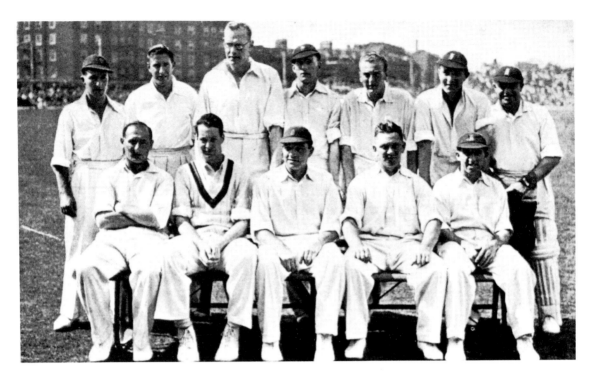

The team that made England's record total of 903 and beat Australia at the Oval in the 'timeless Test' of 1938. *Back row, left to right*: Edrich, Fagg (12th man), Bowes, Hutton, Hardstaff, Compton, Wood. *Front row*: Verity, Farnes, Hammond (captain), Leyland, Paynter.

Hutton and Bill Edrich, who opened the batting in the Oval Test against Australia in 1938. After Edrich was out for 12, Hutton and Leyland put on 382 runs for the second wicket.

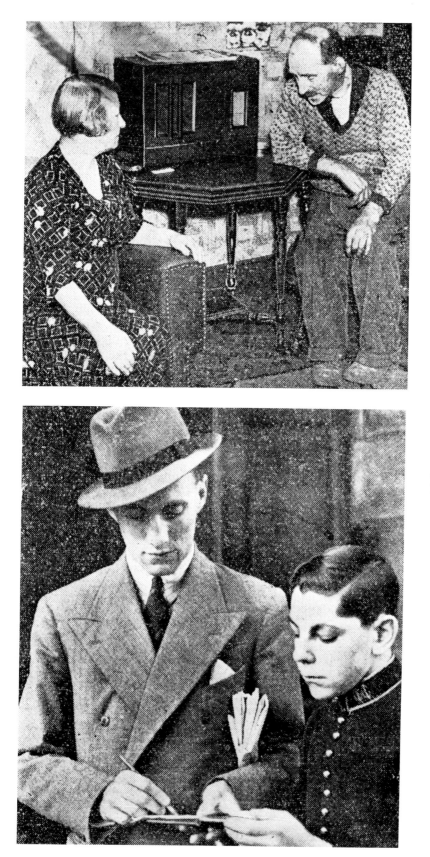

Hutton's parents hear him beat Bradman's record in their house at Fulneck, near Pudsey.

A celebrity signing autographs after his record innings – Hutton was 'overwhelmed by the suddenness of fame and worried about its penalties'.

made. There were runs all round the wicket off any bowler that came on. He was out just before lunch, and it was a great pity that he was, because if he'd have stayed in for any length of time he'd have broken all sorts of records. It was a magnificent short innings, one of the finest I've ever seen. He usually had a quieter approach.

We didn't enjoy facing the short-pitched bowling. You don't enjoy bouncers. We did our best to cope with it. I remember Lindwall bowled a bouncer at me and I hit it for six and he said: 'You're the second bastard that's hit me for six.' I was only the second person who'd hit him for six when he was at his best. Bastard of course was a term of endearment in Australia. It's not like it is here; call someone a bastard here and you're in trouble.

There are no stories of Len off the field because he always lived quietly. I don't remember spending many evenings with him on tour. After six o'clock in the evening you couldn't rely on him to be doing anything for entertainment. If we had to go to a reception he went to them always but usually he kept himself to himself. He only went on things which he had to go on. I can quite understand that.

We did go out together in England because we both worked for the same firm, and when we were in London for a Test match we both had to dine at the Dorchester with the chairman. We were both in the paper trade. It was a very big firm and the chairman was a fellow called Harrison. It was a sort of 'command performance', we had to go out and have dinner with him at the Dorchester.

Old Harrison was very keen on cricket. He employed Herbert Sutcliffe, Maurice Leyland, myself, Len Hutton and one or two others. He was a Yorkshireman. He thought far more of Yorkshiremen than he did of Lancastrians. I'm sure he did. It was very kind of him to provide us with a place on the sales staff in the right area. I was in Lancashire and the others were over in Yorkshire. Then things didn't go so well in the paper trade and we all disappeared.

He was a chap who didn't know much about cricket but he was mad on it; there are rather a lot of those people about. He always had a table booked for us at the Dorchester when we were in London and it was like going on parade. He was a generous man. When you were working for him you'd be having dinner with him up in the north and he'd say: 'London for you next week.' No thought about whether it was convenient for you to do it, but he paid us pretty well so one couldn't be too choosy. Then he died and of course all the cricketers disappeared except for Herbert Sutcliffe. He'd been with them for a long time and I think he stayed on. I was retired and I think Len was too.

Len and I didn't discuss cricket a great deal. We were both selectors on our trips abroad. The captain forms a small group to help him pick the actual Test match side and both of us helped with that on the two trips to Australia and one to South Africa. Wally Hammond was a chap who got his way on every occasion. He was a magnificent cricketer but he was a difficult man to understand. I think he's the greatest cricketer I've ever seen. When he wanted to bowl he could be marvellous and when he wanted to bat he could do the same. I've never seen, in my own small way, a better cricketer in my life, but he wasn't an easy captain to live with. He didn't ask anybody anything. He did everything to please himself.

In 1946, at the beginning of the tour, after we'd played the state side in Adelaide, we were on the train going to Melbourne and Wally Hammond called Len and I in. He told us then that we were going to play until after the first Test in Brisbane, so we knew we were in the side then. After that match the three of us went down to Sydney while the rest of the team went to an up-country match.

The day before we left he told us that we would be starting off at ten o'clock the following morning. He had a Jaguar at his disposal you see, a big, quick Jaguar. He was a good driver too. He drove every inch of the way from Brisbane to Sydney and he scarcely spoke a word except: 'Light me a cigarette.' He was so disappointed with the result in Brisbane, where we'd lost by an innings and 332 runs.

We got so many hundred miles on the way, and when the petrol tank was nearly down he said: 'Right, we'll fill up with petrol and try and get a room for the night.' So we pulled up and he'd hardly spoken a word. In Australia in those days you couldn't get petrol after six o'clock so we went to a small country hotel and asked if there was any possibility of accommodation, but there wasn't. Len and I had to go and knock somebody up to get us some petrol and he drove us on down to Sydney from that moment onwards.

We got to Sydney and there were four days in which Len and I were free, and himself of course. He put us down at the hotel and said 'Cheerio,' and we didn't see him again until four days afterwards. Amazing fellow. He was most disappointed with losing the Test in Brisbane, which wasn't the fault of Len or I at all, though neither of us had got many runs. It was the fault of the wicket. Wally was a difficult man to live with. He never asked anybody their opinion. He always got the side he chose for the Test match too. 'Oh well, leave it to me,' he'd say after you'd talked for an hour or so.

Wally had more power and more stamina as a batsman than Len; he could go on and make runs for as long as he wanted, and he could bowl too, when he wanted to. He was a great cricketer and I admired him for that but I wouldn't say he was a good touring captain because at the end of the day it was: 'Goodbye skipper'. He didn't mix very much at the end of the day, but I can't help but admire him.

Denis Compton was a great stroke-player. He did all sorts of fancy things and he was a very entertaining batsman, but not the easiest batsman to be in with. There was always the great danger of being run out because he hadn't got much idea of what was a short run, and he'd be halfway down the pitch before he'd said anything – very difficult. He was a great fellow, marvellous chap, but a bit unreliable when he was striking the ball, and when you were batting with him there wasn't much ease of mind. You had to be on top of your toes when he was batting. He was much more difficult to bat with than

Len, you didn't know where you were with him, but he was such a popular chap that people put up with it, more so than they did with others, I suppose. He was a great player, a great entertainer, but a very difficult partner to have at the other end of the pitch.

With Len and me, I don't think either of us ever dominated the partnership at all. We just had confidence in each other and accepted that. If he said: 'Come one,' I went one; if I said: 'Come one,' he came one. This thing builds up over a period of time and you have confidence. If he says: 'Come one,' you know that he means it but with Denis, he says: 'Come one,' he'll be half way down the wicket and then go back again. It's a great thing to have confidence in your partner. I had in Len, and I hope that he had with me.

Freddie Brown wasn't the greatest captain in the world either, he was rather difficult. He wasn't in the same street as Wally or somebody like R. W. V. Robins, who was a good captain too. I played under him once against New Zealand in 1937. It would have been very nice to have played under Len as captain.

I think he was very pleased when I was recalled against Australia in 1956 after an interval of time. I'm told he was anyway. I went in to bat at Leeds when we were 17 for 3 wickets. I shall remember that score to my dying day. I stayed with my captain, Peter May, until he got out in the last over or two for 101. I got 98.

Len was a truly great batsman, there's no doubt about that. I was pleased to play with him. Our most successful tour together was to South Africa in 1948/49, where we made more runs than most people did. It was a very successful tour and a happy one too. George Mann was captain. He was a very nice chap and very keen on people doing the right thing, and he got a lot of support from everybody.

Len and I both had a fairly serious outlook on the game and we played it in a sound way. We didn't play shots like Denis did, those sort of shots weren't in our habit at all. You always like to see what the delivery is intended to be, but you can't with a fast bowler, it's not possible. You couldn't tell whether Lindwall was going to bowl a bouncer or not, but you could with Miller because he used to put his head down and tear up. That was why, perhaps, Lindwall was the greater of the two.

They may have thought Len had a weakness against the bouncer. Nobody likes bouncers at all. The great thing about fast bowling, as Maurice Leyland used to say, is: 'None of us likes it but some of us puts up with it better than others.' That's absolutely true. I'll never forget him saying that in his broad Yorkshire accent one evening after a match. I've never met anybody who said: 'I like fast bowlers and bouncers.' I've never met anybody who's been so bloody silly to say that, because it's dangerous. But you get a great feeling of satisfaction if somebody bowls you a bouncer and you hit him for six. It's marvellous then. I went after the bouncers more than Len did, but he was very sound and correct against every type of bowler. He'd got the answer to them all. He was a very great player.

Denis Compton

Born 1918. Middlesex (Joint Captain 1951–52): 1936–58. 78 Test matches: 1937–57. Hutton wrote of Compton: 'His secret is an abundant natural aptitude and a gift for improvisation that amounts almost to genius.' Two of his shots, the sweep and the cover drive, are legendary, as are his time-keeping and precarious running between the wickets. His best season was 1947, when he scored 18 100s and 3,816 runs. Surgery on his knee in 1949 restricted his agility in the field. In Tests he scored 5,807 runs at an average of 50.06. He also played on the wing for Arsenal.

People always think Len and I didn't get on – partly, I suppose, because of this rivalry between the North and South. We were actually great friends, particularly after his retirement. He came to live down in the south, near Coombe Hill Golf Club, and we were on the phone about once a week, talking about present-day cricket.

Len was a little older than me. We both got into the Test side for the first time in 1937 against New Zealand. He played in the first Test and got 0 and 1, and then he got 100 in his second Test at Old Trafford. I came in for the last Test and that's when I started my series of run-outs. I was run out at the Oval for 65 in my first Test innings. It was an extraordinary dismissal. Joe Hardstaff, batting at the other end, hit the ball back to the bowler so hard that he deflected it on to the wicket. That was rather tiresome.

I suppose I must have been playing with Len for the majority of his great innings. I contributed a single at the Oval in 1938. I watched Len get his 364 which, in those days, was a quite incredible feat of concentration; remarkable to spend that amount of time at the crease. Eddie Paynter and I had to sit for a day and three-quarters with our pads on. Eventually we looked up at the scoreboard and it was 400 and something for two and Eddie said to me, 'Denis, I bet you a pound we don't get 10 runs between us.' I looked at the board. Eddie had got 216 not out in the first Test at Trent Bridge and I'd got 100 and 76 not out in the second, and we were both in great form. A pound in those days was quite a lot of money so I said: 'Well Eddie, I'll have to take you up on that.'

When he did go in to bat, he was out first ball to O'Reilly. I went to the wicket thinking: 'Crickey, I've got to get 10 runs now.' I got one off the first ball from O'Reilly. I got up the other end and faced this fellow called Mervyn Waite, whom we'd never heard of. He was quite a gentle medium-paced bowler. It was a wonderful wicket, as you can imagine, and I thought: 'Bound to get 10 runs off this chap'. The first ball he bowled me was a very straight half-volley and I played a charming stroke through the covers: the stroke had charm but no contact. I was out for a single. Every time I went to Adelaide after the war Merv Waite, who's a lovely chap, used to phone me when I arrived: 'Compo, I'm going to buy you a beer.' About the third time this happened, I asked him why he kept wanting to buy me a beer and said I'd like to buy *him* one. 'That's the only Test wicket I ever got in my career', he replied.

I've seen all of Len's great innings. His double century in the last Test in the West Indies in 1954 was a truly remarkable innings. A lot of people didn't realise that he always played for his side and was a wonderful stroke-player. He scored a miniature 37 at Sydney in 1946. Even now, dear old Keith Miller, who's a great friend of mine, says to me: 'I shall never forget that innings.' He was out because his bat fell on the wicket. In that mood, if he'd have lasted another half an hour, he'd have got a 100.

He was such a great player that I don't think the injury to his arm made that much difference. Although he didn't hook after the war, I don't think he hooked much anyway. But he was a wonderful player against fast bowling. Like all of us, he says that if you're playing against extreme pace you must be a player off the back foot. I wonder if, perhaps, one of the reasons Graeme Hick is not succeeding too well against extreme pace is because he plays forward. If you play forward you're committed to the short ball and therefore, I would have thought, you become very vulnerable. Len and I used to discuss that. Len was a wonderful back-foot player and front-foot player; he hit the ball beautifully on the off-side and on the on-side. The hook was the one shot that Wally Hammond never played. Some of us played it, we liked playing it, and others didn't.

Len was the best batsman in the world I've ever known against the turning ball. In the days of uncovered wickets we had a lot of bad pitches, sticky wickets, and the ball turned at right angles. He was a master.

I opposed the change in the lbw rule and the no-ball law. People say it's a minor law, but I think the old rule is much better than the one they have today. A bowler should be punished for a no-ball. In the old days we had time to have a free hit and today there's no time because it's judged on the front foot.

Len used to move back, and then forward. I was different. I'm talking about playing against extreme pace, people like Lindwall, Miller, Tyson, Adcock, Heine, those boys. I would go onto the back foot before the ball was bowled, so my first movement was across. The reason I did that was that it gave me more time, I was there first. I didn't go back and then forward, I stayed back. People say: 'Well what happened if you were bowled a half-volley and you were on the back foot?' Well, I think I used to stroke the half-volley just as effectively off the back foot as I did the front. But that was me. I asked Keith Miller recently, because he's another great pal of mine and we speak regularly, what he didn't like about batsmen he bowled at in those days. He said: 'I hated batsmen who went onto their back foot and covered their wickets and I couldn't see the stumps.' And he happened to say that I was one of those because I went across.

I had the greatest possible admiration for Len in his balance and his stance at the wicket. He was beautifully balanced and you never saw him get off-balance, and he always, somehow, had lots and lots of time to play the ball. That, I always think, is the sign of a very great player, if you've got time to play the ball, you're not hurried in your shot. He was a wonderful judge of length; he knew when to go forward and when to go back, always.

I don't think we shall see the likes of Len again. His ability to concentrate for long periods was remarkable. I couldn't do that. I always used to play for my side, but if it didn't matter if I got out

Old campaigners: Hutton, Bedser and Compton at the dinner in Pudsey in 1988 to mark the fiftieth anniversary of his record innings of 364.

when I'd got 100 I'd give it away. If I had to go in when the score was about 250 for 2, or 300 for 2, I was off the boil before I started. That 300 I got in South Africa in three hours – I was trying to get out after the first 100, but I kept middling it all the time.

Boycott wasn't in the same class as Len. Although Len didn't set out to dominate the bowling, he did so when he wanted to. The difference between him and Boycott? Well, there were many differences. He was a far greater stroke-player than Boycott for a start. All the ordinary bowlers of today could curtail Boycott, but not Len. Boycott had wonderful talent, tremendous concentration, but he wasn't one of the batsmen that I'd want to watch. I'd always want to watch Hutton, even when he wasn't scoring many runs. To watch Len on those uncovered wickets, which Boycott didn't experience, against the turning ball, was fantastic.

When I played with Len he was very, very disciplined. He thought a tremendous amount about the game, so therefore, although he didn't lack a sense of humour, it was slightly less noticeable during his playing days. After he'd retired I suppose you could say that he mellowed considerably, but he was fun. He had a great interest in horse racing, you know. He used to phone me and say: 'What do you think about Ascot, Denis?' He used to tell me some remarkable things about form and all that, which is one thing you wouldn't have associated with Len. He liked a beer or a whisky.

He wasn't a very strong man. He was always on the frail side, and therefore his contribution to the game with the bat must have made it more tiring for him than for me, because I was always a big fellow, strong and all that sort of thing. So that's where he used to like a whisky at night, do him the world of good.

I didn't find him difficult to talk to when he was captain, but he took his responsibilities very seriously. He was always having to think about the game as well as his own form at batting. I never understood why he didn't captain Yorkshire. It was crazy. Captaining your county is almost an apprenticeship for captaining England, you're doing it all the time, but he was never doing it all the time. He was just captain for Test matches. I think he was a cautious captain, didn't really take any chances. Len was one of the captains who slowed the over rate down, but he had a lot of fast bowlers. I think, for a period, he probably had the best England bowling attack there's ever been, and the fastest. He had Tyson who, I would say without any hesitation, for three years, possibly two, was probably the fastest bowler that's ever been – well, the fastest I've ever seen. I played against Larwood, but only in 1936, when he was past his best. I faced him at Lord's, and a nice man he was too, and that was the fastest I'd ever experienced then and he was nearly finished. He had a wonderful action.

Len always recognised Lindwall as perhaps the greatest fast bowler. He also said that the one he found he didn't like, and never relished because of his amazing natural talent, was Miller. Len always used to tell me: 'You never bloody well knew what he was going to bowl and yet he didn't have to practise.' From his toes up to his head he was just full of natural talent. I was batting with Len up at Nottingham, when he got 74 against Australia and I happened to get 184, in the dark in the end. When Len got to 70, but for a disaster, you were very pushed to get him out. I was at the other end and Miller bowled him a delivery which pitched on the leg stump and hit the top of the off. It was the most wonderful delivery. I always remember Len acknowledging that to Keith Miller. He had a lot of respect for Miller's talent.

Miller was as quick as anybody in the world when he bowled a quick one, but he only did so occasionally. He could also bowl a googly, inswinger, outswinger. The point with Miller was that he also had the most wonderful action, everything right, and of course he could catch anything, catch a sparrow in the slips, brilliant fielder close to the wicket. Even though they never really got on and they had a lot of differences, I think Bradman had the greatest possible admiration for Miller's ability.

I played against Bradman in 1938 and 1946–47, and he was the greatest batsman that I ever played against, and saw, inasmuch as he always hit the bad ball for four, no question. He was a terrific player, never hit the ball in the air. I only just saw Jack Hobbs, but he was my idol when I was a schoolboy. My father used to take me to the Oval to see him play. He obviously must have been one of the greatest. Two great innings, apart from Len's, which stand out from 1938

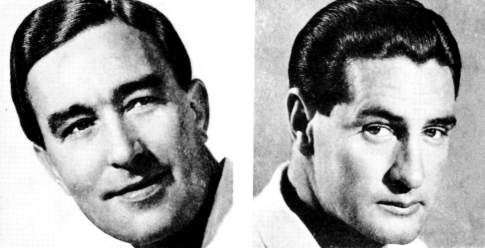

Brylcreem boys Denis Compton and Keith Miller in an advertisement from the 1950s. Hutton promoted cigarettes.

are Hammond's 240 at Lord's and Stan McCabe's 232 at Trent Bridge to save the match. That was when Bradman said to his team: 'Come and have a look at this, you may not see the like of it again.' I'm not sure that he wasn't right.

In the 1953 Test at Lord's Graveney had made 78 the night before, a very beautiful, graceful, elegant innings. The next morning the new ball was due and I was the next batsman in. Lindwall bowled the first ball of the morning with the old ball, but it was as fast as if it had been the new ball. Tom was yorked, out for 78. That's why Lindwall was a truly great bowler; he used to think about it. Immediately I came to the wicket Lindwall took the new ball. For about an hour and a half Len and I were subjected to the fastest sustained spell by two bowlers that I've ever experienced before or since. The ball was fizzing about and they seemed to be upset. I don't know whether or not they were, but they wanted to get rid of one or both of us.

There was a full house and the atmosphere was absolutely electric. In the middle of all this Len called me up the wicket and I said, 'Yes, Len, what is it, old boy?' He said, 'Denis, I've been thinking. I was thinking that there must be a better way of earning a bloody living than this!' And he walked away. He got 145 and I got 57. I'd survived all that and we were playing so well; the very first ball Benaud bowls me, I gave a very lackadaisical push and was caught at slip. I was so angry with myself after surviving all the hard stuff.

I didn't actually know too much about Alec Bedser being dropped at Melbourne in 1954. I knew that Alec was very disappointed. Alec had been a very great bowler, there's no question about that, particularly when conditions suited him, when wickets were slightly green and the ball moved. He could bowl a leg-cutter better than anybody in the world; big hands. But in 1954 he'd had shingles, which you don't recover from too easily, so I don't think he was 100 per cent fit. Len would find it very difficult to go up to a great bowler like Alec and say: 'I'm sorry but I can't really find room for you in my team,' even though it was the right decision at the time.

Surprisingly, I think Len would have been a star in one-day cricket. I watched Botham bowling Border out in the World Cup on television. Everybody said that was one of the greatest balls that's ever been bowled. I said: 'Leonard Hutton would have played that with the greatest of ease in the middle of the bat.'

Another thing about Len was that he could spot players with talent immediately. I always said, and Len agreed, that the best post-war batsman in England was Peter May. He was a magnificent player. Wonderful off the back foot. We always used to emphasise the back foot. You'll notice today that the majority of the players are front foot.

I don't know of any bowler today who would hold any terror for Len. He was a master. I put him down in the first four of the greatest in the world. You've got Bradman, Hobbs, Hammond and Hutton. All round I would put Hutton before Hammond. I think if Wally was slightly vulnerable he would be vulnerable against the real quicks, but he didn't play against too many, not really quick.

The one big partnership I had with Len was in 1939. It was at Lord's against the West Indies. Len got 196 and I got 120. The two of us played against 'Manny' Martindale and I can tell you he wasn't slow, he was quick, a fine bowler. Len played a masterly innings, outstanding.

At the Oval against the West Indies in 1950, it looked as though Len and I were going to have a terrific partnership. Len went on to score 202 not out, but I was run out on 44. He played the ball down to short fine-leg and I said: 'Come on Len,' because the ball went behind him, and off I went. We would both have got in easily but no, he turned me back. It was extraordinary. It was one of those things. I got so used to misunderstandings and run-outs. Someone once said about me that whenever I called my partner for a run it was purely and simply a basis for negotiation.

Len was a good fielder and, whenever he was out of the slips, he could throw. He had a good arm when he wanted to use it. In the early part of my career I was always on the boundary, so I had a good arm. After my knee injury, that restricted me a bit, I had to come close to the wicket. Colin Bland was the best fielder I ever saw, without a shadow of a doubt, magic. Neil Harvey was wonderful too. Bradman was still a brilliant fielder in 1938, a very accurate thrower from cover-point. Bowlers should never field close to the wicket. Most of them can throw a ball and the ideal place for them is on the boundary. Trueman and Statham both had wonderful arms. Miller was a wonderful catcher and so was Lindwall, funnily enough, close to the wicket.

I suppose Len mellowed a little bit after he retired. He'd done England proud, he'd done Yorkshire proud, and he'd done a great service to the game of cricket. A master player. Among the best four batsmen who ever played – and that's saying something.

Godfrey Evans

Born 1920. Kent: 1939–59. 91 Test matches: 1946–59. Godfrey Evans was England's wicket-keeper for thirteen years. A great show-man, he was energetic and acrobatic with boundless enthusiasm. He was the first wicket-keeper to reach 200 dismissals and score 2,000 runs. To witness Alec Bedser bowling with Evans standing up to him was to see cricket at its best. In 1967, eight years after his retirement, he was recalled to play for Kent in place of Alan Knott, who was playing his first Test for England. He became a bookmaker's representative after retirement.

I met Len once or twice during the war when we were both in the army. But it wasn't until after the war that we became friends. Kent played Yorkshire at Tunbridge Wells in 1947 and we beat them. I remember Len making 74 against Doug Wright, who was bowling very well at the time. Len was so correct, he kept the bat so straight. He very seldom played across the line, which was very noticeable to me. He had some very good footwork and he was able to play on bad wickets so well because he had the dead bat. He had the bat slanting so that when the ball came up, when the ball was turning a little bit, instead of travelling fast to first slip it would drop short because he had the bat at an angle. That's why he was so good on bad wickets. His defence was so sound.

He didn't go out of his ground very often. I remember seeing him stumped in a Lord's Test Match once against Valentine. But I didn't see him stumped many times.

Len was a great player of any bowling. When Australia came over with Lindwall and Miller, they were the fastest pair we'd met, and he played them beautifully. He got his regular amount of runs.

I kept against him sometimes in the Test trials when they used to have the batsmen versus the bowlers. I'd usually be on the bowling side, so I had a chance to see him then. There wasn't a much better player than him really.

We went to Australia in 1946 and the first Test Match I played with Len in Australia was in Sydney. Don Bradman and Sidney Barnes got 234 apiece. After they'd put on over 400 I can remember Len putting his hand on my shoulder and saying: 'You know, Godfrey, there's nawt for it but to run buggers out.' His Yorkshire dry humour, it was lovely. He had a lovely sense of humour, very dour, but a lovely sense of humour.

I thought that Len would make a great captain. It was after Freddie Brown's tour to Australia and Len had had a pretty good time out there. One couldn't think of a better player to do it really. He never lost a series. When I look back on my career and I'm asked who was the best, and greatest, captain I played under, I'd say Len Hutton because he was so good. He wasn't always popular with everybody but he had a method of getting the best out of people, which was where I think he had it over most people.

A little incident that I can quote is when he came to me, towards the end of a day, and he said: 'Do you think you can get Freddie (Trueman) to bowl the last two or three overs?' I said: 'Haven't you asked him?' He said: 'Yes, but I've been giving him so much bowling he's just about had it.' I said: 'I'll have a word with him.' I went up and asked Fred how he was doing. 'I'm bloody knackered,' he said. Anyway, I said: 'Look, the fellow batting this end, I think he's fright-ened of you. In the next over bowl a bouncer on the fourth ball and see what happens because I think he's frightened of you.' He said: 'I'm not going to bloody bowl another over.' I said: 'Oh, I don't know Fred. If he's frightened of you I think it's worth it. Only a few more overs to go, the end of the day, and we shall be on the old toot with a gin and tonic shortly.' He said: 'Oh well, all right then.'

I primed the slips and leg slips and told them: 'On the fourth ball Fred's going to bowl a bouncer and whatever ball it is make certain you say "Well bowled, Fred".' So Fred came up, very tired, and bowled this bouncer. It was a little like a tennis ball and the batsman looked disdainfully at it. True to their word, everybody said: 'Well bowled, Fred'. Fred couldn't understand this. 'Well bowled? It must have been a better ball than I thought it was.' The next ball he bowled a super bouncer, it nearly knocked the batsman's head off, and every-body said again: 'Well bowled, Fred'.

At the end of the over I went up and said to Fred: 'It's a pity you're going to come off.' 'Come off!' he said. 'I'm not coming off now. I see what you mean now, Godders.' That was a method of Len's to get the best out of somebody if he couldn't do it himself. I suppose it's called the art of delegation, and he was very good at it.

There were one or two times when it didn't work, when it worked the other way. When he asked Alec Bedser in Melbourne to go and have a look at the wicket, Alec thought that he was in the team. And then, when he came back, he was left out. It was unfortunate because we had Frank Tyson in the team and everyone on the committee had voted that Alec should play. I had pointed out the fact; I said to Len, Denis (Compton) and Bill Edrich: 'Who would you sooner bat against, Frank Tyson or Alec Bedser?' They said they'd sooner bat against Alec Bedser, however good he was, because Frank was very quick.

That was the choice. When Len heard this, that the boys would sooner bat against Alec Bedser, no matter how good he was, than against Tyson, who was much quicker and put the fear of God into a few batsmen, he thought: 'Well, that must apply to the Australian batsmen as well'. So he included Frank Tyson and of course we won the series through that. Alec was a great bowler but he did have shingles on the way out to Australia.

That's why I say he got the best out of people. Len would make his own decisions, but if he got an idea . . . we just planted an idea in his head. He seemed to pick the right idea all the time and that's why I say he was a very good captain. He seemed to be able to sift all the information that he'd got and then pick the best course.

Before the third Test in Melbourne, Len wanted to stay in bed, he wasn't very well. Bill Edrich came to me and said: 'Godders, I think we'd better go up and see Len, he doesn't want to go to the ground.' I said: 'What do you mean. He's got to come; one-all going to Melbourne. He's our captain. It doesn't matter if we've got to carry him out there on a sick-bed.' I think perhaps what had happened was that Len realised that we were one-all and his mental approach was a little bit cautious, having won one against Australia. This was a great feat in those days because we didn't win many against Australia, and he felt he should consolidate.

We got him down there and we told him that he needn't go in first if he didn't want to, but he had to captain the side. Think what a tremendous boost it would give to Australia if he didn't go in. Bill and I went up and literally almost dressed him and got him down to the ground. Basically, Bill was the main instigator of that. He just wanted a little bit of help and I was the best man to go up there. It was a mental strain for Len because he wasn't a very strong individual as such. He was a great player with great technique, but he wasn't all that strong.

An England captain hadn't won in Australia for a long time. Freddie Brown was the last, with just the one Test. To go through the whole tour with pressure like that was getting him down a bit, and I think the press got him down, too. He didn't ever like the press very much when he was playing. He probably thought they were all right when he was writing for them – different story!

We lost the first two Tests in the West Indies on the 1953–54 tour and I think, to a certain degree, without being unkind to Len, it was his method. When things went a bit against us he got worried about it, and because he was a bit worried about it he tried to tell us not to do this or that, not to go to parties. I think that was a mistake.

He suddenly realised after we were two down: 'Oh well, it doesn't matter now, give the boys their heads.' In the end we came out and we drew the series. That was a fine bit of bowling by Trevor Bailey at Sabina Park in the final Test. On a perfect wicket we lost the toss and we thought: 'Oh Christ, that's done it, Weekes, Worrell and Walcott, their tremendous batting side.' And then, all of a sudden, Trevor came along and got 7 for 34. We bowled them out for 139 and that gave us the match.

Driving with one hand against Australia in 1953 – Hassett ducks while Benaud at slip and keeper Langley look on. His left arm often ached after a long innings.

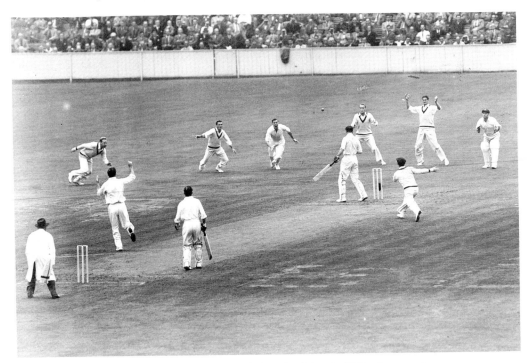

The moment when England nearly lost the Ashes in 1953; a bouncer from Lindwall knocks off Hutton's cap, which falls on the stumps but fails to dislodge a bail.

The victorious skipper on the balcony savouring the crowd's applause at the Oval, 1953.

Cutting the celebration cake with Lindsay Hassett and the England and Australian teams.

People like Bill Edrich, Denis Compton and myself are not people who dislike the opposition just because they win. We want to go and have a drink with them, congratulate them if they win, be friendly with them. Len's attitude was: 'Oh, keep away from the buggers. If we frighten them on the field we don't want to . . .' That wasn't our attitude at all and I think that's what got under the skin of a few players. They thought: 'Who the hell does Len think he's talking to, telling us we mustn't do things like that?' In the end, as I say, he realised he was wrong and he was very clever at putting things right without appearing to do anything. Slowly doing it by saying: 'I didn't mean don't go to parties, just be careful', that sort of thing.

During our partnership in the fifth Test, on the 1953–54 tour to the West Indies, when Len got a magnificent 200, he used to come up and say to me: 'Try not to get out, Godders.' He knew I was a bit of a tempestuous batsman, though I could stay there as long as anybody, as I had proved. When I did get out, I was caught trying to hit Ramadhin over the top for six. I thought: 'Cor, what's the captain going to say to me now?' I shouldn't have done it. We won the match, so it didn't matter, but he could have given me a right rollicking. He didn't throw his wicket away and he didn't like to see others throw theirs away. There were times when I got out and he would quite rightly come and say: 'Not in very good form at the moment, go and get some practice'.

I remember a magnificent cover drive during that innings of 205. I couldn't believe it, off Ramadhin too. Len went down the track and he hit this one like a rocket, straight to the boundary, and it took my breath away. He used to play some good innings during the Scarborough Festival at the end of the season, Gents versus Players, that sort of thing, but that was the best shot I ever saw him play. He used his feet; down the wicket and crack. It was one of the hardest shots that I've ever seen. He was quite a frail individual, but his timing was superb.

He played Ramadhin off the pitch. He'd let the ball bounce and play back or else he got to the pitch of the ball. That's how great players used to play. Wally Hammond used to play it off the pitch. He didn't necessarily know which way it was going, but if it was short he'd go back so that he could watch it turn, and if it was well pitched up he'd cover the spin. Len did the same.

Len was a great admirer of, and always wanted to be like, Herbert Sutcliffe as an opening batsman. And wanted himself to be like Jardine, a strict man, but he wasn't that strict. He had these ideals of people and he thought about them, people who won. He always looked up to people who won. Jardine went out to Australia with the specific purpose of winning and Len was in the same mould, though not quite so dramatic in the way he did it. He wanted to win.

I helped a lot, I think, because Len came up to me more often than he would to anybody else. Because we were friends on and off the field, he most probably had a little bit more to do with me than anybody else. So he could come to me and say: 'Well, what do you think, Godfrey?' That sort of business. Although I wasn't a senior selector I was a selector, so he was well within his rights. He'd still come to me more than anybody else perhaps.

He was a bit of a loner. When we won the Ashes in 1953, everyone went haywire. It was the first time we'd won them for a long time. After the match at the Oval we gave it a bit of hammer and we did the same out in Australia in 1955. Leonard was very good for a party, although he wouldn't over-stretch himself. He wouldn't go out of his way, or do anything wrong to prejudice his position. After all, he got a knighthood for doing the right thing; well-deserved, too.

He didn't relax very much on tour, that's what his trouble was. He was tensed up, praying to God he was going to win at all costs. He didn't bat badly when he was captain, but it must have put a strain on him. I should think his happiest tour was when he won the Ashes in Australia, but that's only because he won. He set out to win and he did what he set out to do. Once you do a thing like that, you've got the confidence of the whole team, to a certain degree, and he was always wary about not doing well as captain because he'd been so successful. That's why he was so upset being two down after two in the West Indies after winning the Ashes in England. The mere fact that we were supposed to win got on top of him a bit and he had to realise that the be-all and end-all in life isn't winning at cricket; so let's go out and enjoy ourselves a little bit.

He was a very good golfer. He ended up with a handicap of three or four, which is good golf. That shows his concentration. He was straight on the golf course. He didn't stray off the straight and narrow very much, rather like himself.

I saw him play such a lot of good innings. I remember him making 202 not out against the West Indies at the Oval in 1950. I wasn't keeping in that match because I was injured, but I saw most of it. That was a fine innings, but Len hadn't got enough batsmen to stay with him.

His 37 at Sydney in 1946 was a magnificent innings, it was fantastic. It was the first time, really, that I saw Len go for the bowling from the start, against Lindwall and Miller, those two greatest bowlers of their time. He was driving and cutting. He was only there for about twenty minutes. The whole of the Sydney Cricket Ground stood up to him when he got out and it was mainly due to his weak arm that he did get out. He said: 'If only I'd been able to hold onto that bat. It was due to my weak wrist that the bat came out of my hands and went onto the stumps.' I think he just wanted to prove that he was the best opening batsman in the world, and I think he was at that time. He had no responsibility. He wasn't captain. He just went out there and cracked the ball all over the place. It really was superb.

We always used to have a pre-match dinner. Shortly after Len had been made captain, we had this dinner and he tried to change his accent from a broad Yorkshire accent to rather an Oxford-type accent. I remember him saying: 'Now lads, I do not wish to see you flail your bat outside the off stump to Lindwall and Mr Miller.' And then, in broad Yorkshire: 'Just cut out the cutting, or if you cannot do anything else just bloody duck!' He got the accents muddled up and it was very funny.

He was always amusing. He'd come out with stories of days gone by, of Abe Waddington who played for Yorkshire and had a bit of money. You could listen to Len for quite some time and reminisce about days gone by. Often, we used to sit down in the evening, ten of us round a table, and he'd come out with these wonderful stories about 'Ticker' Mitchell of Yorkshire.

I used to see him at Lord's for the Test matches after his retirement. 'I've got lunch with Paul Getty today, Godders', he'd say. 'Well you'll be all right, then, you won't need to buy a drink', I said. 'He's got a few bob hasn't he?' he said. He had this lovely knack of not saying much, but you couldn't help laughing at what he said. It was this dour Yorkshire humour that he'd got. It kept him a bit aloof, I think, but when he let his hair down he was as good as anybody at it. He liked his Scotch; he was very fond of a drop of Scotch.

He was a great player, so he had an advantage when he was captain. Everybody, didn't matter who it was, looked up to him. If someone like that makes mistakes you don't criticise them too much. I think he got away with a few things because he could foresee a method of winning a match. And, all right, if he had to slow the game down, so he slowed the game down. Then he'd say: 'Well, I think we can try and get a few more runs than normal because the bowling isn't all that clever', or: 'The wicket's nice and true.' In that way he'd always give you a helping hand. He wouldn't say much but he'd drop a little hint, and it's those hints that keep on being dropped that let you get the gist of the fact that we've got to score runs quickly; or we mustn't get out; or this, that or the other.

It was his dry humour, I think, that got him over all the problems, and he was one of the great players. A very important thing. Everybody knew that he was a great player, therefore whatever he said was taken quite seriously. I think that because he was such a great player he was made captain.

He thought about the game a bit. He thought about the game more for himself than for other people. He worked out what he should do and how he'd go about it, but he sometimes found difficulty in passing information on without it being bravado, if you see what I mean. He was a bit quiet about passing information on, but it got to you in the end by this lovely type of accent that he'd got. That gave you a little bit of confidence, even though it wasn't said in such a manner. He was very popular in life after he'd finished playing.

Trevor Bailey and Alec Bedser

(talking to Donald Trelford)

Bailey: *Born 1923. Cambridge University and Essex (Captain 1961–66): 1946–67. 61 Test matches: 1949–59. Trevor Bailey was a genuine Test all-rounder – a steady, often slow-scoring batsman and a right-arm fast-medium bowler. He opened the bowling with Bedser in the late 1940s and early 1950s and then supported Tyson and Statham. P. G. Wodehouse once wrote of him: 'Bailey awoke from an apparent coma to score a boundary.' He had an astute tactical awareness and would have captained England but for a newspaper article he wrote on returning from the West Indies in 1954. He is now a cricket writer and radio broadcaster.*

Bedser: *Born 1918. Surrey: 1939–60. 51 Test matches: 1946–55. Off an economical run-up, Alec Bedser bowled right-arm medium-pace with great control and a variety of late movement. During the post-war years he carried the England attack almost single-handed and during the 1950s he helped Surrey win seven consecutive Championships. Both Bradman and Hutton rated him among the best they faced and it was one of the hardest decisions Hutton had to make when he dropped him in Australia in 1954/55. He was the longest-serving England selector from 1962–81, chairman from 1969. In 1987 he was President of Surrey.*

AB: When Len was younger, he took a bit of understanding. No one knew him in the early days, not when I first played, he just kept himself to himself, very private.

DT: People say he developed more of a personality after he retired.

AB: He was like a lot of cricketers. They suddenly realise that you rely on a lot of other people to get you a living. And when you go out into the world and try and sell something, or try and represent someone, you've got to be a bit different from when you were a batsman playing for yourself.

DT: Neither of you played with him before the war?

AB: I met him before the war, but I didn't play with him. I was at the Oval for the last two days of that 364.

DT: Was Len's technique very obviously different after the war because of his injury?

AB: I saw him before the war and the main thing he did that he never did after the war was hook.

TB: He never hooked. I never saw him before the war, but I suspect that he was a back-foot player. After the war he was primarily a front-foot player. He was one of the very few great front-foot players.

By and large, the great player, as distinct from the ordinary player, is either a front or a back-foot player. The majority are back-foot players. Len was a front-foot player; so were Tom Graveney and Graeme Pollock. Len was probably a back-foot player before the war. His mentor was Sutcliffe, who was certainly a back-foot player.

AB: I remember him in 1946. He always used to go back a little bit first, ready to play forward. Unlike Hick, who's forward before the ball's bowled.

DT: How did you rate him to bowl against?

AB: He was a fine player of course, but I never really wondered where I was going to bowl next to him. That is what I always say was the difference between him and Denis Compton. When Denis was on song you wondered what you were going to do next, but not with Len or with Colin Cowdrey. If you bowled them a good ball they played it as a good ball, so I never felt they'd take me apart. Denis was a different type of player altogether.

TB: Mind you, Alec, you were basically an in-swing bowler.

AB: He didn't like in-swing or off-spin.

TB: Because he was a front-foot player. Denis was a much better player of in-swing or off-spin, but I'd say that Len was a much better player of away-swing and the left-armer.

AB: I don't know whether it was because he couldn't extend his arm enough, but there was always a bit of a gate there really. Len always had a bit of a gate.

TB: I was a front-foot player. Len wanted me to open and I opened a lot as a result of that, because I was a front-foot player. I always found it more difficult to play off-spin and in-swing than away-swing and left-arm. Normally the outstanding player (and I wasn't an outstanding player) is worried by the ball which pitches and leaves them. That one never really worried me – not that I didn't get out to it sometimes.

AB: You'd have missed it!

TB: I'd got a fair old chance against that one, but the in-swing I found more difficult. And Len, who was a different class, had exactly the same problem. Ian Johnson got him out quite a lot.

AB: Reggie Perks used to get him out. But he played the slow left-handers and the ball going away from him. I should think it was the same before the war, because Jack Cowie, the New Zealander, used to get him out and he bowled in-swing, made the ball come back. He was definitely a wee bit suspect to the off-spinner.

DT: What was it that distinguished Len? Was it his Yorkshire character, the grit, the concentration?

AB: I don't accept the bit about Yorkshire grit. A lot of blokes outside Yorkshire had tons of grit. In a way there was a bit of Boycott in Len. They were the same type of people.

TB: Exactly the same.

AB: The difference is that Boycott was objectionable and Len wasn't.

DT: Was Len technically superior to Boycott? His record's better.

TB: He was beautiful and Boycott's never been beautiful.

Hutton massages the back of his knee as he is trapped lbw by Alec Bedser
after scoring 104 for Yorkshire against Surrey at the Oval in 1952.

AB: I think Len was a far better player than Boycott. Boycott's a made player, Len was totally different. I couldn't compare the two really. Boycott's done a fine job, but he just wasn't as good a player. Len was a natural player.

TB: And a beautiful player to watch. Len's forward defensive was worth watching, everything he did was always elegant, he was a beautiful looking player. He had grace. He got 196 when he was about 18. You'd got to be very good to get into that Yorkshire side before the war, because it was a very tight-knit little community. The sad thing was that just before the war we had the four best young professional batsmen this country has ever produced: Hutton, Compton, Hardstaff and Bill Edrich. They were all just coming to their peak when the war started.

AB: You could put Gimblett into that list too, almost.

DT: How old were you during the war, Alec?

AB: I joined up in 1939 when I was twenty and I was twenty-seven when I came back.

DT: The key years for a bowler.

AB: Well, I'm not sure about that. I often look back and think that probably one of the best things that happened to me was that for two and a half years I didn't play. When I did come back I'd stopped growing. The important thing was my ligaments and my tendons, which a specialist told me don't finish growing and developing until you're twenty-five. So if you don't really strain them . . . I just wonder what would have happened to me if I'd have been asked to bowl 1,300 overs in a season when I was twenty-three.

DT: It's a criticism I hear of Gooch, that he doesn't nurse bowlers, whereas Len did, didn't he?

TB: Len certainly nursed Tyson but he was the only one he really nursed. He let the others go.

AB: You talk about Gooch. A captain asks a bowler how he feels and if he says he feels a bit knackered, you don't bowl him and that's it. I watched in Australia last year when Gooch was captaining Devon Malcolm. First of all he had him running round the Sydney Cricket Ground at ten in the morning and nearly killed him before they started. Then he put him on to bowl and he bowled for an hour and a half.

Len had a better understanding of bowlers. Wally Hammond understood as well. Sometimes, if I'd been bowling hard in county cricket, I'd say to Len: 'I don't want any nets, just a few balls.' And he'd say: 'Fair enough'.

DT: How do you rate Len as a captain?

AB: I thought he was very conservative really, particularly in picking his sides. In 1953 we went into three matches against Australia with only four bowlers. Len never told me anything, he'd never confide in me at all.

DT: What about that famous time when he left you out in Australia?

AB: No, he didn't tell me. I don't mind being left out, but I want to be told.

DT: Why didn't he tell you? Could he just not bring himself to do it?

AB: He didn't like to tell you, that's what it amounted to really.

DT: You had been unwell, though, hadn't you?

AB: I should have gone home. I had the shingles. I shouldn't have played in Brisbane, that was my big mistake.

DT: So you're not querying the rightness of the decision, but the way it was done?

TB: Actually, it was a wrong decision.

AB: I was getting better then. I shouldn't have played in Brisbane. It was a curious thing because I had shingles and I didn't know what shingles was at all and nobody said, 'You shouldn't do anything for three months.' When I played against Queensland in Brisbane, it was wet and the ball moved around all over the place. I got a couple of wickets and we bowled them out fairly quickly. But it dried up for the Test match and after I'd bowled for about 50 minutes I was knackered.

DT: Why was it wrong to leave Alec out at Sydney then?

TB: It happened to be a swing bowler's wicket as distinct from a seam bowler's wicket. It was one of the very few Test matches when I bowled swing as distinct from seam. I was really a seam bowler rather than a swing bowler and I got quite a few wickets in that game. It swung around from the word go. Alec was a different class as a swing bowler and would have had an absolute field day. We'd have won a lot easier and I very much doubt if I'd have got on to bowl. But whether we'd have won the next Test at Melbourne, which was won by Tyson's pace, is an entirely different story. His pace was tremendous and he got through on pace, but at Sydney Alec would have had a great Test match.

DT: Trevor, you went on Len's tour to the West Indies in 1953–54. I gather it was an uncomfortable tour socially.

TB: Yes. The MCC, in their wisdom, picked a captain who'd never captained a touring side, a vice-captain who'd never been to the West Indies before and a manager who was a player/manager who'd never been to the West Indies. It was not the ideal get-together for a tour when the West Indies was just approaching independence and in a very political mood. No, that wasn't an easy tour.

DT: I gather Len didn't like his players socialising with the opposition off the field.

AB: That's what he said to me. In 1946 there was six o'clock closing in Sydney. You couldn't get a drink after six so what used to happen was that Lindwall, Miller and Hassett used to get a barrel of beer and three or four of us used to go into their dressing-room and sit there and polish it off before we went home. We'd have a really good sociable evening with them and we all became great mates. You've got to realise, too, that I was in the war with Miller and one or two others, so you're not going to refuse to have a talk to them, are you? We'd all been in the services and the fact that you'd been in the war gave you a totally different outlook on life. Anyway, I used to go in there every night, and sit there until we'd polished off the beer. It wasn't a very big keg of beer so it didn't take very long to drink and we'd be away by a quarter past seven. And then in 1954, when he was captain, Len said to me that he didn't want me to go into the Australian dressing-room. 'Bollocks,' I said. The majority of the younger ones, Peter May and people, just cleared off because they thought they would upset Len.

DT: Did Fred Trueman misbehave in the West Indies and was that why he didn't go to Australia in 1954?

TB: Yes and no. A bit of both. He was very young. It was Len's first tour as captain. I was a very inexperienced vice-captain and Charlie Palmer had never been to the West Indies. If you want a recipe for disaster, that was it. Basically, you want a manager who can mould with your captain, otherwise you've got nothing. Charlie Palmer was pretty ineffectual. Len was very good *on* the field but off the field . . .

AB: Len never bothered. He was a chap who didn't communicate to anyone at all, all the time I knew him. When he played, he was so absorbed in what he was doing himself . . .

DT: About his game?

AB: Everything. Just to give you an example, I had these shingles and I lay in a bed in Perth for ten days and he never came to see how I was all the time I was lying there. Only because he didn't think about it.

DT: How did Len treat you as bowlers?

TB: I set my own field. If he'd set a field for me I would have been very annoyed.

AB: So would I.

TB: There wasn't very much wrong with Len as a tactical captain. He was very shrewd in the field. He was probably a little bit too pace-conscious.

DT: The Australians say that Len was the first to slow the game down deliberately as a ploy.

AB: The first to do so obviously. In 1954 my brother Eric was broadcasting and it took fourteen minutes once for Tyson and Statham to bowl two overs. Eric timed it because he used to have to sit and try to fill in. Len came to me once, when we were playing New South Wales, and said: 'You bowl your overs too quickly.' I knew what he meant, of course, but I claimed innocence and said: 'Why? What do you mean?' He said: 'The less balls you bowl the less runs they're going to get.' So I said, 'Have you ever thought that the more balls I bowl the more wickets I'm going to get?' And he walked away then. He was a funny mixture old Len was.

DT: But there was a brain twinkling away there.

TB: Oh yes, there was no shortage of brain about Len. One of his problems, and this probably applies to Boycott too, was that he couldn't believe that anybody wanted to be the friend of Len Hutton without an ulterior motive.

AB: He always wanted contacts with money. When he had his first contract with the *Evening News* the opposition had signed up

Bradman, so they signed up another knight to compete. They gave him an Armstrong Siddeley and he went to pick the car up. It was full of petrol, this gleaming new motor car, and he looked in the glove box and said: 'There are no dusters in here.'

TB: This bloke in Johannesburg had looked after Len, loaned him his car and given him everything. This chap came to see Len off at the station and asked if he could have one of these miniature bats that Len used to get for nothing. Len produced it from his hand luggage and said: 'It'll be a fiver.' Five pounds was a lot of money in those days and he'd stayed with the bloke, been taken to golf with him and so on.

DT: Did he inherit all that from the Yorkshire dressing-room?

TB: Oh yes.

AB: Boycott's just the same now, so it must be a Yorkshire trait.

DT: I asked Len what Bradman was really like as a man and he said: 'Like Boycott'.

TB: The one thing you could always say against Boycott was that he could never actually dominate. Len could dominate. One of his great dominating innings was a flash, a little cameo of 37 at Sydney in 1946–47. Australians still talk of that as a cameo of brilliance. Boycott hadn't got the temperament to do that and it was certainly unusual for Len.

AB: That 37 was a fine innings. He hit his own wicket, his bat went over his head. I don't know why he did it in the context of the game. He got out, that's how I looked at it.

TB: On the tour to Australia we left behind Willie Watson, who actually could bat. He'd scored a century on every island on the previous tour. Len's one complaint about Willie was: 'It's too easy. It's too easy for him. He doesn't take it seriously enough.' Willie was a natural, a beautiful mover. He was rather like Gower, though not as flamboyant. Len's complaint was that it was too easy. It was extraordinary that Willie didn't come to Australia in 1954–55.

DT: I bumped into Peter May in Barbados in 1986 when Gower's team were really going down the tube and said to him: 'Nobody could have played these bowlers on these pitches. It's just not possible.' Peter turned to me quite crossly and said: 'Len did. Len did.'

TB: There wasn't anyone that fast bowling at him in 1953–54. Len got a marvellous 205 at Sabina Park. I opened with him. I played King and he played Gomez.

DT: What he meant was that it needed one innings to show everybody else that it could be done.

AB: Len was very good at making sure he was at the right end. In the early days I can remember two or three matches when he did that.

TB: That is class batting.

AB: That's selfishness. You wouldn't get Jack Hobbs doing that, he'd have taken the bowling.

TB: And 'Compo' would have.

AB: At Manchester against the South Africans in 1951, it was dark when Len went in with Ikin and McCarthy was bowling very fast. I reckon Len only had about fifteen per cent of the balls. Ikin faced them and he was a chap struggling to get into the side.

DT: Len took against certain players. He took against Graveney early on.

AB: He said he'd no guts. Tom was a fine player but it took a long time for him really to become a Test player.

DT: So Len was right in a way?

AB: Oh yes, I think he was right.

DT: Somebody said that Len thought the problem with Graveney was that he had a red face, meaning that he was a bucolic, relaxed sort of person, not taking things seriously enough.

AB: Well that's a funny remark to make and typical of old Len.

DT: And why did he take against Reg Simpson?

TB: Back-foot player. Len was always worried about the ball that was going to nip back, that's why he was on the front foot and that's why he wanted me to open. It was as simple as that. Simpson was a marvellous player of fast bowling because he was a good back-foot player.

There's one thing we haven't mentioned at all about Len so far. When we first played, the real criterion of a good player was if he was good on a bad wicket. To be called a good player on bad wickets was the supreme accolade, because you'd got a lot of players who could score a lot of runs on good wickets when the sun was shining, but it was getting runs when the ball was turning square or lifting.

AB: The other question was: 'Who did he get them against?'

TB: It was the bad wicket player who was always rather special and Len was a superb bad wicket player. In Brisbane 1950–51 we bowled Australia out for 228 on a beautiful wicket in the first innings and then it rained. Len came in at number six and he was the best player on a bad wicket by far. I eventually joined him and I reckoned I could bat on a bad wicket occasionally. It was lifting and it was very, very unpleasant. I batted with Len for about seven overs and he made it look easy. This, to my mind, was one of Len's great assets; he was a magnificent player on a bad wicket. He had the ability to adjust. As a result of getting his hand round he could come back, he could go forward, he went forward then he could come back and drop it dead. He was a beautiful bad wicket player.

DT: Len could never understand why Colin Cowdrey didn't make full use of his ability.

TB: Much too nice. He never really believed he was as good a player as he was. He lacked belief in himself.

DT: Not selfish enough, perhaps. Bradman was selfish, Hammond was selfish, Boycott was selfish.

AB: Any great batsman's a bit selfish. Frank Woolley, even Jack Hobbs, were selfish. In order to be a great run-getter you've got to be selfish. Ken Barrington used to be selfish.

TB: Bradman was a very selfish player in 1930. We've only known him when he's mellowed.

AB: They had to be selfish. There was another great thing in Australia pre-war. Don was Protestant and O'Reilly, Fingleton and all the people who criticised him, were Catholics.

TB: It was rather like Northern Ireland now – in cricket terms, that is.

AB: You look at the Australian side in 1938 and the people who were anti-Bradman were McCormick, O'Reilly and Fingleton . . .

TB: They wanted Grimmett and he'd brought Ward, who was a Protestant.

AB: I'll tell you a funny story about Len. The first ball after lunch at the Scarborough Festival I bowled the orange at Len, a full toss. He came forward instinctively and it covered him. It brought the house down, couldn't have gone better. He wanted to send me the cleaning bill.

AB: Old Len, there are so many stories against him, but he was a fine cricketer.

TB: I never had a cross word with him.

AB: Neither did I.

TB: We haven't discussed the fact that he was brought up in pre-war Yorkshire and this was before a social revolution. I played for the young amateurs of Essex when I was 14, before the war. The professional was meant to call me Mr Bailey. This was the set-up pre-war, and it overlapped to a certain extent post-war, and Len was brought up in this atmosphere.

AB: Len never got over it. He had this fixation. Boycott had it when he came to see me, that he was there under sufferance and that they didn't want him really, he wasn't an amateur.

TB: This must have affected Len. He was brought up in this very tight-knit atmosphere of the Yorkshire dressing-room.

AB: This was one of the things that Len never got over really. He always felt that he wasn't treated on the same plane as the amateurs. He used to think that he sat in the selection meetings because he was there under sufferance.

DT: He had a chip?

AB: Oh yes.

TB: On the other hand I can literally say that I never had a disagreement with Len the whole time I played with him. I think we probably both played the game with the same sort of outlook.

AB: I never had a disagreement with him about what we were going to do, because he never talked to me about it at all. I don't know why it was. On the 1954–55 tour Len asked me to be senior pro and I said: 'What for? You're the captain, you're a professional. What the hell do you want a senior pro for? It's pointless. What are you but the senior pro?'

DT: Did you have an edgy relationship with Len generally?

AB: No. I never said much to him, simply because he never came to me first. Once he became captain I thought that as captain he should promote himself to me, which he never did. But that didn't mean that I didn't do everything that I possibly could.

DT: I heard a story about Bobby Simpson playing for New South Wales against England on that tour. He'd got to 98 and there was just the very slightest sign of rain, nothing really, then he saw Len leading the team off the field. He was left standing in the middle. The batsmen hadn't been asked. There was an interval and when they all came back Simpson was out the next ball. He said that he'd always admired Len Hutton's captaincy after that.

TB: Len was a pretty good, shrewd captain. A little bit defensive; a little bit too pro-pace because he played spin better than he played pace, rather like Gooch.

AB: He's not the only one. Everyone's pro-pace.

TB: He didn't like Australians; understandable.

AB: I think, in the back of my mind, that if Len Hutton had been controlling my destiny I'd never have been any good at all. He'd never have thought I could have bowled – because I wasn't fast. But when Len matured, he was a totally different bloke.

DT: I never knew him when he was the hard figure you're talking about.

TB: He wasn't all that hard.

AB: He kidded himself that he was hard. He was uncommunicative. I never really knew him until after I finished playing.

TB: Len married a particularly charming woman and she made a hell of a difference. Dorothy was very, very good indeed for Len. She was marvellous. Two great cricketers with two great wives, one is 'The Don' and the other is Len.

One last story about Len. He comes in at tea at Sabina Park in Jamaica and he's about 180 not out. He's been batting for about a day and a half and as he comes up the steps a figure sways in front of him. Len pushes him to one side and comes into the dressing-room and we take his pads off, we smoke a cigarette for him. 'I'm so tired, I'm so tired,' he says. 'Come on Len, a few more runs,' we say. We drank a cup of tea for him and everything is fine until there's a knock on the door. I go to the door and this chap says: 'Your captain – he's insulted our Prime Minister.' We never told him and out he went and got a few more and we won the match, but that was an extraordinary performance.

He used to say to me: 'You're lucky you are, you're an all-rounder.' I couldn't understand and then I suddenly realised. 'When I'm playing for Yorkshire and I don't get a hundred I've failed,' he said. It was rather the same for Fred Trueman, if he didn't get five wickets he'd failed. As an all-rounder if I got fifty I was happy and if I got three wickets I was happy. With Len they wanted a hundred.

Colin Cowdrey

Born 1932. Oxford University (Captain 1954) and Kent (Captain 1957–71): 1950–76. 114 Test matches: 1954–75 (Captain 27 times 1959–68). Colin Cowdrey started his life in cricket by playing for Tonbridge at Lord's when he was thirteen and then playing for Kent while he was still at school. The first of his six tours to Australia was with Hutton in 1954/55 and his first Test century, 102 out of 191 in the third Test at Melbourne, was striking in its maturity. He was a beautiful stroke-player who had poise and balance but introspection led him, on occasion, to doubt his own abilities. He scored 22 Test 100s and has played in more Tests than any other England player, except Gower. After retirement he continued a distinguished career in cricket as President of MCC and chairman of the International Cricket Conference.

The first time Len and I ever played together was, I suppose, in the University Parks in Oxford, but my first real memory of him was when I watched him play four consecutive innings. He got a hundred against us at Canterbury in 1952 and then we drove together, with Godfrey Evans, to Scarborough, and he got a hundred in each innings for Yorkshire against the MCC, that's three in a row. The next match (Gentlemen v Players) was on the following day and he was out for 99. I ran him out, which was most unfortunate; I wish I hadn't. I was only a tiddler. Godfrey Evans was the chauffeur; I used to go with Godfrey a bit. I sat in the back with Godfrey and Len in the front. That was a wonderful eight-hour journey up, full of cricket chat, an insight into the oldies, as they were then.

Len, for me, had this deadish pan face but the most incredible light blue eyes. He had this twinkle when he smiled, his eyelashes went up, and then he looked at you. He had the most wonderful sense of humour, but he was always feeling his way with you as to whether you were really on his side. He had to establish that you were a good chap, and you were not trying to denigrate him in any way, or knock him. He had these defence mechanisms which could make him very difficult with people. Once I'd got past that, and I got past that pretty early, he took enormous pains to help me in all my cricket.

I played two innings in front of him which probably got me my place to Australia in 1954–55. I got 70 odd at Dover, when he was playing, in a Yorkshire v Kent match. It was a slightly dull game but I batted well and he had a brief word with me about certain shots I was playing. Then I got a hundred against him at Scarborough, against some quite good bowlers. It was the little things which attracted his attention about my game and the fact that I took it pretty seriously.

He was a tremendous friend to me, full of wit and wisdom. Not many people knew more about the game than he did. Obviously you could keep quoting Bradman, Hammond, Hutton, Hobbs. He was in a very top bracket as a batsman. I think he's possibly underestimated a bit, as we look back, because he was not so debonair as Denis Compton, who caught the eye. There's no doubt in my mind that he had the stiffest examination of any batsman in the history of the game: to come back, after six years of war, and to have opened the innings for England in 1946, 1948, 1950–51, 1953 and again in 1954–55, against the relentless attack of Lindwall, Miller, Johnston, all fast, hostile bowlers, absolute top exponents of their art. Just look at his record: it got better. In 1950–51 no one came up to his measurement at all. He averaged something over 80 in the Tests.

At that moment, I think, he stood out as one of the supreme batsmen the world has ever seen. He was different from the 'Don'. The 'Don' just kept scoring, kept moving the scoring along. Len got stuck a bit more. He was a terrific technician. His secret, like them all probably, was to think early and go late. That would be the thing I learnt from him: get your antennae out. He always used to say about me, very kindly, that I saw the ball early, earlier than most. I don't know quite what that meant, but he certainly saw the ball as early as anybody, but he then moved later than anybody. The more average the player the more he sees the ball a little later, and goes too early and gets bogged down.

I remember playing against Western Australia in my first innings with Len. I took a leg-stump guard. There was a left-arm quick bowler on and after my first over Len came down and said: 'No fine-leg. If he's got no fine-leg he's not going to bowl at leg-stump.' I moved my guard across and played easily. It was the first time I'd taken a centre guard. He also told me that when you do that, when you make any adjustment, you unhinge a bit, you unbalance, so you have to watch the gap you've left. He was a university don tutor rather than someone from the parade ground at Sandhurst, or the prep school teacher. I was a very interested pupil and he realised that. I wasn't just there grabbing the beer from him; I was very proud to be associated with him.

I was absolutely petrified running with him because of the fear of running him out. He didn't call very much. If he ran, he ran when he felt like it, so you had to be rather quick off the mark. I just had to watch and see and then go.

He was an outstanding character in a very passive sort of way. We didn't talk much when we were batting together. We'd meet in mid-wicket and he'd say: 'Well done, well done'.

I was so junior that I didn't know that there was any question of him not playing in the Melbourne Test in 1954, when he felt unwell. I think he found it difficult at the end, when he wasn't quite as good a player as he had been. He was struggling a bit at the end, not struggling badly, but when you've been as good as he was it was disappointing when he couldn't quite be the master again. I think he was just getting older, and that sharpness leaves you. The 'Don' was marvellous in 1948 when he came over here, he was a very sharp little man, but he would say he didn't play so well after forty, and Jack Hobbs would say the same, and yet Jack Hobbs made nearly a hundred centuries after his fortieth birthday. When I talked to him he said: 'You should have seen me when I was younger.'

My father died when we were on the boat going out to Australia in 1954. Leonard had been talking to my father at Tilbury, and before

we'd got to Perth he'd died, and I think that rather moved Leonard. I was the young man in the side and Len had said to my father: 'Don't worry, I'll keep an eye on him,' sort of thing. I think that may have influenced my relationship with Len, though I don't want to play it up too much. The fact that I showed him due respect, and was a bit of a fan/disciple, also played a part in establishing a rapport with him, though it's terribly difficult to say. I didn't spend a lot of time with him because he was much more senior than me. Funnily enough, we'd find ourselves playing golf together on Sundays; he loved his golf and there weren't a lot of us who played on that tour.

On the *Orsova* to Australia in 1954, flanked by the young Colin Cowdrey, George Duckworth and Alec Bedser. The tour brought triumph for Cowdrey, disappointment for Bedser.

He could be very difficult, especially with people who he felt weren't toeing the line, people who thought they knew it all. There were those who didn't have the same regard for him as others did. He had a great intuition as to whether someone liked him or not, and if they didn't he was liable to go back into his shell and be quite evasive. I was a youngster and he'd go out of his way to help me a bit. He wasn't too keen on the good-time lads and he could, well, cold-shoulder them a bit.

I had a partnership with Len in Adelaide, in the fourth Test in 1955, and then Denis Compton and I had a partnership. I think then Len was getting a bit weary, and he was a bit disappointed with himself, that his own form was but a shadow of his great period before. I won't say that it got him down but I think he found that disappointment a bit hard to bear. He knew how he could play and now it was just beginning to elude him. He wasn't all that strong a man, funnily enough. I don't know how strong a man he was when he got all those runs in 1938. He was a bit on the fragile side physically.

The second Test, after we had lost at Brisbane, was terribly tight. It was a wonderful game of cricket and it could have gone either way. We won by 38 runs, which is a bit too close for comfort really. I think the decisions over Alec Bedser were very difficult for Len, frightfully difficult. Alec in his prime would have bowled beautifully on the Melbourne wicket, and who's to say that if Alec had been given a go he wouldn't have bowled well, you just don't know. I think Len felt, rightly or wrongly, that Alec had lost a bit of his zip because he'd been unwell with shingles: 'In theory he could do quite well, but I think I'd better go for the quicker man.'

Those are very tough decisions, and of course Alec Bedser never really got over it. It was the end of a great career for him really and was one of his last chances. He might have come up with 7 for 50, you never know, a wonderful finish; it's one of those things the story book will never tell you now. Alec felt very bad about it and one could understand that completely. I felt sorry for Len, as captain, having the final decision. Although you discuss it with your senior players, it's your burden. I think that was probably one of the most crucial days of his life.

Although people might think he was hard, it was not true. Len was a very sensitive man. He'd have taken a lot of that decision into old age, I think, that dreadful decision to make. And although, in the end, we were justified, you couldn't say that Alec might not have made it easier for us. I always think of that episode as a sort of Banquo's ghost. It was a desperate thing for Len's life that day, he could have done without that decision. It must have taken a great deal out of him because he had respect for great cricketers, as we all have. It was a brute, that one.

Had he been a slightly more outgoing personality, and been seen to flick the ball around the park a bit more happily, he'd have had a quite different image as a batsman. People have tended to underrate his stature because of that. I was batting with him when he got a big score (145) against Western Australia and he played some amazing shots, quite uncharacteristic. All technically good shots, but he was taking a bit of a chance, lifting the ball on the up. He was such an amazing middler of the ball. At the other end I was amazed at how the ball used to find the middle of his bat; he used to go so late.

I don't know that one can ever tell how good a captain he was, because he didn't captain very much. He captained Yorkshire only rarely and it's easy to be a good captain when you're winning, and he won three series. It's like Stuart Surridge – everyone says he's a great captain, but they won five years running. You don't know what he'd have been like captaining the lowest county. There was no doubt about his knowledge of the game and, like a bridge hand, weighing up how to play it, tremendous. Maybe he was short on lifting up the troops who were down – I'm not sure about that, you'd have to ask them. On the field of play it really was like playing a bridge hand; he didn't miss much.

Len used to think standing up, standing tall, was important. I tended to crouch a little bit and get hit on the glove. He used to say: 'You don't want to get hit on the glove and hurt your fingers or break your fingers.' Rather than go down with the ball, he told me to keep my hands high, which was very helpful, although not something I found easy. Len was very rarely hit on the hands, or anywhere. He was remarkably adept at getting out of the way. Standing high and staying still, that was a great lesson.

I think he was an underrated player. I think people tend to think of the three Ws (Worrell, Weekes and Walcott), Viv Richards, Denis Compton, Wally Hammond, and obviously they'd think of Hutton, but I don't think people realise just how good he was. I was lucky enough to play with him, albeit at the end of his career, and I could see for myself how he was able to be as good as he was. I don't think I remember anyone else, a right-hander anyway, play the new ball as well as he did. He was in a different class from anyone else I've ever seen. It was because of this lateness. The good Lord had given him something different. He was a very natural games player, a natural striker of the ball. Ted Dexter was a freak player but Ted didn't go to school on it as much as Len had done. He was correct and played the quick bowling well but I don't think that he ever gave it the same thought as Len.

He hoped I'd open against Australia in 1956 and do that job well. I didn't ever enjoy it and there were reasons why I felt that. I'd never done it until I did it with him on tour. In the end I think I opened thirty-nine times for England, which is more than most people play in a lifetime, and I got better at it. He was very keen that I should open. I think he thought that I would take over from him. My style was a bit different really. If I'd known then what I know now about the game I might have achieved it, but I tended to make my final decision a fraction earlier than he did. He was so brilliant about going late. I got better at it as the years went by. I found out for myself. It's not something which can immediately improve your game when you hear it – these are very high-level things, rather like Faldo being taught by David Leadbeater. Len was a bit unusual, he was a bit of a one-off really. He was a true master of his art.

He sent out two bananas with the twelfth man, Vic Wilson, in the Adelaide Test. The crowd were barracking me in a big way and I had quite a reputation for having a big appetite. I was obviously getting a little rattled by the crowd, I'd got a bit stuck, and Vic Wilson suddenly appeared in his blazer. I hadn't sent for him. 'The skipper thinks you look hungry,' he said. 'Would you like a banana? What's going on? You're getting a bit itchy.' I had about a quarter of a banana and he said: 'For God's sake don't throw your wicket away. Get down to it. The skipper says to keep concentrating.' That was quite funny in a way, it was a way of making me think about it.

He was a marvellous player in difficult conditions. Maybe not such a killer, although he could annihilate attacks. His way, really, was to carve success out of quite hard granite, not to flash the rapier around. Light blue eyes and an enchanting smile and a very, very tough opponent.

Peter May

Born 1929. Cambridge University and Surrey (Captain 1957–62): 1950–63. 66 Test matches: 1951–61 (Captain 41 times 1955–61). 6ft 1in tall, Peter May was a hard-hitting right-handed batsman who played very straight in defence and was a classical stroke-player, especially off his legs. In the latter half of the 1950s, he was arguably the best batsman in the world. In 1955 he took over the England captaincy because Hutton was ill and became, in Richie Benaud's words, 'a ruthless, determined and courageous leader'. He led England in 35 consecutive Tests. He was an England selector from 1965–68 and chairman from 1982–88. In 1980–81 he was President of the MCC.

I first played for England when I was still at Cambridge. That was the first time I had close contact with Len, though I had played against him for Cambridge v Yorkshire. England had a Yorkshire opening partnership in 1951, Hutton and Frank Lowson. We fielded for a couple of days while South Africa got 538 on a lovely Headingley wicket. Our opening partnership put on 99. I was number three, so I had quite a long wait for my first Test innings – and it seemed a very long time, as you can imagine.

When I went out to bat it was the last ball of the over. Athol Rowan, an off-spinner, was bowling – the Rowan brothers, Athol and Eric, were very successful for South Africa. He bowled at me from the Pavilion end. There were no sightscreens in those days, and he tossed the ball up and I lost it in the background. My dear old coach at school, George Geary, had always said: 'When in doubt, push out', and I duly pushed forward and got an inside edge. It went down the slope for four runs so I was off the mark and mightily relieved.

The great man was at the other end, on 40 or so, and he came down the wicket. I walked up and he looked at me and said: 'Are you all right?' 'Yes, thank you, Len. Yes, I think I'm fine,' I said. The point of the story is that we didn't speak again for the rest of the innings. As a young undergraduate I didn't expect the great man to talk to me. Why should he? I watched him play. He made 100 and I went on and made 138 myself, which was lovely. I ran his runs and watched. He ran my runs. But once he was batting he was batting and he had no time for anything else.

I got to know him extremely well afterwards, being his vice-captain in Australia in 1954–55 and playing with him in the West Indies, watching him make 205 in that great heat. He batted for ten hours in British Guiana and in Jamaica, two amazing innings. He had wonderful concentration and he played every ball. Unlike Denis Compton, he'd say: 'Whatever you're going to bowl at me I'm going to play with the middle of the bat and wait for the one I'm going to hit for four.' A bit like Boycott actually. Denis was different. He could take charge and he took risks.

Len was a marvellous judge of a run to mid-on. He was always looking for a single. I remember fielding at mid-on against him – and I was fairly quick in those days, surprisingly. I thought: 'Well I'm going to stop that single.' I crept up a little bit, got a bit wider, and every time it was just out of my reach. I'd come roaring in and just miss it. He didn't charge between the wickets but always had enough time. It would be interesting to see how many times Len was run out in his career. I bet it wasn't many.

When I was vice-captain to Len in Australia, he was quite inscrutable, never gave anything away. I saw him after a fairly important press conference and said: 'Well, they all came out smiling, Len. How did it go? What did you tell them?' 'I just baffled 'em,' he said. What he said I don't know. He used to say: 'You know what I mean, don't you?' and you hadn't a clue what he was talking about, bless him. You hadn't got the heart to say: 'Well, no Len, I really don't know what you mean at all.'

I think it was caused by his shyness actually. He was a very shy person and suddenly to be the first professional captain of England was a hell of a job for him, being the person he was. To achieve the success he did was a remarkable achievement because it was very, very hard work. The man-management was very hard for him. He knew what he wanted. He thought the only people who would win Test matches were quick bowlers, that was his philosophy, because they were the only type of bowlers that worried him.

The Alec Bedser thing on the Australian tour of 1954–55 was just sad. Len hadn't got the confidence to say to an old friend: 'I'm sorry Alec.' Alec had shingles and he should never have played at Brisbane in the first Test, that was the thing. If he'd played at Sydney in the second, the wicket could well have helped him, but he should never have played at Brisbane.

Len had always got at the back of his mind the idea that we needed two quick bowlers. If you look at the great, successful Test sides they've always had two quick bowlers, with notable exceptions like New Zealand with Richard Hadlee. There's been Lindwall and Miller, Gregory and McDonald, Tyson and Statham, Trueman and Statham, and it goes through history. When you get an Alec Bedser . . . Think of the opening bowlers he had, dozens of them, incredible. He opened the bowling at the Oval in 1948 with Alan Watkins. Incredible. He never had the support at the other end, so it was amazing what he did himself.

I wonder why Len came to live in the South. He could have done so much by being in Yorkshire. In the end he accepted the Presidency, which may have brought on his death, with all the trouble. Yorkshire needed people like that to be there, didn't they? I thought it was very strange that he should leave Yorkshire. He must have spent half his life out of Yorkshire, which is quite extraordinary when you think about it.

I went to see the Lord's Test against the West Indies in 1939 at the age of nine. My great hero then was Wally Hammond. It was wonderful to watch him walk out: he walked out like a king. He made 14 in that match and when he was out I was so disappointed that I said: 'Well, we better go home then.' It was too much to take. He used quite a light bat. We all used lighter bats in those days – 2lb 4oz, 2lb 5oz. Gooch uses a 3-pounder.

Wally was a supreme slip fielder, of course, and Len was very good there too, very good pair of hands.

Len didn't like Reg Simpson much. He used to go and sit out with the crowd in the sun, which annoyed Len. Len wouldn't sit in the sun, would he? He didn't like sunbathing. Len thought Tom Graveney was a little bit casual too.

Len was right in wanting Colin Cowdrey to be an opener. Colin had more time to play the ball than almost anyone else I played with. He played the moving ball so easily. Colin didn't realise how good he was. If he'd gone out saying: 'I'm the king,' and taken people on . . .

The thing today is that not many players play back; they're all half-forward. I always thought that the best players actually played back. If you go back you can go forward, if you go half-forward you can't. Len went back then forward. For the spinners you've got to be going forward, but for the quicker bowlers you've got to give yourself a little more room.

Len was a great theorist, and a very quiet person, even when he was captain. What I learned from him in the field was that he summed up the opposing batsmen's weaknesses. He knew exactly what field to set for Neil Harvey when he came in. He never hurried to reset the field once the chap had taken guard or was taking guard. He might make a little tactical move, just to upset the chap or make him wait a bit longer for his first ball. It was very clever. He knew exactly how each batsman played. His success record as captain must have been pretty high.

People have described Denis Compton as an amateur professional, me as a professional amateur because I used to try and play a bit like Len sometimes. I tried to combine the two really.

I hit a six in Jamaica on the 1953–54 tour, quite unintentionally. I think it was Gomez bowling and it was just short of a length and I went for the ball. I went straight through with it and it just dis-

'People still argue whether Hutton's cover-drive or his on-drive was the more sublime.' This picture captures his perfect balance at the wicket as he drives past mid-on.

appeared over mid-on. Len came down at the end of the over. 'What are you doing?' he asked. 'I wasn't quite there, so I just went through with the shot,' I said. 'You mustn't do that. You keep it on the ground,' he said. I don't think I got many more.

He was a very shy person and you never really got to know him, or if you did it was only a bit of him. I don't know what he said about me, but whatever he said he never gave you an inkling of what he was thinking about you.

Brian Statham

Born 1930. Lancashire (Captain 1965–67): 1950–68. 70 Test matches: 1950–65. Fast and consistently accurate, 'George' was universally respected and admired for his undemonstrative dedication to bowling. Between 1953 and 1963 he formed a formidable opening attack with both Tyson and Trueman. He was perhaps at his fastest bowling with Tyson in Australia in 1954/55. Noted for his rhythmic run-up, his accuracy often set up wickets for his partners.

My first Roses match was in August 1950 and that is when I first played with Len. From memory he didn't get many in that game. I was an extremely raw young man and great names didn't mean anything to me at that stage. To be honest, he was just a bloke at the other end with a bat in his hand.

Len was a very great technician, probably as fine a technician as I ever came across, but being technically correct does occasionally have its drawbacks. Basically, regarding body position, you can get all tucked up in places, which happened to Len – and, I think, to a similar degree to Geoffrey Boycott as well. They get tucked up with the short rising delivery coming sort of middle and leg direction. They really can't avoid it, they have to play it. It didn't mean you were going to get them out, just that they had technical difficulties there, not that they didn't play it reasonably well.

Len was always reputedly susceptible to the ball coming into him. I think that this was probably so, particularly in the early and middle 1950s when we were playing on uncovered wickets. Perhaps the off-spinner was more likely to get Leonard out than the slow left-arm. He played slow left-arm orthodox bowlers very well. Bowling to Leonard was really no problem because he treated every ball on its individual merit. He would certainly tuck the bad ball away for four. But if you bowled Leonard a reasonable ball, it wasn't going to get hit for four. Unlike Denis Compton, who would manufacture a shot and hit even a reasonable delivery for four, Leonard would never do this. If you bowled a line and a length to him, you kept him reasonably quiet.

I probably didn't bowl a tremendous number of maidens to him, though, because he had the ability to time his strokes and control the power of the shot to enable him to take singles. He was able to work the ball around and keep the scoreboard ticking over, even though he wasn't murdering an attack. With Denis Compton, you never knew when he would manufacture a shot and unleash it and the ball could go sailing for four or six. So you were easier of mind with Leonard.

Once Leonard got in, you knew he would eventually take his toll on the bowling. He was capable of playing very long innings. So it was essential that you got him out as quickly as possible.

Leonard, like many other England captains, proved to be a hard taskmaster. I think, probably, that stems from 1948, playing against the Australians and Lindwall and Miller in particular, when he and Cyril Washbrook had to face the brunt of the attack and England not having the big guns to fire back at them. We were desperately short of somebody quick and reasonably hasty to reply with. And I think Leonard, once he found he'd got one or two quick bowlers at his command, made sure they earned their corn.

At Headingley in 1953 I was twelfth man and I spent all day going from third man to fine leg. He organised that tremendously badly, unless it was a deliberate ploy to slow the game down and slow the over rate. It was an awful long way to go, and to do it for a day I was, of course, quite exhausted at the end of it. Literally all day.

He didn't say a dickie bird to me about it. Leonard was a very difficult man to get close to. He wasn't a tremendously verbal man and very often talked in semi-riddles. I didn't always understand what he was talking about and these little conversations invariably ended in: 'You know what I mean?' which was a pet phrase of his. And you'd say: 'Yeah, I know what you mean,' but quite often you didn't understand what he was getting at. But he was a very shrewd captain.

I think he came to appreciate me as a player gradually rather than as a result of one outstanding performance. I know that he was impressed when he saw me in that first Roses match in 1950. I think Leonard was partially responsible for Roy Tattersall and I flying out to Australia in January 1951 to help the MCC when they were badly hit with injuries. They lost nearly all the bowlers in a couple of weeks or so. Even though I'd only played about a dozen first-class games, I know that Leonard did put a good word in for me, so he must have seen something he liked.

I was in a peculiar situation, inasmuch as I didn't know anything about the opposition and very little about my own team mates. I'd probably met half a dozen, not much more than that. I'd never seen them play. It was a bit like breaking into a new school. The climate didn't help. We'd left snow on the ground in England and the first game we played in it was 102 degrees. The change was just too dramatic, too sudden, because we were playing within ten days of being asked if we could go out there.

Denis Compton had a particularly bad trip, I remember, averaging only about eight. He was getting centuries in the state matches and none in the Test matches. Leonard played pretty well and Reg Simpson played pretty well. Reg was somewhat underrated as a player and perhaps in a different era he would have played more Test cricket than he did.

The opening partnership was pretty unsettled at that time and I'm sure Leonard felt more settled when he had a regular opening partner at the other end. His most stable partner was Cyril Washbrook, of course, and Cyril was certainly a good judge of a run and mix-ups in calling were few and far between. They were positive and they took the runs as called.

On the West Indian tour in 1953–54 Len didn't get on too well, I believe, with Godfrey Evans, but that was not an on-the-field situation, it was more an off-the-field situation.

I remember Leonard's 205 at Sabina Park in Jamaica. It was a match-winning innings, and a very tiring innings as well. There was an incident there which shouldn't have happened. Leonard came in at tea-time on the second day of our innings, having batted for five sessions, and was a very exhausted man. He came through the crowd towards the dressing-room, head bowed and not looking at anybody, and Bustamente, the Chief Minister of Jamaica, said: 'Well played Leonard,' and Leonard ignored him. Unfortunately there were press men around at the time and the headline the following day was: 'Hutton snubs Bustamente', which was very unfortunate and I believe Leonard had to apologise for this so-called snub. It wasn't that Leonard snubbed him, he never saw him or heard him. It was just an incident that was blown up out of all proportion.

Leonard basically treated me the same on that trip as he did on any other trip. He extracted his pound of flesh and we had to work hard, but really no harder there than anywhere else. We very rarely had tactical discussions before the day's play. Leonard gave his bowlers credit for knowing what they were doing and left it to them. You could make suggestions from time to time, which perhaps he wouldn't accede to unless you could quantify it very strongly, e.g. moving one fielder somewhere else. But in general you had the field you wanted and he expected you to bowl to it. He would always consult you if he wanted to change the field. In general he didn't change the field much. He would always start with a very attacking field and only reduced it if they were getting too many runs too quickly, then you had to set a more defensive field and slow things down a bit. As long as runs weren't coming too quickly, Leonard was quite happy to have quite a strong attacking field.

One of his pet theories was to make the opposition wonder where they were going to get the next run and generally to slow the game down and make them think about it. He slowed the game down with extremely tight bowling and defensive fields, but not ultra-defensive, not a field where half your fielders are on the boundary. They were fields to stop the single, to stop them pinching runs. It wasn't unknown for him to slow the game down in other ways and, to be honest, I didn't feel one way or the other about it. Whatever was being done I knew was being done in the best interests of the side. In general, I'm not in favour of long discussions in the middle during field changes or taking drinks every five minutes.

Even when I was playing I felt exactly the same way and I was very conscious that all you were doing basically was depriving the public of seeing a little bit more cricket. I did feel for the man who had paid at the turnstile, because, when all is said and done, it is only a game and you are relying on those people to pay your wages, so it's in your best interests to see that they get as much cricket out of the day as you possibly can give them.

You never know what's being said in the opposition dressing-room. I'm sure that these little bits of gamesmanship didn't go unnoticed, as indeed they didn't go unnoticed when the opposition were doing the same thing to us. I don't feel that in our playing days there was the same amount of animosity on the field that perhaps shows through today. There certainly wasn't the same amount of chit-chat.

Leonard wasn't in favour of very much social activity with the opposition. He wasn't over-keen on you going out and having a drink with them at the end of the game. It wasn't a hard-and-fast rule, by any means, it was only a suggestion, and I used to go and have a drink with them. Invariably one didn't discuss what had gone on during the day. It was really more of a social drink and social discussion. You might mention in passing that someone had taken a good catch or bowled well or batted well, but really it was left at that; no deep discussion about what was going to happen in the match or anything.

Team meetings as such were not held very frequently. If Leonard had something to say, he would do it as a generalisation in the morning prior to the day's play. He expected people to read the game as it was progressing, and if you've reached international standard you ought to be able to do this automatically. There were brief discussions that went on between captain and bowler from time to time, in between overs in general. He'd ask you how you were doing and if you were all right, meaning physically. 'Can you do another couple of overs?' or: 'How do you feel?' He would have a damn good idea, from the way you were moving about, whether you were ready to put your sweater on or not.

During those brief interludes he would also say: 'They're getting a few too many runs, do you think we should take a slip out and put him at extra cover?' or: 'Do without a leg slip? The ball isn't going there. Put him on the off side?' And he would expect you to have the answer for him during that over's rest. He would want to know at the end of that over what you wanted.

The Brisbane Test in 1954 went drastically wrong, really from the word go. Leonard was mainly instrumental in the format of the side, which was to play all his quick bowlers and virtually nobody else. But Alec Bedser had had shingles the moment he'd set foot on land and even by that game he hadn't fully recovered. In fact, I don't think he fully recovered on the whole of the trip. Shingles really knocked him and took its toll out of him.

I think Leonard based his side on the wicket we'd had in the previous match against Queensland – quite a quick wicket which had a little bit of grass left on it and the odd ball moved around a bit as well. We beat Queensland fairly handsomely, and the Test wicket was right next door to this wicket we'd played on. I think Leonard thought it was going to be a similar sort of wicket with a little bit of bounce and a little bit of movement. He based his side on this and then really he'd no option but to go in the field first if possible. If he lost the toss, he would have to hope that the opposition would bat first.

It worked out that we did go in the field first and I got a wicket after about twenty minutes, Favell, and that was virtually the last wicket I got. They made around 600 and everybody got runs. Godfrey Evans had gone down with a throat infection and Keith Andrew played, and missed one or two very difficult chances, low down on the leg side, off Neil Harvey in particular. I'm not sure whether he was leg-glancing very fine or whether he was getting inside edges very fine. But these things were only reaching Keith at ankle height and he couldn't hang on to them. So Keith had a very disappointing game.

We followed on. Denis Compton found himself running round the perimeter at one stage, for some reason or other, and went to chase a ball, stuck his hand in the fence and broke a finger, which meant really that we'd lost a batsman.

Alec Bedser only played in the one Test, at Brisbane. If he'd been bowling fully fit, I would have missed him, but bowling as he was, no, I didn't. It does get extremely hot out there. Not perhaps the first two Tests, although it's hot enough, but certainly the Tests around Christmas are very tiring. It's very hot. It was always 100-plus in Adelaide, which is not too clever for bowling quick.

In Melbourne Leonard nearly didn't make it to the ground. This was not common knowledge on the morning, certainly not among the majority of the players. It only emerged via whispers and rumours a little later. He must have had an attack of the nerves. It was surprising for a player of his stature, but I don't know that it affected his play.

That was the extraordinary weekend when the groundsman was thought to have watered the wicket. On the Saturday night it was very much like a pale asphalt; you could kick away at will and only make little scratches in it and on Monday morning, when we got down there, you could draw a beautiful black line, with very light pressure, with your spikes. He said it had sweated under the covers over the weekend. Somewhere around the 100-mark all weekend and not a cloud in the sky, never mind any moisture. We found it extraordinary.

The general consensus of opinion was that Appleyard, on what turned out to be the last morning of the game, would be the chap to do the damage. In fact, he didn't get on to bowl. Frank Tyson and I bowled through that morning and Frank whistled them out as fast as they walked in. It didn't really surprise me that Appleyard didn't

bowl, because in general you would always start the morning with
your two quick bowlers, and really it all stemmed from that. Everything went well, so we were allowed to get on with it, and in the
event bowled them out; bowled them out by lunchtime.

Leonard was never what you'd call a robust man. He was always
slight of build but he still had the tenacity to play a very long
innings when required. There were no signs that Leonard was tired
on that trip, though it may have been apparent to the more senior
players.

It was a great moment when we won the 1955 series at Adelaide,
but there again Leonard had a touch of the jitters. Keith Miller had
us at 18 for 3, and Leonard's remark was: 'The buggers have done
us.' Godfrey and Denis went in and smacked one or two around and
saw it off. There was tremendous relief then. Although we hadn't
got to panic stations and we had plenty of batting left, we were all
well aware of the capabilities of Lindwall and Miller.

The atmosphere on that tour was very good and the atmosphere
in the dressing-room was tremendous. There was a lot of confidence.
It came from the manner in which the tour had progressed and the
way we'd tackled the Test matches and got stuck in and had a real
go. It turned out in our favour fortunately.

There was always champagne in the dressing-room at the end of a
Test match, but only in the victor's dressing-room. The one thing that
Leonard did like was to have the opposition drinking our champagne.
He was not too keen to go into the opposition dressing-room and
drink theirs. I must admit it is a bit galling, going to drink the opposition's champagne having lost the game, but it was the thing one
had to do and that was it.

Leonard was a man who contemplated very frequently. He could
be having a conversation with you and all of a sudden he'd look
straight through you and you knew he wasn't hearing what you were
saying. One of the little sayings we had among ourselves was: 'He's
back home on the moors with the missus.' Miles away. He was the
same with cigarettes. He was the only man I ever knew who could
bring them out lit. Most peculiar. He'd buy you a drink but he
wouldn't give you a cigarette. Very odd. He was sponsoring filter tip
but wouldn't smoke them and would gladly swap 200 filter tipped
for 100 plain ones. He'd do that regularly. He would gladly accept
cigarettes around the table and then bring out his cigarette case and
light one himself but not offer them around, even though he hadn't
paid for them.

He was a very serious man, Leonard, whimsical maybe. He played
his cricket very hard. I don't think he genuinely found anything
funny about it and he had a very dry sense of humour. He had very
set little theories and abided by them; pet hates. I think he was thinking about cricket most of the time. I don't think he was the sort of
man who could genuinely leave the day's play on the field and not
take a bit of it back home with him. I don't know whether he ever
worried a lot about his own general form. Everybody gets flat patches
where you're not taking wickets or you're not getting runs. I'm sure

L. HUTTON

A Hutton cigarette card
– the players joked about
his tight-fistedness over
sharing cigarettes.

that Leonard had played long enough to realise that this was only a flat patch and sooner or later it would come good.

He was such a correct player that he was always in the right position, and close to the ball, which meant that any smallish deviation was highly liable to find the edge of the bat. Rather than play and miss, he was so close to the line that he was going to play and edge it. It depended largely on the wicket as to whether it carried to the slips or not. You can put the top hand down, to a degree, playing the forward defensive shot against the quick bowlers, to stop the ball carrying, but it doesn't work on the back foot. Leonard basically was always looking to play on the front foot. Other players basically always want to get on the back foot to give themselves more time to see it. Cyril Washbrook always wanted to play on the back foot. It gave him that split second longer to look at it. Leonard liked to stop any deviation at the source if possible. Sometimes he was lucky, sometimes I was lucky

Leonard was one of the very few players who would change his bat in the middle of a long knock. He always carried a Harrow size bat around with him which was slightly shorter, and an ounce or two lighter, than a normal bat. During a long innings he would use it when he was getting tired and it wasn't detrimental to his strokeplay at all.

He was a fair captain. He always treated his bowlers well. As I said earlier, he hammered his quick bowlers, but I found all other captains did exactly the same, so it really wasn't out of the ordinary. He wasn't a captain who was prepared to make a declaration, to give his own side a chance to win, if there was any danger of giving the opposition a chance of winning. Declarations would be absolutely concrete safe, sometimes not quite giving you the opportunity to bowl a side out again. I was never particularly happy in long stints of defensive bowling, i.e. keeping runs down. But it is part and parcel of the game and one had to do it. If you look at it sensibly, you're not going to get wickets unless you've got the ball in your hand and you're bowling; so yes, I was always happy to bowl. There are always going to be occasions when you feel that you have been over-bowled. It depends to a degree on how successful you have been during that spell. If you've picked seven wickets up, no, you don't think you've been over-bowled, but if you're 2 for 100, well, you do.

Leonard was always sort of money-conscious. If we hadn't seen each other for a few years (this is after cricket had finished), we'd just talk as though we'd met yesterday. All of a sudden he would come out with something like: 'How're you doing anyway? Are you making it pay? Are you making plenty of brass?' He was always interested in whether you were making a quid or two. He used to talk about stocks and shares now and again with people like Godfrey Evans and Denis Compton. At that stage I wasn't into shares. I hadn't the money for shares. This was a major problem in our era. You basically made a living wage but there really wasn't any money about. Denis Compton, and indeed Keith Miller, did these Brylcreem ads and it was £1,000 per annum, which is basically peanuts.

I think that captaincy weighed relatively heavy on Leonard. There was the situation where the MCC thought that he was the man to skipper England, and Yorkshire didn't consider him the man to skipper Yorkshire, which was a somewhat invidious position for him to be in. I think this weighed on him very heavily. I think he would have liked to have been asked to skipper Yorkshire.

Roy Tattersall

Born 1922. Lancashire: 1948–60. 16 Test matches: 1950–54. Tall, slim, right-arm off-break bowler who varied his direction, flight and speed. In 1950 he was top of the national averages with 193 wickets at an average of 13.59, and he and Brian Statham were flown out to Australia as replacements in 1950/51. Unlucky to have been a contemporary of Jim Laker's, he took 58 wickets in Tests. After he left Lancashire, he played for Kidderminster in the Birmingham League.

I first encountered Len in 1950 and played in eleven Test matches with him and in 'Battle of the Roses' matches, as well as for MCC against Yorkshire and the Scarborough Festival.

It was a great honour bowling to him. He was 'the great Len' even then. Fortunately, I managed to get him out quite a number of times, including twice in my first game against him at Bramall Lane, Sheffield. I think I had him about ten or eleven times altogether, but against the left-armers he was absolutely devastating. If he had a weakness, it was against either the in-swinger or the off-spinner, but he proved himself against all sorts of bowlers.

I got him out in various ways. I think really the main thing that got him was my variation of pace. I used to vary it a lot, not noticeably, but bowling faster balls, slower ones, a variation. I don't think he settled too well against me for that. And then, as we all know, he had one arm a little bit shorter than the other, his left arm. I think that's where he might not have been able to play the off-spinner, the ball coming on to him, quite as well as he could the one going away from him. We had some good bowlers in Lancashire in those days, players like Bob Berry, Malcolm Hilton and Bill Roberts, but they were no trouble to Len at all. He crashed them to the boundary, beautiful shots.

In the second half of 1950 Brian Statham came along. Brian got him a few times, being extra quick and so accurate. I used to be the first change and sometimes I did him and sometimes not, but Len only hit one hundred against us in 1952.

The Roses matches were played hard and fair; you didn't try and cheat anybody out, like they do today. It was always played in a friendly spirit: you had a drink or two afterwards, and a chat. Once battle commenced you were trying to get them out, of course, which was the right thing to do. I enjoyed those games. I think I took 90-odd wickets against Yorkshire. You seem to get more wickets against some teams than others.

I didn't mind bowling to Len. You'd get far lesser batsmen, not fit to lace Len Hutton's boots, who might give you a hammering, but Len never did. I don't know why it should be. The only thing I can think of, and looking at it over the years, was my variation of pace. Of course it was spinning sometimes and other times you'd try and spin it and it'd go straight on, which you don't know and the batsman doesn't know. And I could always bowl a good length, and have a close-in leg trap as well, and any mistakes he made he was snapped up there.

His reach was a little bit shorter in the left arm, they always mention this against the in-swing. His arm seemed to be slightly bent as well, and when you had enough ball movement he might have been a bit restricted.

Len was a very good player against spin. Generally speaking, on turning wickets he was a good one, there's no question about it. When you were playing with him, you saw good spinners against him and he had this happy knack of making the ball appear dead. As he was going to make contact with the ball, he came back with his bat a little bit to take the force off it. Some push forward quite hard and there's a big resistance there and it goes to the leg trap. Len had this happy knack of just going back a little and the ball would hit against a limp bat.

You've always got memories of your first Test. Mine was in Adelaide in 1951. The heat was terrific. Len batted right through the innings for 156 not out. He was great to watch, without ever taking command, because we weren't in a position to take command of the game. They tried all sorts to get him out.

The fifth Test, in 1950–51, was the first time we'd beaten the Australians since before the war, 1938. That was a great occasion for us and we celebrated in true style. Lindsay Hassett took it very well. A great sportsman, he came over with champagne for us. It was also Reg Simpson's birthday and he'd got 156 not out in the first innings. Len got 79 and 60 not out.

I never really batted with Len. I didn't remain long. He never was a man of a lot of words, wasn't Len. He'd come down and say: 'Play a straight bat', or: 'Try and keep your end up', but he didn't give you any precise details of what to do or how to play. He'd just let you get on with it.

I could never understand Len really; sometimes he was a bit funny. Not altogether sarcastic, but he'd a sense of humour. I always remember a funny incident when we were at Scarborough. This was on a good wicket and all the bowlers were getting a lot of stick. Len came along and he said to me: 'Are you tired?' I'd only bowled two or three overs and normally I could bowl thirty or forty. I mean, I'd bowled fifty overs in a day. I'd not taken a wicket and it was just his way of doing it. I looked at him and I said: 'No, I'm all right, Len'. He gave me another couple of overs and he said: 'Are you sure you're not tired?' 'Len', I said, 'I'm buggered'. He smiled because he knew very well that I'd rumbled him. That was his way of trying to make you want to do better, of getting more out of you. It was all in fun. He didn't say anything afterwards, he just let me carry on. That was the way he was.

He was an astute captain. If he thought that you were going to go through a side he'd keep you on, and if he didn't he'd make his changes, and that's a good captain. He weighed it up pretty quickly. He'd give you the field you wanted and if he wanted to move a certain player he'd usually come and say: 'Do you mind . . .', and you didn't argue with a fellow with such experience. He knew the game inside out and he was a good captain, he proved that. I wouldn't say he was always the easiest captain to understand, but his motives and everything else were right. He didn't lose many games when he was captain. He proved his point.

You hear some players say that he was the best captain they had, especially as a professional captain, but you've got to speak about people as you find them. I found him a fine chap and I enjoyed his company and never felt ill at ease with him or anything like that. I soon got his sense of humour and I quite liked it. I think the fact that I'd got him out would always be at the back of his mind, but he never said anything to me.

You get used to certain players. Willie Watson was a very, very good stroke-maker. He always gave me more trouble than Len Hutton did in the Roses matches. Willie was a devil to get out but Len, he wasn't the hardest one for me to get out. The figures prove it, don't they?

Len was a dependable player and got his runs with no big hitting. He had all the strokes, a graceful player. I remember him playing some beautiful, effortless shots in a 91 against us at Old Trafford in 1950.

He was a very astute player. When we played the South Africans at Old Trafford in 1951, the wicket was hard underneath and soft on top. Cuan McCarthy, a very fast bowler, was playing for South Africa. The day started at about 4.30 and there were only about two hours, at most, to play, so the fast bowlers could keep going. The wicket was dangerous and Len Hutton opened with Johnny Ikin from Lancashire, a gutsy player, a tough left-hander.

Cuan McCarthy was really letting them go, some short-pitched ones, and it was nasty to bat on. At the end of the day they were both still there; how they managed to survive God only knows. Johnny Ikin was hit black and blue. Most players would have retired hurt, but Johnny was the sort of player who didn't. At the end of the day we all said: 'Well played Johnny and well played Len'. It was an achievement to stay there, and Len came out with the remark: 'If Johnny had been a better player he'd have got down the other end a bit more'. That's what Len did, he let Johnny take most of the strike. Whenever he could, he got a run, away from Cuan. It made us all laugh in the dressing-room; it was the way he said it.

That was a masterful innings really against those bowlers. Don't forget there were no helmets, all you had on was a box and a thigh-pad, and thigh-pads weren't like they are today. There were times when you went in with a towel and socks in your pocket.

Len played forward a lot and this is where a good batsman soon picks up your flight and your length and everything else, whether to go forward or back. He was very, very quick, even against leg-spinners. He was a very good player against them. The ball didn't carry from his bat so much, that was the beauty of it, with a resistant bat it shoots off. Later on different techniques turned up. The batsmen used to put their bat in front of their pads playing forward and if it got the edge it could go to your leg-trap, but Cowdrey and May, against Ramadhin, put the bat behind the pad and the ball hit the pad and went down instead of carrying to the leg trap. Len had this technique of softening the blow by taking the bat back a bit.

He always went back slightly before he went forward, his first movement was back and then he picked up your flight and length and then he came forward or he might stay back. That's where he was so good, he was quick at picking it up, and he could bat on all types of wickets all over the world. Figures speak for themselves; wherever he was he got runs.

Like so many Yorkshiremen, Len didn't throw his money around, but that's the way they are and good luck to them. Len used to smoke Black Cat cigarettes; he advertised them and of course he used to get them free. There wasn't much sponsorship then, but he was one of the exceptions because he was such a good player.

I used to smoke in those days as well. I used to smoke either Senior Service or Players. Len would come along sometimes before a game and say: 'What are you smoking?' and so on. He'd have his free issue. 'Try one of these, let's have a change', he'd say. There was no doubt about which he preferred. Because he'd got his free ones, he wanted to swap with you. It was just the way he used to do it: 'Try one of mine', like, 'and I'll have one of yours'. He smoked quite a lot did Len, between an innings and that sort of thing – usually as soon as we came in we lit up. It's not like it is today. In those days a lot of sportsmen used to smoke.

Len should have been made captain of Yorkshire, there's no question about it, but Lancashire and Yorkshire always preferred to have an amateur captain if at all possible. Traditions die hard, but there's nothing wrong with a professional captain. Len was captain of England after all. I was surprised he was not made captain before Ronnie Burnet and people like that. Mind you, there were difficulties at Yorkshire then, with different schools pulling different ways, and Ronnie Burnet was put in to sort it out, which he did.

Tom Graveney

---

*Born 1927. Gloucestershire (Captain 1959–60), Worcestershire
(Captain 1968–70), Queensland: 1948–71. 79 Test matches: 1951–
69 (Captain in 1 Test, 1968). Tom Graveney was an elegant front-
foot batsman. In his early career there was a question about his
ability against fast bowling and his temperament for Test cricket. In
and out of the England side for nearly 20 years, he was recalled in
1966 after an absence of 3 years and scored a memorable 96 at Lord's
against the West Indies. After that he continued playing Test cricket
well after his 40th birthday. He moved from Bristol to Worcestershire
in 1961 and helped them win their first Championship in 1964. In
an outstanding career he scored 47,793 runs in first-class cricket
and 122 centuries.*

I played for England first in 1951, when Len was the senior batter.
That Test was an astonishing game. We were playing South Africa at
Old Trafford and it was a square turner, nobody got many runs at
all. In the second innings we wanted about 140 to win. John Ikin
went out and opened the batting with Len and blocked, to let Len
score all the runs. Len was trying to get his hundredth 100 in the Test
match at Old Trafford.

It was my first Test and I couldn't believe what was going on. The
clouds were gathering and in the end he'd got 94 and we wanted
another four to win. Cuan McCarthy bowled a slow long hop down
the leg side which he tried to slog for six, miscued slightly and it only
went for four. So he was 98 not out at the end of the match, which
we won by nine wickets. I wondered what the devil was going on
because we won, I think, just before lunch and after lunch the
heavens opened. I thought it was a very strange first Test match.

I remember McCarthy bowling to Ikin and Hutton in the first
innings. He hit Len on the pad at about twenty past six and he didn't
bowl another ball for six minutes. Len was down, pad off, massage.
Cuan was steaming, he wanted to get at them. Len was shrewd, very
shrewd.

Len was very sound as a captain, he didn't take many chances. He
wasn't an outgoing character like Denis Compton and he kept very
much to himself. The younger players had very little to do with him.
He'd say hello and pass the time of day and be quite friendly, but
from a tactical point of view, he kept very much to himself. There
were four or five senior players like Godfrey Evans, Alec Bedser,
Denis Compton, Trevor Bailey, and everything centred on them
rather than anyone else.

I think Len felt I was a little bit flippant about the game, because
basically I just used to enjoy playing, and although a Test was obviously that much more important, it was still a game of cricket as far

as I was concerned. I think he felt that I was a little bit of a David Gower. You know, I just went and played the game.

I played in all five Tests on Australia's tour here in 1953 – somewhat fortunately, I think. I had a wonderful partnership with Len at Lord's, where we put on 168 after Don Kenyon had got out when the score was nine. Len and I completely dominated. We were going very well, but about ten minutes to six Len said: 'Just take it quietly, we don't want to lose another wicket'. As a young player going well, I felt that both of us should have got a century that night. I think we let them off the hook. I got out third ball the following day, which didn't improve things as far as I was concerned, but it was a wonderful partnership, wonderful bloke to bat with. He made everything look so easy, beautiful cover drives. Technically he was streets ahead of anyone.

Len made everything look so easy. The bowlers didn't fancy bowling at him, so you were that much better off batting with a man of that standard. Because of the contrast between Len and Denis, a lot of people looked on Len as a dour, uninteresting player, and he certainly wasn't that. He just used to pick his spot and go ping, and the ball used to go through the gap. A master player, especially against the slow left-armers; against the turning ball he was absolutely superb. A perfect technician.

I felt as a youngster that it was a definite war between North and South with Denis and Len. If the Northerners could have a go at 'Compo', they did, but it wasn't quite so bad when Len came South. I don't think the Southerners minded because he was doing a job for England.

Len could play how he wanted. If he wanted to take the bowlers apart, he took them apart, he was that good. I've seen him take Gloucestershire apart a couple of times, though Gloucestershire were not his favourite county for getting runs against. He just dominated when he felt like it, and in Test matches too. When we went to the West Indies in 1953–54 we lost the first two and we had to win the third; he got 169. We played the fourth on a jute mat, so that was going to be a draw. We had to win the fifth and he got 205. That was the sort of thing he did, he did what had to be done, terrific player.

That winter we were all lined up at the Queen's Park Oval, Trinidad, being introduced by Len to the Archbishop of York. He came to me and said: 'This is Tom Goddard', so I couldn't have made too great an impression on him. I think that on that tour he was a bit disappointed with the younger batters. P. B. H. May didn't really play as well as he could, and neither did I.

We were chasing, not an enormous total, about 380, at Barbados on a good track and were 70 for 3 when I went in. Ramadhin was bowling. I hit the first one like a rocket at mid-off, next one like a rocket at mid-on, and at the end of the over Len came down and said: 'We've got to get our heads down and battle through.' I just fell apart actually, I didn't look to strike the ball or anything. I batted about two hours for 15 runs and ended up hitting a full-toss from Ramadhin straight back to him. Trying to work it on the leg side, I got an outside edge and it went straight back to him, which was terrible. Len had put me off my natural game.

Some of the senior players felt that we should be able to play our shots and they said to Len: 'Come on, we've got good shot-makers, we must let them play.' And it worked for me in the second innings, I got 64 not out, but we lost and we should have won. There was an appalling lbw decision against Denis Compton when he was on 93 and he and I were really going and it looked as though we would get the runs. It was a terrible decision. It completely changed the game and the last five wickets went down for less than 60 runs.

What I found disappointing on that tour was that a number of the upper level of the press were very 'anti' before the tour ever started,

The England team 'in training' for the 1954 tour of Australia: Graveney, Hutton, Evans and a fourth man at play, watched by Wardle, Statham and Loader.

because Len was the first professional captain. They were looking to pick holes in him for everything he did. We only had a limited administration staff, because Charlie Palmer was the manager and also a player. He had an enormous amount to do and a lot of responsibility was put on Len, but I felt he handled it pretty well really. In the end we squared the series, which was a tremendous performance. A tough trip for Len.

There was an episode, I remember, in the final match, when Len got 205 at Sabina Park and Trevor Bailey had bowled them out for 139 in the first innings. Len wasn't a strong man physically but had wonderful application. He used to come into the dressing-room and just sit down in a daze. We'd take his pads off, give him a cup of tea and with five minutes to go we'd say, 'Pads on, get ready'. I reckon he did a wonderful job on that tour. I don't think the MCC and the hierarchy really wanted a professional captain. He had the backing of the players. Trevor Bailey, Peter May and Charlie Palmer were the only amateurs on that tour.

We always had problems finding a partner for Len once Cyril Washbrook retired. Willie Watson went in, then Trevor Bailey. He never really had a settled partner when I was playing for England. John Ikin started, David Sheppard came into the side, Reg Simpson, Don Kenyon, it even ended up with me going in first. I was never an opening bat, though I did get my only hundred against Australia when I went in first. That was Len's last Test against Australia, in 1955.

Len had to carry the load himself and he was the sort of man who took it all on himself. He didn't share it with anyone, which was the way he was, it was the man he was. Some people chatter away and talk, I've been accused of that, talking to people while I'm batting, but you can't help the way you're made. Len kept everything inside.

I struck a purple patch on the 1954–55 tour of Australia. I was in great nick, the ball kept whistling off the middle of the bat, which was very nice. I played in the second Test because Denis had broken a finger, and I might have got in the first Test but I got the flu up in Queensland.

I felt that I'd just about done enough to get back in the side for the fourth Test in Adelaide, which was going to be the clincher. I think Len and the selectors talked it over and decided to go for Bill Edrich for experience, an old war horse, an old fighter, rather than take a chance with me. I was very disappointed about that actually, very disappointed. For the first time in my cricketing career I'd gone out and trained, worked hard to get fit, run up and down the sands at Adelaide, and I wasn't picked. I was livid actually, but that didn't matter because we won the match, though Bill didn't contribute a great deal.

I only got my chance in the final Test match because we'd had a lot of rain. What happened was that there were thirteen players picked, as Colin Cowdrey hadn't been well and that's why I was standing by. Len went out to toss and nobody knew who was playing. Obviously he had to declare the side in the middle, tossed the coin, lost the toss. Ian Johnson said: 'You'd better bat.' Len came into the dressing-room, walked by me and said: 'Tom, put your pads on and come in with me.' That was the first time I knew I was opening. It must have worked because I got 111.

The 'Don', Bradman, had seen me get a few runs here and there and he'd said that I ought to go in early. I'd never looked on myself as an opening batter at all. I don't know whether he'd said it to Len or not. Knowing Len's in-built distrust of the Australians he might have thought they were trying to pull one over on him, but that was Len. I don't think he trusted the Australians very much.

It was a hard trip for Len, having lost the first one at Brisbane so badly, and once again not having a settled opening partnership. He started with Reg Simpson. In many ways Len gave Reg away, and myself, before the tour had got underway. I don't think he got on very well with Reg Simpson and he decided that I was a little bit too loose a player.

It was a pattern of the 1950s that we couldn't find a regular opening partnership. I remember in 1956, when Len had retired and the Australians came over, Gubby Allen, who was chairman of the selectors, said: 'Watson will open for Leicestershire, Cowdrey will open for Kent and Graveney will open for Gloucestershire', and we had to. The message came round after a week to forget it, because Cowdrey was going in first with Richardson. That wouldn't happen now.

Batting with Len, when the going was good and things were going well for him, you had to get ready on the fifth or sixth ball because he wanted to keep the strike, which is fair enough, he was the best player. I remember the first time I ever batted with him, which was in 1949 at the Scarborough Festival. It was neck and neck for who was going to be top of the averages and he and Joe Hardstaff were right up at the top, averaging about sixty each. There was nothing in it, nip and tuck.

They were both playing in the match and I had the misfortune to bat with them both and I never got a bloody ball. I hardly got strike. I remember in the second innings, batting with Len, he hit the last ball of the over straight at cover. 'Yes', he called, and it wasn't there. I must have been run out by about two yards, quite comfortably. Old Emmott Robinson was umpiring and he said: 'Not out'. Then he said to me: 'Son, get on with your game, don't take any notice of these two'. He'd known what was going on with Joe Hardstaff in the first innings. 'You get on and enjoy your game, have another knock', he said, which was fabulous really. I didn't get many runs but it was a wonderful thing for Emmott to do.

As a captain Len was sound, solid, greatly concerned with the quickies, particularly on the 1954–55 trip when we had Frank Tyson. And of course the bloke at the other end was a magical bowler, Brian Statham. Everyone talks about Frank Tyson whistling down the hill with this 40 mph gale behind him and knocking seven over. Brian Statham bowled for two hours straight into the teeth of that gale, never gave a run away, absolutely marvellous.

Len knew all the basic things about the game. He never made any mistakes, basic mistakes, was very sound, and when trouble was there the old quickies used to come on and shut it up. He was possibly one of the first men to start delaying things to upset the youngsters, to upset the Simpsons, the Davidsons, the Archers and Harveys, who were young men wanting to get on with the game. Frank Tyson used to take more than five minutes to bowl an over. Len would walk from slip, in the middle of an over, to Tyson who was sixty yards away, just to slow things down.

I think he wanted to win a lot because of what he had to suffer in 1946 and 1948. England dropped him in 1948, which was unforgivable. How could you leave Hutton out? In Australia in 1954–55 he liked having the boot on the other foot. And he made it work; he really did make it work.

Len obviously loved getting runs, but at times he gave the impression that it was very hard work. I think a great deal of that was because of his physical frailty. But I think he really enjoyed it afterwards. He got the hard work in but afterwards he really enjoyed it. His left arm used to get tired.

I remember playing with him at Scarborough in 1949. Len had had a wonderful year after a bad start. His arm was aching a bit and he used a Harrow bat and got 100 in two consecutive games at Scarborough – 147 for Yorkshire v MCC, 101 for the Gentlemen v Players and 75 for the Leveson-Gower XI, with a little bat, one that a 15- or 16-year-old would play with, weighing about 2 pounds maximum. The ball still went off because he was a stroker of the ball, a timer of the ball. There was nothing brutal about anything he did. He sort of caressed it, beautifully placing the ball. He was such a good player, the sort of player who when he got in it seemed so natural that he just kept going. What always amazes me is that he used to say: 'I was a player before the war.' He reckoned he was a far better player pre-war than he was afterwards, and he was a great player afterwards.

Apart from the genius of Compton, there wasn't anyone to touch him and with all due respect to recent people, like Geoffrey Boycott and others, they're not in the same street as Len Hutton, couldn't lace his boots, no way. He was just a better player than they were. Yorkshiremen are always being criticised for their attitudes, their selfishness, long pockets and short, sticky fingers and that sort of thing, but Len always played for the team. Superb player.

The two matches we had to win in the West Indies, he just set himself in; he set his stall to win. He just said: 'I'm not going to get out. I'm going to put the platform there and make sure that we're in charge.' And that's exactly what he did and he was good enough to do it. We all have these aims; you know you can play well but you can't always play well when you want to. But with Len, you always felt that if he really wanted it, in the same way that Denis used to, if he really wanted to do it no one would bowl him out. He was an astonishing player.

We used to get on all right together, but I'm sure he felt I should have done better. In the end-of-term report, I think he would say that I had the talent but didn't use it to his satisfaction. A reasonable player, nothing like the Huttons or the Comptons, but he felt deep down that I should have done better. And then when I did, late in my career, that's when he said: 'Good player, you are, good player'.

We always talked later on, once he'd retired. He was a nice man.

He had that feeling that I had the talent to contribute more than I did, which is fair enough, but when you play cricket you have your own attitude. Cricket is different from any other sport because it's got to be part of your life. You spend so much of your life on the field. It's not like playing soccer; cricket has got to be a way of life and your own personality and feelings come into it. To me it was never a war, the way some people look at it. I think on occasions, purely because of what happened in the 1940s and early 1950s, Len was inclined to take it very seriously, which perhaps I didn't. Obviously I wanted to do well, but it wasn't the be-all and end-all of my life. Sometimes you surprise yourself at how well you can play at times, and Len felt that I should have surprised myself more often.

On the West Indian tour of 1953–54 we were sitting round a table, Brian Statham, Jim Laker, myself and Len. Len asked Brian if he wanted to go to Australia the next year. 'Well, of course I do', he said. Then Len asked me the same thing. 'I've never been', I said, 'and it's the pinnacle of cricket to go on a tour of Australia. I'd love to go.' Then he turned to Jim and he said: 'Have a drink, Jim?' Jim never went. Once Jim had made his comeback in the West Indies, people had even more respect for him and I always have the feeling, one way or another, that the captain's got to have the last say. Having said that, although Jim didn't go to Australia in 1954, Bob Appleyard did and he did a wonderful job.

Len was a little bit of a leg-puller; he used to take the mickey out of people; he upset Keith Andrew. Good golfer. He liked to be on the winning side. In the early days, he used to get me to play golf with him, against the Governor of Bermuda and people like that. He was a fine golfer. He was never unkind to me. He'd just look and you'd think: 'Oh bloody hell, I shouldn't have played that shot'.

When batting, Len did like to get on the front foot. His first movement was forward, but he was such a good player that he could play from anywhere. He never missed a half-volley from a spinner. He was always in the right place and he used to hit the ball a bit late to miss the fielder. He gave the impression that he put it exactly where he wanted to put it.

Frank Tyson

Born 1930. Northamptonshire: 1952–60. 17 Test matches: 1954–59. Known as 'Typhoon Tyson', he was at his fastest and best in Australia in 1954/55 when Hutton thought him as fast as any bowler he had seen. After the disastrous first Test, he was persuaded to shorten his run and took 10 wickets in the second after being hit on the head by a bouncer from Lindwall, and his Test best, 7 for 27, in the third. Hutton thought he was a yard faster after being hit. A graduate from Durham University, he emigrated to Australia and became a teacher in Melbourne and coach to the Victorian Cricket Association.

Was Len Hutton good as a captain in handling his fast attack? His attitude changed somewhat when we first came out in 1954–55. He had anticipated that the brunt would be borne by Al and Boil (Bedser and Bailey), established bowlers, and Brian Statham. I don't know whether he expected myself and Loader to contribute much; we were the apprentices. But very early on his opinion changed.

In Perth we played on an extremely quick wicket rolled down about an inch below the level of the square. In later years, he told me why he changed his mind. I hit a batsman on the pad and they had to carry him off; he couldn't continue. Hutton realised he had a couple of quick bowlers in myself and Statham, and with us he could regain the ground lost between 1946 and 1954.

He did understand how to use fast bowlers. He didn't bowl me in very long spells; he used me as a shock bowler, and rested me when he could. He deliberately slowed the over rate down, but at the end of the day we generally got them out. He understood a bowler's psychology. He'd walk from slip to the end of the bowler's run and say: 'How are you, Frank?' and then walk back again, which would enable you to have a breather.

Originally, in League cricket, I'd bowled off ten or fifteen yards. Then I strained a back muscle and wasn't moving quickly enough into my delivery stride. I went to Alf Gover's cricket school while I was qualifying for Northants in 1952 and 1953, and at the same time felling trees for Stuart Surridge to strengthen my back. So Gover knew I could bowl off a short run, very quickly.

We got to Australia. By then in England I'd lengthened my run to 25 yards, so that I was arriving more quickly at the wicket. Gover, who was in Australia as a journalist, suggested after Brisbane that I should go back to a shorter run. I tried it and realised that if I pushed my acceleration in my approach to the wicket I was just as quick. So it was a reversion to what I'd done before.

Lindwall hit me on the head in the Sydney Test. That served me right, because I'd dared to bowl him a bouncer in Brisbane, but it made me a little angry. Thereafter Lindwall never scored a run because he was always expecting a bouncer and I got him with half volleys and yorkers.

Did I ever bowl at Hutton? Not very much. The first time was when I was at Durham University and we played against Yorkshire at Redcar as a pipe opener for them at the start of the season; thereafter our paths didn't cross. It was interesting at Redcar; he was such a superb judge of where his off stump was. He knew exactly which balls to play and which to leave alone. And he moved pretty early; he was a great technician.

Often nowadays I tell the kids, with their helmets and gear, that no one ever hit Hutton. His positioning was so good. He moved first on to his back foot: a slight shift backwards of his weight and across slightly. If your weight is on the front foot you can't move it. Then he was in position, if he wanted, to move further back and across. Or he could move forward. He could play with the swing and still be balanced. He hated Miller because he swung it so late. Miller puzzled him, the way he bowled an outswinger, inswinger, bouncer, wrong 'un. That was not in the Yorkshire handbook of bowling.

Len was a great psychologist. It wasn't what he said, but what he didn't say. I remember at the Windsor in Melbourne, four of us and some girls, at ten o'clock one night; Len poked his head in. 'Are you

The victorious skipper with fast bowlers Tyson and Loader in Australia, 1954.

all right?' he said. It was what he didn't say that counted. 'I'll see you in the morning.' Within an hour we were all tucked up in bed fast asleep.

He had a wry sense of humour. He said to Peter Richardson on the boat out: 'Be careful; they all come from robbers here, you know.' In Sydney once, he was taken to Tattersalls Club and watched people playing poker machines for an hour; then he told his host: 'You ought to teach them to do something useful, like playing cricket.' Sometimes you would expect him to be about to say something deep, and he'd come out with something intensely banal like: 'Are the trams still running in Melbourne?'

Mentally, he was a very convoluted sort of person. He was in a mess with fibrositis. I remember his state of mental agitation about whether he should play in the third Test in Melbourne. It was George

Duckworth, the baggage man, who persuaded him to play. If we hadn't had him, as psychological leader, we would have been in difficulties; but he was in severe pain.

He really wanted to beat Australia in Australia; he'd been so often on the losing side. That was his driving force. He was very perceptive, but sometimes found it very difficult to communicate; he wasn't quite on the same wavelength as some people. I don't think Fred Trueman found him easy, for instance.

I was present in Adelaide when he said: 'The buggers have done us.' He was reflecting his heritage, particularly as it was Miller who had taken two wickets, him and Edrich, and brilliantly caught May. Miller had put on a marvellous performance in Melbourne when in England's first innings he took three wickets in nine overs for five runs. But in Adelaide we only needed 94 to secure the Ashes, and even Len didn't really believe that we wouldn't get them on a perfect wicket. It was a kneejerk reaction. He was so strung up; and he was in pain, as I recall. Besides, he'd been out for 80 in the first innings hitting a ball from Johnston plumb in the middle of the bat and getting caught, so he was not feeling in a very lucky frame of mind. Compton went out and stayed there and that was that.

Afterwards we went to Sydney and nearly beat them in three days. The funniest part was Richie Benaud being bowled by Hutton, who bowled the last over of the game. That was the match in which Ian Johnson made a classic error. He thought Australia had saved the follow-on because they were exactly 150 runs behind, but they hadn't because they needed one more run when Johnson carelessly ran himself out. Len made them follow on, to his great delight. They'd lost six wickets in their second innings and were still behind when the match ended.

The Australians didn't understand Hutton at all, though they had great regard for his technical ability; that 62 not out he made in the Brisbane Test in 1950 is still talked about as one of the best innings ever seen up there. As regards his character, they didn't have any idea at all. He was Yorkshire in his temperament, character, and makeup. He had been brought up, in his early days, in a Yorkshire side that literally ate, drank, and slept cricket, and talked about it till the small hours: people like Bowes, Leyland, Verity: a worthwhile list of people.

As a tactician, Hutton rarely missed a trick. He wasn't a genius at innovation, but he knew when to bring a bowler on, when to press home an advantage, and when to attack. There was an interesting example in 1955 in Adelaide. At the end of the fourth day, in Australia's second innings, they were 69 for 4 and Appleyard had taken 3 for 13; the ball was turning, Appleyard was magnificent. He bowled Harvey with a ball that came really fizzing across him from outside his leg stump. The following day everyone said spin would decide it.

But Hutton never bowled Appleyard at all. He realised that after Sydney and Melbourne he had the advantage with his pace men; and in one and a half hours we had them out for 111. It was quite remarkable, really. Everybody said he should have used Appleyard. But the result of the decision was that we only had to chase 94 to win the Ashes.

In Auckland, we bowled out New Zealand for 26. I had two for ten, and Len thought that was too expensive. When we batted he went in at number five and I came in when we were 160-odd for seven. He said to me: 'Stick around, and we'll beat these fellows by an innings.' I thought it improbable, but we were out for 246 and his prediction turned out to be true.

It wasn't Hutton slowing down the over rate that unsettled the batsmen. The fast bowlers would do that for him, once we were on top. The scores were quite illustrative of that. They wouldn't have got as many runs as they did if it hadn't been for Maddocks and Johnson. They were 151 for 8 in Melbourne and got 231. In Adelaide they were 229 for 8 and got 323: again Maddocks and Johnson. It was the tailenders who got the runs. The top order weren't got out by the over-rate, but by the bowling. You can't get distracted by over-rates.

If he didn't have to play the ball, he didn't. He never really chased a ball wide of the off stump. He never hooked. Bowling bouncers at him was just a waste of time. I sometimes wonder how many balls he would play from the West Indian attack these days; it would be extremely tedious to watch.

He never mentioned the injury to his arm.

He hardly ever seemed to hit the ball. He transferred his weight. It was stroking, not punching. May was the opposite: he used a lot of right hand.

Peter Loader

Born 1929. Surrey and Western Australia: 1951–64. 13 Test matches: 1954–59. Right-arm fast bowler who swung the ball, varied his pace, and had an effective bouncer. He opened the bowling with Alec Bedser at Surrey during their run of seven Championship wins from 1952–58. His only Test with Hutton was his debut, against Pakistan at the Oval in 1954, though he did tour Australia in 1954/55. He left Surrey in 1963 and emigrated to Western Australia at the same time as Tony Lock, his team-mate at Surrey.

Len was never renowned for putting his hand in his pocket, but coming out on the boat to Australia in 1954, about a week out of England, he asked Tyson, Statham, me, and, I think, Appleyard for liqueurs and coffee in the lounge after dinner. Len said to me: 'You'll have a good time on the tour, and the experience will be good for you. But you won't play in a Test match.' Imagine saying that to anyone! It wasn't very encouraging; and if you look at the statistics I think you'll find that before the first Test in Brisbane I'd taken more wickets than anyone else. Len had this dream: he wanted to blast Australia off the map.

There was an awful lot of unhappiness on that tour. Len spoke to very few people: Denis Compton, Godfrey Evans, Trevor Bailey a bit. He was a very shy man. After we'd won the Ashes in Adelaide, we were all invited to different parties to celebrate, and I went to the toilet and Len was next to me. 'Hello lad,' he said. 'Did you have a good trip?' It was almost the only time he spoke to me off the field for the whole tour. He was the most extraordinary man.

Years later, here in Perth, my wife answered the phone, our business phone, and said that someone called 'Lyn' wanted to speak to me. So I took the phone and said: 'Can I help you?' and the voice said: 'It's Leonard here.' We never ever called him Leonard or Len; only the top echelon did that. We called him skipper. I instinctively said: 'Oh, hullo skipper'. Then I said: 'If you're here, we must get together.' He said: 'What about a game of golf?' 'Fine', I said. 'When?' He said: 'Now'.

After we'd won a Test match, he'd sit in a corner with a bottle of beer that had been kept warm for him on a shelf. We saw so little of him. I'd be bowling and go back to the end of my run; Len would be fielding in the gully, and he'd waddle – he was a most unathletic person – from gully to the end of my run. I'd think: 'Now here comes some classic of cricket thinking; some adjustment of the field perhaps.' Then he'd say: 'You all right?' I'd say: 'Fine' and he'd say: 'Oh, good', and then he'd walk back to gully.

It was dreadful the way he slowed down the over rate. I'd been brought up at Surrey under Stuart Surridge, where the idea was to get on with it, because the more balls you bowled the more people you got out. Hutton was a most superb batsman, but his cutting down the overs was a bloody disgrace. I was embarrassed. I'd think to myself: 'Here is one of the great cricketers of the world, and he's got it wrong.' We didn't have the best attack, because we'd left the two best spinners in England at home, but we had a pretty good attack and we wanted to get people out.

I wasn't the bravest of batsmen. In those days we used to play all the states twice and we played New South Wales in Sydney. When Miller came in to bat, Len said: 'Give him three or four an over.' Bouncers? Me? I hit Miller a few times and eventually got him out. He knew I'd been acting under orders, but as he went out he said: 'You'll bloody well keep'. That was fair enough. Len said: 'Well done lad, well done. You've done a lot for England today. And don't worry. You won't ever bat against him.' Well, we went to play New South Wales again later in the tour and their captain was K. R. Miller. We started our innings late in the day and Hutton said: 'Put your pads on. You're night watchman.' Hutton got out and I had Miller bowling at me; he didn't bowl bouncers, but he hit me in the backside a few times. But making me night watchman . . . it was unbelievable.

He had this lovely waspish sense of humour. There were no curfews in those days, but you were supposed to go to bed at a reasonable hour, and it was understood that if you had a late night and didn't perform well the next day you were liable to find yourself on a tramp steamer bound for home, and miss out on your £150 good conduct bonus. In Sydney, Statham and I went out and came back late to the Hotel Australia, and thought, we won't go in through the front door, we'll go in the back. Somebody, the team manager I think, saw us. Next day was hot, very hot, and I bowled a very long spell. Finally Hutton came up and said: 'Did you have a good night last night? Have a couple more, lad.'

PART THREE

The View From Yorkshire

J. M. Kilburn

Ellis Robinson

Ted Lester

Vic Wilson

Billy Sutcliffe

Michael Rines

Bob Appleyard

J. R. Burnet

Fred Trueman

Brian Close

Arnold Silvester

Yorkshire, the champion county, at Scarborough in 1937. *Left to right*: Verity, Bowes, Yardley, Sellers (captain), Sutcliffe, Smailes, Barber, Wood, Leyland, Turner, Hutton – 'one of the finest county teams of all time'.

J. M. Kilburn

Born 1909. Jim Kilburn played for Barnsley in the Yorkshire League and Bradford in the Bradford League. He was the cricket correspondent for the Yorkshire Post *from 1934–76, and knew Hutton better than any other journalist. His many books include:* In Search of Cricket *(1937);* Homes of Sport: Cricket *(with N. W. D. Yardley) (1952);* Cricket Decade *(1959);* History of Yorkshire Cricket *(1969);* Thanks to Cricket *(1972).*

I knew of Leonard Hutton before I knew him because he had a tremendous reputation as a schoolboy player in the Bradford League for Pudsey. At the age of fourteen or fifteen he was one of their star players. He used to come up to the Yorkshire nets for coaching from that age, which is very unusual. At about that time, 1935, Herbert Sutcliffe wrote an autobiography, in which he said that Yorkshire had, waiting in the wings, a wonderful boy batsman who would certainly play for England within a year or two. This was a pretty big thing for somebody like Herbert Sutcliffe to say and so everybody knew of Hutton who didn't actually know Hutton.

In 1934, Leonard, at the age of seventeen, played in his first first-class match. Yorkshire went to Cambridge to play the University. In his first innings, he ran himself out for nothing. You can imagine what a youngster of seventeen would feel in circumstances like that, absolutely down, but at that time, when Yorkshire were a great side, nobody patted you on the back and said: 'Well, never mind, it'll be all right old chap.' The only consolation he got was from Maurice Leyland, who very kindly said: 'Never mind, Len, you've started at the bottom'.

Leonard's character was formed in that way and he didn't expect any nannying or babying. His business was to learn cricket and he was the best learner, I think, I've ever met in my life. He didn't say anything, he'd sit down quietly and if something new occurred to him he'd think it out. In his second year in first-class cricket he had a very ordinary season because he was ill; he wasn't really fit and Yorkshire were very careful with him. They didn't push him too hard.

In the winter of 1936–37 he had an operation on his nose, and his health improved enormously. From 1937, when he played in his first Test match, there he was: he was great without any argument. Not only George Hirst and Herbert Sutcliffe thought so. I remember Plum Warner saying: 'Well, you can't fault him.' This was a lad of eighteen! His method was so good.

George Hirst tried everything to find a weakness. That's why he sent for Bill Bowes, just to put a bit of pace and a few bouncers at him. George, who was a great personal friend, never suspected a weakness in Leonard. I can imagine Ellis Robinson bowling at Leonard's leg stump all winter. When you first come into top-class cricket, someone who can turn the ball, bowling at the leg stump with a leg trap, wants a bit of playing unless you're pretty good with your feet and you know what you're doing. I don't think Ellis found any weakness either. Against a turning ball Leonard was at his very best.

He had an awful lot of fast bowling to deal with because he was the number one batsman. Immediately after the war, when his reputation was so enormous because he held this world record of 364, the Australians got at him and tried him out for all they were worth. People like Miller and Lindwall, who weren't babies when it came to bowling. Against fast bowling you've got to fight all the time. It's not only a question of technique, it's a question of getting out of the way as well. These bowlers came along and they were very quick and, although they weren't in any sense nasty-tempered, they were very quick and they had no mercy. If they saw the slightest flinching on the part of the batsman, they were after him like nobody's business.

I don't think Leonard ever had any doubts in his own mind that there was anything else in the world for him than to play cricket. It never occurred to him that he was great; all that concerned him was that he was a cricketer. In his first season, 1934, I travelled with him by train from Hull to London. You weren't allowed to take a car, even if you had one in those days. In one corner was Leonard Hutton and in another corner was me.

I had a few things to read, paperbacks, that sort of thing, and I passed them over to Leonard and said: 'Have a look at those if you want to.' He looked at those for a time but he didn't look for very long. He was sitting back and after about forty minutes, just as we were getting towards Doncaster if I remember rightly, he suddenly burst into a little chuckle. I said: 'What's the matter with you, Leonard. What are you laughing at?' 'I'm laughing at playing for Yorkshire,' he said. It had dawned on him, the life before him opened out, and he couldn't help but chuckle at the idea of Leonard Hutton playing for Yorkshire, while everybody else was looking at it the other way around: aren't Yorkshire lucky to have Leonard Hutton coming up to play for them.

In that sense he never got a swelled head at all. Never – and I got to know Leonard very well, I was just a few years older than him. I never, never knew him to be in any way conceited. Confident – yes, full of confidence, believed in himself, believed in his batting, wanted to be a leading cricketer, but didn't want to be a leading cricketer for the sake of it. I never knew him say a boastful word about himself, never once.

He was a little bit, what shall I say, reserved in his praise for others, but when he gave his praise, he gave it very wholeheartedly. He'd have cleaned Wally Hammond's boots for him if necessary, he thought so much of Hammond. I never heard him express any jealousy at all, against any player, even against players who were getting a bit more limelight than he was, Denis Compton if you like, doing the Brylcreem stuff.

He didn't know what to do with all the attention he received after scoring his 364. He was completely flabbergasted. Bear in mind that he was only twenty-two and he had never had anything like this before. We stayed in the same hotel, the Great Central, pulled down now, at Marylebone Station. That was the headquarters for the England team at that time and some of the major press people stayed there as well. On the morning after his 364, Leonard rang from his bedroom to one of his companions and he said: 'I don't know what to do. I can't get out of my room, the corridor's full of people with bits of paper and pens and they're all wanting me to sign things.' He was as naive as that. We said: 'Don't move Leonard, stay where you are and we'll send somebody up to handle all these people.' Leonard hadn't the faintest idea what to do.

That was the foundation of his financial fortune. He got a lot of advertising from it. He also got £1,000 from an Australian chap who had also given Bradman £1,000 when he got his 334. £1,000 was a lot of money in the 1930s. It bought Leonard his house. In those days you could buy a nice little house for £800 or £900.

After the war, when he had become not only a great young cricketer but a cricketing personality as well, he could mix with people outside cricket who were nevertheless, well, lion-hunters if you like. There was one particular chap, a paper manufacturer, who took Leonard into financial circles that he never got anywhere near before, and being a very good listener, he didn't waste the information that came his way over the dinner table. He just quietly went round to his stockbroker and said: 'I've been told about this, what do you think?' He made quite a lot of money that way and he also had a lot of money offered to him for sponsorship. He got a little bit of a reputation for chasing the money: 'How much is there in it for me?' – that sort of thing.

He wasn't a teetotaller, but you'd never find him in the bar after the match until he became captain and then he more or less had to go and buy the others a drink. There's lots of others who'd be pretty hard pushed before they'd pay up, you know. Leonard wasn't a social cricketer in that sense. He would go and have a quiet dinner on his own, go to the pictures, something like that. He wasn't a bar man in any sense. He probably would appear pretty quiet, especially if you were at the other end of the scale; someone like Miller would buy anyone a drink at any time and have two for himself.

He was a responsible chap, Leonard, very responsible. In his cricket, private life and in all his affairs he was pretty shrewd. I can tell you a little story: when he was negotiating with the *Daily Mail* and three or four other people at the same time, he was offered a certain amount of money and various perks, which included a car. He said yes, he would need a car and they asked him what kind of car he was thinking of. 'A Bentley's a good car', Leonard said. They sat back in astonishment and said: 'Well, I don't think we can run to that, Leonard.' That's the sort of shrewdness that Leonard had.

In his cricket, in his captaincy in particular, his whole strategy was never to get into a position that he couldn't get out of. In other words, he would never burn his bridges. When things were going against him, he had to work very hard to think of some way of stopping the rot. That was the origin of this slow over-rate. He said: 'Well now then, they're getting runs like fun, we shall have to stop this. We'll bowl two overs instead of three in the next ten minutes. They can't score if we're not bowling to them, can they?'

With his batting, bowling and captaincy, he always tried to ensure that the situation never got out of his control. He had a lot of disappointments in that way, because some of his players were a bit irresponsible, in the sense of saying: 'Well, all right, if I've got out I've got out.' Leonard couldn't bear that, the thought of getting out when you didn't have to get out, or when you shouldn't get out. He was very disappointed by that attitude and he carried his England responsibility to a point of excess, I would say. He nearly broke his own health carrying the responsibility.

He didn't enjoy the England captaincy, but he wanted it very badly indeed. In that year, 1954, when there was doubt as to whether David Sheppard or he would take the side to Australia, poor old Leonard nearly finished up in a mental home. I can remember driving to one of the Essex grounds from our London hotel with Norman Yardley, who was then on the England Selection Committee and saying to him: 'Look, are you going to make Leonard captain for Australia?' 'Oh yes, I think so, no question about it.' 'Well', I said, 'for God's sake tell him or you'll have him in a mental home. Put the chap out of his uncertainty.' They did and all was well.

Leonard relished the captaincy. He always wanted it because he thought he could do it better than any of the other candidates, which was quite right, he could. It was pretty sensational at that time for a professional to be captain of England. It was a tremendous thing for Leonard, but while he was doing it it was very hard work indeed. He was thinking for ten other people as well as for himself and he'd got a lot of social obligations that he didn't particularly want.

He was very, very conscientious about fulfilling these obligations, which he absolutely hated. He didn't like public speaking at all, for instance. I remember when we were in Australia and we'd gone upstate to play a country team. The country club we were playing wanted Leonard to dress up as a jockey for the trots and get on a trotting horse to have his photograph taken. Leonard was terrified of horses but he thought it was his duty to do this, good publicity for the England team, friendly with the natives and all that sort of business and so he got onto this trotting horse's sulky. They gave him the reins and the fellow stepped away from holding the horse's head to get out of the photograph. The horse moved slightly, and I could almost see Hutton going paler and paler underneath his sunburn in case this damned horse ran away. Anyway, he got out safely and with great alacrity, but that was the sort of thing he would do although he hated doing it.

Between you, me and the gate-post, he was a bit lucky with the press on that tour (1954–55) as he had quite a good adviser. This chap (J. M. Kilburn) was appointed by the English press to be a liaison man between the press and the players, so if Leonard wasn't certain

what to do about some things he knew where to come, because he'd
got a pal on the other side, so to speak. There was never the slightest
difficulty with the press at all, throughout the whole tour. We dealt
with the Australian press by saying right at the beginning: 'Look,
Leonard, when you have a press conference, when all these fellows
are waiting there with their pencils and their questions, take the

initiative, tell them something, even if it's only the date. Give them
something, if you give them something they'll forget about what it
was they wanted to ask you. All they want is something – that Leonard Hutton said it was a nice day on Friday, that's my quote.' He
followed that and got away without any trouble at all.

Hutton with Yorkshire
journalist J. M. Kilburn
on their way to Australia
in 1946. Kilburn, who
followed him for over 20
years, wrote: 'Hutton's is
a very romantic story,
but Leonard wasn't a
romantic.'

I glowed during Leonard's innings of 37 at Sydney in 1946. It was
incredible; a magnificent performance. When he was out it was a bit
unlucky. He played a forcing shot, a shot off the back foot with a
follow through and the bat slipped from his hand. Well, it didn't slip
from his hand, but he had to reach for it over his shoulder and it
touched a bail and out. It was just before lunch and I saw him during
the interval. 'That's a pity, Leonard', I said. 'Well,' he said, and it's
the only time I ever heard him talk about his own batting: 'Well, it is
a pity because if it hadn't happened, we might have seen something
this afternoon.' In other words, we might have had a display that

was beyond belief because he never in a Test match batted like that before or since.

It was absolutely wonderful, it all took place in about twenty minutes against the new ball. Where somebody bowled a beautiful in-swinger, Leonard would send it off for runs down to fine-leg. The crowd sat with their mouths open, they didn't believe it. The other players didn't either. It was one of these astonishing things. It was literally a moment of cricketing inspiration. He'd played a shot or two in the first over which came off and he simply couldn't stop playing shots. He really was inspired.

Leonard's greatest batting, speaking purely in terms of batsmanship, was on the South African tour of 1938–39 and the English season of 1939, when the West Indies came, just before the war broke out. He was free, he was a young man, he had no responsibilities, he wasn't captain. All he had was the joy of hitting the ball and because he could hit it so well the greater the joy. It was absolute joy to see him at that time. You got little thrills down your back. He batted as Frank Woolley batted in those two seasons and if he hadn't been injured and his career hadn't taken the sort of course that it did, he would have done just the same after the war. He would have been brilliant to a degree.

The Australians eventually thought he was the finest defensive batsman they'd ever seen, but they insisted on the 'defensive'. It was circumstances that made him the finest defender. If circumstances had been different, he'd have been one of the finest attackers too, he'd have been rather like Stan McCabe, only more reliable. His injury literally limited his movement. He never hooked after the war. There wasn't any stroke that he didn't play to perfection, technically, before 1939. If you can't hook, the only thing to do to people like Miller and Lindwall is to duck.

They were a very Yorkshire Yorkshire before 1939. They'd got people like Arthur Mitchell, Sellers himself, Maurice Leyland, Herbert Sutcliffe, whose motto to the younger player was: 'Well, now look, you can't get any runs in the dressing-room, the longer you stay out there the more likely you are to accumulate some runs, but the first thing to do is to stay out there. Don't do anything flashy, Leonard, stay out there for as long as you can.' And so, in that sense, he was encouraged to be defensive. He was told: 'Now, never mind what we're doing, we're chasing runs for a declaration, but you needn't, you stay in if you can.' That was the way he was treated. They didn't force him. They treated him like a younger brother.

Frank Dennis played in the Yorkshire side and when they went to Scarborough Leonard got to know Frank's sister, Dorothy, and that was it. And I might tell you, that *was* it, literally it. I never saw Leonard, and I went all over the world with him, look at anybody else at all. In fact, I remember after his 364 there was a photograph which appeared in one of the London papers of Leonard at a round table in a nightclub with perhaps half a dozen people. Somebody had taken him out, lion-hunting I suppose. Next to him was an attractive-looking girl and Leonard said to me: 'Do you think this picture will

Len arrives with Dorothy for a wartime charity match. He scored a hundred, then found his broken arm had failed to set.

appear in Yorkshire? I just wondered if Dorothy might see it before I could tell her what was going on.' I never saw Leonard interested in any other girl. I think she was tremendously helpful to him. She had a strong and a very well-balanced character that complemented him absolutely. She was a damn sight better as Lady Dorothy than he was as Sir Leonard. He said: 'It's all right this Sir Leonard business, but it's another ten shillings on the bill every time.'

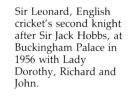

Sir Leonard, English cricket's second knight after Sir Jack Hobbs, at Buckingham Palace in 1956 with Lady Dorothy, Richard and John.

In ability he was unmatched, nobody better. He was the absolute epitome of the orthodox. You never saw him in what you might call a rough, uneducated batting position. He always looked right in whatever he did. Even if he missed the ball he looked right in the shot he played, and he never attempted anything unorthodox at all. He wasn't flowery and it didn't matter what stage of his innings it was. Naturally he forced the pace when it was necessary, and he could. Nearly all this time after the war he was the only reliable batsman that Yorkshire had and he was the only reliable batsman that England had, if it came to that, as well. All the time he'd got this burden of responsibility, so he couldn't afford to be flowery and flashy.

There was no vacancy for the Yorkshire captaincy, so it didn't worry Leonard or anybody else at all. Norman Yardley followed on quite naturally from Sellers. If there had been a question of a vacancy and somebody else had got it, then Leonard would have been offended and hurt. When Leonard came back from Australia his career was finished and he didn't care then. Once he became captain of England, Hutton played with Yorkshire but not for Yorkshire. He had great sympathy for Norman. He always said of Norman: 'You know, Norman's too nice a fellow to be captain of this lot', and he was quite right too, they were a very awkward lot at that particular time: Appleyard, Wardle and one or two others.

He gave up because he was exhausted mentally, and he really had a very bad back indeed, terribly bad back, and he'd carried that bad back for many years before he retired. I remember we were in a hotel in Oxford at the beginning of the season. We were having breakfast and Leonard said: 'I wonder if you'd come down to the shops with me?' I said: 'Of course, Leonard, where are we going?' 'Well,' he said, 'I want to go to Marks and Spencers.' 'What do you want in Marks and Spencers?', I said. 'Well', he said, 'I want to buy a lady's roll-on and I don't like to go by myself.' That was one of those stretch things, so that he could wear it under his shirt to keep his back from getting damp. If you bat for a long time, you want to stand up and rub your back. Well, if you're going to make 364, you're going to be doing a lot of back bending.

Leonard had to deal with quite a lot of Australians and he didn't really understand them, they were a bit brash for Leonard, who was the sort of bloke who'd rather sit in the corner with his beer. He'd have liked Australia if it hadn't been for the Australians, so to speak, but he got on very well with the Australian players. He wasn't a typical Australian sportsman; he wasn't the sort of fellow to dash onto the beach. He wasn't a drinker; he was no good in the Sydney six o'clock swill for instance.

I think Leonard's most enjoyable tour was to South Africa in 1938–39, when he was a great player and when to be a cricketer in South Africa was just about all you could ask. All the girls came round, it was a white man's paradise just before the war. He didn't get on frightfully well with the West Indians; the 1954–55 tour was difficult. It added to the general tiredness which gradually grew over him. I think I once wrote that he retired with relief rather than regret.

He'd talk to you about cricket only if you displayed to him that you knew what you were talking about, but not if you didn't know the difference between a banana and a bosie. He talked very obliquely, he never told you something straight, he told it you half-way and left you to fill in the other half, to make clear to yourself what his meaning was. When Leonard became captain, as a professional, he went into the holy of holies of the amateurs at Lord's. He had to tread very warily so that he didn't do or say anything wrong. Naturally, not wanting to say anything wrong, he would tend not to say anything at all. He would hint at what he wanted to the Selection Committee, he wouldn't say: 'I'm having so-and-so in my team', to Gubby Allen or somebody. He'd say: 'Well, I should have thought, with that little bit of extra height, Bob Appleyard would do well in Australia.' All the time he had to talk like that and behave like that to avoid putting his foot in it and yet to get his own way at third hand, so to speak.

He would hint rather than state because he was never quite sure how much you knew. If he knew that you knew, then, of course, he didn't have to say the thing straight out. It might seem odd to an Australian who's a bit inclined to call a spade a bloody shovel and no nonsense about it, but Leonard would probably have said: 'Well, there are one or two gardening implements that are quite sharp at the edges.' You see, again, you've got to be a Yorkshireman to under-stand this. You could have gone to a cricket match in Yorkshire and sat on the pavilion balcony and they'd have been very astute watching the game. 'He's bowling well, three farthings.' 'Oh, I don't know, don't you think he'd be better at the other end, nay a halfpenny.' What they're doing is bargaining for wool prices between watching the cricket. Now, if you didn't understand this, you wouldn't know what they were talking about, but if you lived in Bradford it was perfectly normal ABC to you.

By the time he moved south Leonard had lost his shyness, his Yorkshire reserve, because he was in business then and it was his job to make himself clear and get on with people. When he went to Australia and South Africa selling his goods he traded on his name. If you were a buyer and your secretary brought in a card saying 'Sir Leonard Hutton', you'd see him, wouldn't you, even if you weren't going to buy anything. So he always had the entry and he used that, and without making an oration he'd got a pretty shrewd idea of how to present his case: 'Well, we do so-and-so and we do it rather well. Anyway, think it over and see you again later on.' He wasn't a pushy salesman, he was quite confident in his own ability to represent the firm with dignity. He had great dignity. No one ever saw Leonard do an undignified thing on a cricket field. He had tremendous dignity without thrusting it at you; he just never did anything which was objectionable on a cricket field.

I never knew him really angry, but sometimes he went silently cross. I never heard him swear at people or be bad-tempered. I remember him being very annoyed one Sunday in 1950. I'd been out to play golf with Leonard and we were going back to London in the car. At 6 o'clock we turned on the radio to listen to the sports news and hear the touring party to Australia announced. Freddie Brown was made captain and Denis Compton had been appointed vice-captain. I felt the car slow down and Leonard gripped the wheel. 'All right, Leonard, what's up?', I asked and he said: 'As soon as I get back to London, I'm going to write the MCC a letter and tell them that I'm not going on the tour.' I made him stop the car and told him not to write that letter and told him that he would captain England long before Compton ever would. Leonard wouldn't have gone on that tour if I hadn't made him stop the car and see the consequences of writing a letter like that. As soon as he realised what the consequences would be, he didn't write the letter. That was the one occasion on which I saw Leonard badly hurt. Compton and Hutton had to share a cabin on the boat out to Australia too.

Being made President of Yorkshire was a great honour, but I don't think it was as important to Leonard as being made captain of England. He talked to the England players when he was the captain but he didn't lecture them. He'd get a player and say: 'Let's have dinner together tonight', and he'd tell them what he thought could be done. He would also say to another player: 'You know, I think Tyson's run is five yards too long, do you think we could persuade him to cut it down? Anyway, let's have a talk with him, come and have dinner with us tonight.' He'd do it that way, he wouldn't go to a fellow and say: 'Now look, I'm not having this business, you attend at 9.30 in the morning and we'll practise your run-up.' Never dreamt of that. I should imagine, if he'd been playing today, that he would have told Micky Stewart several things about himself and his ancestors because he wouldn't have undertaken that sort of discipline. He'd have thought it was daft, idiotic.

He wasn't always as tactful as he might have been because he was shy of doing what he had to. When they had to drop Bedser, I knew he was being dropped before Bedser did. Leonard didn't actually say to Bedser: 'Look, we're going to drop you from this next Test match because you're not bowling well and you never recovered from your shingles. Anyway, that's the team that's going to play in the next match.' Leonard couldn't bring himself to do it. It might have been better if he'd had that cup of tea or that beer or that dinner with Bedser and said to him: 'We're going to leave you out, you're not doing your stuff and you can't get the Aussies out, but Alec we still count you because you're the most experienced bowler in the world. We do want you, particularly, to help this fellow, Tyson, who's raw. See what you can do; cut his run, help him out.'

That was his way of captaining. He was an introvert. He took things in, thought them over, grinded the machinery very slowly and eventually came out with what he thought was the right answer. It wasn't a consensus. He found communicating to the players very difficult indeed.

He couldn't understand why people couldn't take a hint. If he suggested something and the other fellow didn't take it up, then Leonard couldn't understand that. That's where he got cross with the

Yorkshire side in the 1950s. They'd got plenty of fairly good players but they never made a team and they always said: 'Well, Leonard doesn't help us, he's such a great batsman and we're so far below him that we don't like to ask him anything. We don't like to communicate with him.' Leonard, at the other end of the spectrum, said: 'Well, they never come to me, these fellows; I could help them, but they never come and ask me.' A great deal of Leonard's enormous talent, in that sense, was wasted. All he could do was to show them and he showed them. If you look at the figures you'll find, for four or five seasons, Leonard Hutton top of the batting averages and so-and-so next and there's a difference of 20 to 25 runs between the top man and anybody else. He was carrying the whole thing. If the pitch was turning, then you could bet your life: Hutton 75 not out, Yorkshire all out for 110.

He never played about with his cricket. Even if he was playing in a festival, he was playing properly, he wasn't being funny. Leonard could never have played cricket in a funny hat. The game meant so much to him that he couldn't do it badly if he tried. I remember a wonderful performance he gave at Sheffield in 1946, when they were playing Glamorgan on a nasty wicket, a turning wicket, and a fellow called J. C. Clay was bowling and he and Hutton had a duel that lasted nearly a whole afternoon, Leonard countering him with 99 not out.

Leonard once said to me: 'I think that fellow Laker's a good bowler, he's one of the very few that make me think.' That was something important to Leonard and to bring the best out of him you had to have somebody good at the other end. Lindwall and Miller got at him in a different way and he had a very high respect for both of them. He always said that Miller was a much better bowler than batsman. He said Miller had the finest bouncer and that he was the only one to frighten him with a bouncer. He bowled it so far up the pitch, he hit the pitch so hard from a good length to get a bouncer, whereas with all the others you could see them coming. He never confessed which other bowlers made him think.

The whole game meant so much to him that he wouldn't do anything to hurt it. When he was captain of England in England, he said to me: 'You know, I've had lots of offers, advertising and that sort of thing, but a lot of them can be turned down straightaway. I don't think that it would be quite right for the captain of England to be doing that sort of thing.' So you see, he wasn't altogether a money-grabber.

His great model and idol in a business and social sense was Herbert Sutcliffe. I don't think Herbert Sutcliffe ever stayed in a hotel twice in a season, he always had an invitation to stay with somebody in an away match. Herbert was a very shrewd fellow when it came to financial matters. A lot of Leonard's secondary character, as distinct from his cricket character, came through Herbert Sutcliffe. Leonard admired him enormously and learnt from him. Sutcliffe carried tremendous authority. Leonard asked me to help him with his autobiography, but I wasn't a ghost writer. I haven't written a biography because Leonard has already written his own autobiography, which I don't think is much good. Hutton's is a very romantic story, but Leonard wasn't a romantic.

There is one story I remember about Leonard keeping away from the strike. In 1951 England were playing the South Africans, who had two fairly handy fast bowlers. England went in one evening and opened with Ikin and Hutton. Ikin was not really out of the top drawer, which is unkind but true. Anyway, the bowlers bounced and threw everything at the batsmen, but they survived. At the end of play, someone who'd noticed that Leonard hadn't had much of the bowling said to him: 'Didn't Ikin play well?' Leonard looked up and said: 'I'd have thought a better batsman would have been down the other end a bit more.'

Ellis Robinson

Born 1911. Yorkshire and Somerset: 1934–52. Born at Denaby Main, Ellis Robinson is the last surviving player to have learnt his cricket in the hard school of the pre-war Yorkshire side. He bowled his off-breaks to the young Hutton in the Headingley Winter Sheds. He was also an attacking tail-end batsman, and toured Jamaica with Yorkshire in 1935/36. He was an outstanding close fielder. During a match in the 1930s, after taking an acrobatic catch in the slips, 'Ticker' Mitchell turned to him and said, 'Get up. Tha's makin' an exhibition of tha self.' After leaving Yorkshire in 1949 he played 90 games for Somerset.

I first met Leonard when we both went to the Winter Shed at Headingley together in 1931 or 1932. He was a natural. It really wasn't an effort for him, it just came. George Hirst had me bowl all one winter at his leg-stump. His concentration was natural, it was there. He was a bit dour, he had to be. Well, not so much dour but dedicated.

He got better and better as a batsman, on all wickets. He was probably the best I've seen, on all wickets, when the ball was turning. The wickets weren't covered in those days, of course. He could bowl when he wanted. A useful fielder. He was a quiet sort of a chap. He had a dour sense of humour. He wasn't a flamboyant character by any means.

Leonard wasn't a very strong man in those days. He was a stroke-maker; he didn't hit the bowling, he placed it, like all good batsmen do. For two seasons he didn't make many shots, he was just there to learn the game, and then eventually he was told to start making shots and from then on he developed into the great player he was. If he occupied the crease for a long time it meant, well, someone else had to go and force the pace and probably get out. It's difficult to explain the Yorkshire discipline. You knew what to do and if you didn't, you didn't last very long. You had to produce results; if you didn't, there were two or three others to take your place in those days. I got 13 wickets in one match and at half past six I was told that I was not required for the next match, that I was playing in the seconds. You couldn't sort of fathom why; it was probably to stop you getting big-headed.

At Bristol one year – I'll never forget this – Tom Goddard had got forty-odd wickets in the first month. We get down there, there's thirteen of us and they won the toss and put us in to bat. I was made twelfth man and I was an off-spinner, just like Tom Goddard, and I'd got loads of wickets too. That really upset me. That wicket was made for me, a dry turner. Our chaps knew it, and we lost the match

A rare picture of the young Len with his coach George Hirst at a Yorkshire celebration dinner.

easily. The lads probably couldn't understand why I'd been left out. You couldn't say anything. The captain, chairman of selectors, chairman of the committee, was a virtual dictator.

We got about with great difficulty by train. It was a hell of a job carting the baggage about. If you were a junior you had to take all the cricket bags and suitcases, get them on the train, get taxis, pay the porters, and you'd probably been bowling all day. Hell of a job. Should have been done by a scorer or somebody, but it wasn't in Yorkshire's day.

You had to pay everything out of your own pocket and then get it back from everybody. Leonard, he dodged it quite a lot. He had to do it once or twice but he didn't do it very often. We always reckoned that he made a new suit out of us. He always questioned the cost, in banter: 'Cost us how much?' you know, 'Oh, Leonard's got a new suit.'

If you had been playing away from home, it was an especially difficult job. I lived locally and coming from London you'd probably dump the bags in Sheffield, get up the next morning, pick them up and get to Leeds. Very difficult. The established people, they didn't have to do it. You wouldn't expect Herbert to do it, would you? It's easier now, with cars, and they don't have cricket bags now, do they? Suitcases would have been a lot easier. We used to have to look after thirteen cricket bags and thirteen suitcases and the press used to stick theirs in too.

When we changed stations in London you'd have to get a taxi and stick the stuff in beside the driver. Sometimes you'd have to get two taxis which, of course, was expensive and you had to pay. You got paid a match fee but everything you had to pay for, and then get it back from the players, which was a difficult job for a junior. You had to pay for your boots to be cleaned, tips for that, and waitresses in the dining room. Two bob for this, two bob for that.

When he was young, Leonard was a big eater, I tell you that. We all knew that he could really eat. Put him and Paul Gibb on a table and they'd go through it like a plague of locusts.

Leonard didn't use a lot of bats; you don't if you hit the ball in the middle. I think that I used more bats than he did. I got the edges, lots of edges, and that ruins your bat, but Leonard, he used to hit them in the middle.

Ted Lester

Born 1923. Yorkshire: 1945–56. By the end of the 1940s, Ted Lester had established himself in a strong Yorkshire batting line-up, often opening with Hutton. An amateur turned professional, he came top of the Yorkshire batting averages with 73.00 in 1947. Hutton was close second that season with 70.50. After retiring he was Yorkshire's scorer for more than 25 years.

I went in first with Len at Scarborough in 1945 and I always remember it. I was clean bowled by a chap called Nutter, who played for Lancashire and then went to Northants. He bowled me one outside the off stump and I just let it go. It knocked the off stump out and Leonard came afterwards and said: 'If you're ever going to leave one outside the off stump, always make sure you put your pad in the way.' That is the only thing that Leonard ever volunteered in all the time I knew him.

I think you learnt more from watching him than talking to him. I spent hours padded up waiting to go in while he was batting, so I had every chance to judge him at first hand. I played in an entirely different way from Leonard. He would never have condoned the way I played, so I never really had a conversation with him about how to play. He said very, very little in the middle. He kept very much to himself, unless you approached him. He would very rarely approach you. I've always felt, though, that if he'd got the Yorkshire captaincy and had had the extra responsibility, it would have opened him out: he would have come to you, expressed his opinion and tried to advise you, because he would have felt responsible for the side, whereas he felt it was somebody else's responsibility, not his.

I always thought he was disappointed not to get the Yorkshire captaincy. People have said that he wasn't, but I'm sure that he was. Captaining England he must have felt that he ought to captain Yorkshire. It was the amateur/professional relationship, I think, that probably stopped Len getting the Yorkshire job. I'm sure he'd have made a good job of it.

He was, I won't say a strange man, but he was the sort of man that you never really got to know. After the game you never saw him, probably because he played before the war and he was that little bit older than most of us. He'd made his friends before the war and they still wanted to entertain him when he played after the war. We very rarely saw him after the close of play. He was virtually apart from the team and he was very quiet in the dressing-room. Occasionally he might make the odd caustic remark if somebody had got out in a silly way, but he very rarely said a lot.

I always found he was most talkative when he was doing badly and it wasn't often he was doing badly, so he wasn't often very talkative. When he had a bad run, he was looking for sympathy more than anything else, I think, so he would open up a little bit. He always said that it was a struggle being a cricketer. If you were playing for England you were struggling to keep in the England side, and if you were only a county cricketer you were struggling to keep in the county side. So he said that whatever level you play at you're always struggling; why he should say that I really don't know. Different from Geoff Boycott, who always enjoyed batting. I often got the impression that Len didn't enjoy batting. He thought it was a bit of a toil. I remember once at Sheffield we were crossing over, it was the middle of July, and he said: 'You know, there's only 35 days to go now', as though he was looking forward to the end of the season, which seemed rather strange.

He suffered a lot from lumbago, which may have influenced the Yorkshire captaincy in some way, because the committee, I'm sure, felt that he was swinging the lead. One of the committee was heard to say: 'Well, I wish lumbago came out in spots.' They thought it wasn't right.

The captaincy of Yorkshire was in the melting pot that season (1954), because Norman was waiting to finish and take a job. I remember that Norman said: 'You know, if they'd give Len the captaincy I'd pack up tomorrow', but they wouldn't, so Norman had to carry on. I distinctly remember him saying that at one time about giving Len the captaincy. It may have had some bearing on the fact that he didn't play an awful lot in 1954.

In 1968, about thirteen years after he'd finished, he came and played at Huddersfield in a centenary game for an International XI and he scored 77. It was just like turning the clock back. Although he'd been out of the game for 13 years, it was just incredible, every-thing was still there. I'm sure that he could have continued. That's the great tragedy really. Players like Geoff Boycott never saw him and if he'd have carried on for another three or four years, it would have given a lot more people the chance to see what a good player he was.

If he'd got the Yorkshire captaincy I think he would have carried on playing for another two or three years. Quite honestly, I think that he'd lost interest really and sometimes he didn't look as though he was enjoying it. It was probably no longer a challenge to him. I think he just needed something to gee him up a little bit, give him a bit of a boost, and if he'd got the captaincy I'm sure that would have done it.

Nobody can tell how his left arm affected him, but he didn't do so badly after the war. With regard to his running between the wickets he was a good counter, I'll say that. If the conditions were favourable he was not averse to taking a single off the last ball and similarly, if the conditions weren't so good, he might take a single off the first ball. He was such a good player that he could dictate in that way. He ran me out two or three times when he said 'Yes' and I never had the price of getting in. Most great players tend to be a little bit selfish and they tend to monopolise the strike and to run a little bit for themselves, and Len was no worse than a lot of the others.

I always felt a bit of an inferiority complex batting with him. The worst feature was if you were waiting to go in and you saw Len playing and missing, you'd think: 'Oh hell, if the greatest batsman in England is playing and missing, what chance is there for me?' I used to go in feeling a bit down when that happened. I always felt happier when he wasn't playing because there was nobody to judge you at his level.

He wasn't a bad bowler of leg-spinners. He didn't bowl them a lot, but he used to tweak them occasionally. Today he'd be useful, because there aren't many about, but Johnny Wardle used to bowl then, so Len didn't get much opportunity. I think that he could have taken a lot of wickets if he'd had to bowl. He bowled more before the war when Yorkshire hadn't got a leg-spinner. It was a different game before the war. The pitches were quicker and more helpful to leg-spinners.

I remember a great innings at the Oval in 1953 when he got 76. I remember going in with Laker bowling at one end and Lock at the other. I'd never a price to play Lock when the ball was leaving the bat, but I had more of a chance playing the off-spinner coming in. Len was making it look dead easy, everything in the middle, and I thought that I'd try the same way. I set about Jim Laker and got 30. It went all ways. Anyway, nobody got many runs except for Len, who made it look dead easy. That was as good a knock as I ever saw him play. When you are at the other end and see it turning you appreciate it, whereas if you're in the pavilion you think it's doing nothing because he made it look so easy.

There was also an innings at Harrogate I remember, against the

Combined Services in 1954. Len got a hundred and then started, I suppose, a bit of exhibition cricket. There was a left-armer bowling and he packed the off-side, as they normally did, and Leonard got so far round with his left shoulder that he was nearly driving to third man, it was absolutely incredible. I think there were seven in the covers and he couldn't get it through, so he went that bit further round and hit it behind point, incredible. He's the best player of left-arm bowling that I've ever seen; he could drive it so well through the covers.

I can't remember Len chasing runs. Obviously he scored quickly enough in the first innings, and in the second innings when there was no great urgency. If there was a left arm bowler on, he'd score

as quickly as anyone because he had this knack of hitting the ball where the fielders weren't, just bisecting the gap through the covers. I'm not so sure he'd have done so well against medium-pacers dropping it short of a length. He was, however, a great player and great players can adapt.

Hutton the leg-spinner – he took 173 first-class wickets, most of them before the war.

They all hated the new lbw rule, the ones who had played before the war. I think Len felt that it was a little bit unfair to judge him alongside Herbert Sutcliffe, because the new rule certainly made life more difficult.

Brian Johnston once told me that someone had asked Len why he had gone to live in the south. Len said: 'Oh, they're too fond of their brass in Yorkshire', which is probably quite true. There was probably more chance for him down there. He worked for Fenners, who were a Hull-based firm. I think he had a good number there because all he used to do was play golf; he used to entertain overseas visitors by taking them on the golf course.

He was very shrewd and very self-contained. I know that Frank Lowson, who went in first with Len for a long time, used to say that Len never offered him any advice and Frank was a little bit upset that he never volunteered anything to him. He would help you if you asked him, though. Boycott's exactly the same.

Len had a very placid nature. He never seemed to get terribly upset outwardly, although if he didn't get any runs I think inwardly he was upset. He used to come in and put his head in his hands and he'd stop like that for fifteen minutes. If there was anybody else about, he just didn't want to know. When he got runs there was no sign of elation about it, he wouldn't be jumping up and down saying how well he'd done, he'd just sit around and you didn't know whether he'd got runs or if he hadn't. He was very shrewd, tactically, about the game, but he kept a lot of it to himself. I think he helped Norman Yardley, when they used to inspect the pitch together and that sort of thing. Not that Norman needed a lot of help because he was a very shrewd tactician. Norman's biggest fault was that he was too nice a bloke. I'd have thought that if Len had been captain the other side of him might have come out and he wouldn't have been quite as genial as Norman. The professional image would have come out and he'd have been a lot harder. There were one or two who needed it as well.

I've nothing against Len at all. He was the sort of chap you could go round with for a year but you'd never know him. Indirectly he'd say one or two things and you'd wonder what he meant by them, but he very rarely said a lot. It seems silly really, when you look back, because we travelled everywhere by train and where Len got to I honestly couldn't tell you. We used to play cards but he never played and all I can assume is that he must have sat in a corner reading a book or wondering where he was going to make his next pound from. Strange really, he was that sort of person, he could just fade into oblivion, disappear. It wasn't as though he was a ladies' man, he wasn't chasing a bit of stuff or anything like that. When some of them disappeared, you knew where they'd gone.

He was a Test selector for a few years, but I'm afraid that he didn't do very well. It was a pity, I used to get stories back from players in the England side that some used to make fun of him because he didn't know who the players were. I can appreciate that he didn't really want to watch cricket, but he didn't want to lose touch with cricket either. He still wanted to meet his old pals and talk about the game but he couldn't be bothered to watch it. Mainly, I suppose, because when you've been as good as he was, you don't like looking at inferior quality. He should never have been a selector, that was a mistake. If you're going to do a job you've got to do it properly and if you are a selector you've got to go round and watch. It's no good looking at the paper and saying: 'He's a good player, he should play.'

Len could never have used a bat the weight of some today; he could never have lifted it, he wasn't very strong. The way he could time the ball with a light bat, he could hit it as hard as anybody, just through timing. His footwork was so good as well, to slow bowlers he used to dance down the pitch and hit it on the half-volley, where-as today people don't use their feet. The last I saw play slow bowling like Len was Colin Cowdrey, at Scarborough, playing against Phil Carrick. He got fifty or sixty and I said to him: 'This is taking me back a long way, seeing you play like this.' It's something that's gone out of the game. It's a great pity because it was a great spectacle seeing Len driving through the covers. He wasn't quite such a good player of off-spin because he wasn't quite so good on the on-side, but through there he was pure magic.

It wasn't very often that he got an edge, even when it was turning, and if he did he'd got this left arm that was so loose that the ball never carried. He wasn't often done at slip. It would be interesting to be able to compare him before the war and after the war. I'd like to see films of him before the war and see how far forward he played and whether the left arm made any difference. After the war he played a lot of half-cock, he didn't get right there and whether he did before the war I don't know. If your left arm is a bit shorter you're not going to get as far forward. When he was driving, of course, he went the whole way, but when he was defending he never went the whole way, he went half-way. It worked in his case, obviously. Off-spinners caused him more trouble than left-armers, which is really the hardest ball to play, the ball leaving the bat. The one coming in he had a little bit more difficulty playing, he just got a bit tucked up, not that he had any trouble, but they were more likely to get him than left-armers.

I once saw Jack Walsh, who used to play for Leicestershire, tie Len in knots when he'd got into the 70s. He used to bowl chinamen and googlies – nobody in the game, I don't think, could tell t'other from which. I once asked Jack if there was anybody in cricket who could tell his googly. 'Well', he said, 'I thought that Laurie Fishlock was the only one who could. He got a hundred against me at the Oval and I went and asked him and he said that no, he couldn't spot it.' He bowled two googlies, one which was obvious and one which wasn't, to lull you into a false sense of security. Len once asked me, after I'd been playing for about a year: 'Who's the best bowler, the most diffi-cult bowler you've ever played against.' I said: 'I've got to say its Jack Walsh,' and he said: 'Aye, not a bad bowler is he.'

Len got 202 not out against Ramadhin at the Oval in 1950 and somebody who'd talked to him about this said that he couldn't spot Ramadhin, but he still got a double century, so it didn't make any difference. He used to play them off the pitch; there's a touch of genius about that really. If you can tell which way it's going it's easy, but when you can't it's very very difficult.

Len didn't like running about an awful lot and he tended to field at slip when he could, and a bit at short-leg. I remember he was at

Bradman is caught by Hutton off Bedser at Trent Bridge in 1948. The Don was caught in the same leg trap in both innings by Hutton, who had 'a good pair of hands' when fielding at slip or short-leg. But he once missed a crucial catch from Neil Harvey.

short-leg in 1948 when we played the Aussies at Bradford. He dropped Neil Harvey and we had them at 19 for 5; they only wanted about 60 to win. Neil Harvey came in, Johnny Wardle was bowling, and pushed forward and Len dropped him and he went on and just slogged. They got the runs and beat us by four wickets. If he'd caught that, we'd have beaten them.

I don't think he was all that strong at any time; if he had been, he'd have probably been even better. He always looked very fragile and there were quite a few occasions when I'm sure he got out when he'd got a hundred rather than go on to get the 200 which he could have done, simply because he got tired. It's difficult to know whether he was tired of batting or just tired; my guess is that he was tired. Physical tiredness – I don't think his concentration would ever worry him.

I can't remember Len having a lot of net practice; he might have had a couple of minutes knock-up outside the pavilion but serious net practice I can't remember, not once the season had started. How he'd have got on today with all this pre-season training, I just don't know. He'd have just laughed at it for sure.

Vic Wilson

Born 1921. Yorkshire (Captain 1960–62): 1946–62. Vic Wilson, a farmer, was a reliable left-handed number three batsman, and is still noted in Wisden for taking 61 catches in 1955. Taken by his friend Hutton to Australia in 1954/55, he was twelfth man in all five Tests. He was Ronnie Burnet's senior professional in 1959 and succeeded him as captain in 1960, thereby becoming Yorkshire's first elected professional captain since Tom Emmett (captain 1878–82). In his three years as captain the team won the Championship twice and came second in 1961.

If it hadn't been for Len, I'd never have gone to Australia in 1954. He's one of the best friends I've ever had in my life. I wasn't good enough to go in that side. That was the finest side, possibly, that's ever gone to Australia, certainly in my period of first-class cricket. I was extremely fortunate to go. The only reason why I went was because Denis Compton had this dodgy knee and Len wanted somebody there just in case Denis broke down, so he suggested I made up the party. It was because of Len that I went.

The previous summer, 1954, I think I would probably have played in a Test match against Pakistan. Len was the skipper, but unfortunately he was ill for that particular match and David Sheppard took over. I didn't play, but if Len hadn't been ill I think I should have played in that Test match. He took me to Australia purely and simply because he was the captain. He was the only one who would ever suggest me going, even though Norman Yardley was chairman of the selectors. He was extremely kind to me on the tour.

It was a shattering blow to lose the first Test in Brisbane. We were hammered. When you read the papers today about losing the first Test match, you notice they write you off for the tour. We'd dropped twelve catches in the match, so it was just a one-off situation and Len certainly wasn't dismayed by it. His head didn't go down or anything like that. He just started planning more and more and resolved it with this wonderful partnership of Tyson and Statham, which won us the series. He organised that and planned it down to how many balls they bowled in a day, and how many overs and such like. He slowed the over rate down, without a doubt. He knew how many overs they were going to bowl before we went on to the field. If somebody came on as a change bowler, he had to bowl as Len instructed him. He had to get through his over in however minutes, to give Tyson a rest, and that was the only reason why he was on, whoever it was. And his strategy worked. It didn't please everybody, far from it, but it certainly worked.

Colin Cowdrey started his Test career on that tour, an unknown university player, a raw student. He came to the fore, with Peter

May, on that tour. Peter was in the top rank at that time. It was obvious to everybody that he was one of the top stars in the world, but Colin came from nowhere, and Len must have done an enormous lot for him. Len didn't go out of his way in the nets, I never saw him do that. He talked about the game, studied it and watched Cowdrey play. He had everything at his fingertips and he was a great tactician. It seemed as though he could put his finger on what was necessary. He expected everybody to do what was required.

His policy was that Tyson and Statham should bowl as few overs as possible. He used them as a spearhead and he broke through the Australian batsmen in that way. When you look back on our last full tour of Australia (1990–91) and you see the overs Devon Malcolm bowled and you think about the overs Tyson and Statham bowled, you realise Len used them completely differently and far more successfully because he was a great captain. He wasn't a strong captain, but he was a great tactician and a very shrewd man. Whether he was the most popular captain ever to go to Australia I won't say, but he was certainly one of the most successful.

Len Hutton, if he'd been as strong as Boycott, would probably have out-pointed Boycott in every record department, but time after time Len made a hundred and he gave his wicket away, because he was absolutely shattered. As I say, he wasn't a strong man.

He put his all into that tour to Australia and you've got to be pretty strong to stand up to the pressures of such like, haven't you? We all celebrated and I presume he was celebrating as well. He certainly enjoyed the triumph. He was never one of the boys. He wasn't a Compton or anything like that, he was a man to himself and what he enjoyed probably wasn't what other people enjoyed. Or what other people enjoyed probably wasn't what he enjoyed. He enjoyed that success. It was his over-riding ambition to beat the Australians. He'd suffered so much over the years, he'd been the only man who could stand up to the Australians singlehanded over a long number of years. He had to put up with an awful lot. He took some hammer. The Australians aren't the politest type of people by any means, and when they were on top they would let him see they were on top. He'd had no one to support him against Lindwall and Miller, so he was naturally elated by the success on that tour.

Len was a very quiet type of person and what struck me was his intense concentration when he was playing. During his batting, when he was in the middle of an innings, you could speak to him and he wouldn't even know you were there. His was such intense concentration that he was oblivious, really, to anybody else who was in the dressing-room. The only time he really opened out was if he got a duck and he would chat and be fairly relaxed. He said to me: 'I make news if I get a duck, I don't make news if I get a hundred.' He was relaxed when he got a duck, but when he was building his scores and building his totals up, he had intense concentration. I didn't go out with him and have a meal in the evening or anything like that.

I remember one very famous occasion in 1949, when Close and Lowson had just come into the Yorkshire team and I looked to be the one who was on his way out. We were playing Scotland at Hull and Len and I were batting. We made a hundred each and I was walking off the field and Len said: 'Well, that's put the cat amongst the pigeons.'

He didn't talk a lot during the innings. What he did say was: 'Keep your head down', that was the principal thing: 'Keep your head down', two or three times in a session. Probably that's the reason why I didn't go on to amass totals like he did, because I didn't have the intense concentration.

He got very het up at times in Australia. It wouldn't do for me to say what they were, but without a doubt he was very aroused on occasion. He was the captain and he was entitled to crack the whip, which if he thought necessary he did do. If somebody stepped out of line, he said what he thought. He didn't suddenly look at somebody and give them a good cursing like Brian Sellers would have done. Brian Sellers would look at somebody and say: 'Well, you want a cracker up your backside', or something like that. Len would go about it in a totally different way, but he'd let them see that he considered they were in the wrong and that it wasn't suitable.

I dare say that people who were not Yorkshiremen found him hard to understand. For myself, I understood him perfectly and I never found anything remiss at all about him. He was a very shrewd man on the cricket field and I think he applied some of that shrewdness off the field as well. He worked for Fenners, Mr Hainsworth's firm at Hull, and I came across him on numerous occasions after he'd retired from cricket.

Whether he was disappointed not to be made captain of Yorkshire is something no one knows really, but you'd have thought so. Personally, I think he would have gone on playing longer if he'd been made Yorkshire captain. He was such a good player that he could coast through the matches really. He didn't have to exert himself to that extent. He was such a fine player that he'd have got by in county cricket without really doing himself any harm, even though he wasn't a strong man at any time. It rather looks as though he was a bit disappointed.

I'm greatly indebted to him for the wonderful thrill of my life going to Australia in that wonderful side. Purely and simply because of him. I looked upon him as a personal friend who bestowed upon me the good fortune to take part in that tour, for which I shall be everlastingly grateful.

Billy Sutcliffe

Born 1926. Yorkshire (Captain 1956–57): 1948–57. William Herbert Hobbs Sutcliffe, or Billy, was born in Pudsey, son of the great Herbert. As an amateur and an attacking right-handed batsman, he succeeded Norman Yardley as captain in 1956, when some thought

Hutton might have been appointed. Yorkshire, without Yardley and Hutton, finished seventh and third in the championship under his leadership. He resigned the captaincy at the end of 1957 for business reasons. He still runs the sports shop in Leeds that his father once owned.

I knew Len from the time my father used to take me round with the Yorkshire team. I was born in 1926 and it was from the age of roughly seven or eight that I would have met him. My father was very enthusiastic and he was the one who brought the public's attention to this great prospect. Of course he fulfilled that and added more, didn't he?

I played first-class cricket with Len in 1948 but I played with him before that, during the war. My father used to run a lot of matches for the Red Cross during the war and I used to take my bag along as a teenager, and if somebody didn't turn up I was only too delighted to stand in. I saw quite a few people, like Learie Constantine, Bill Copson, George and Alf Pope; they were all playing at this time and Len was too.

Before the war, my father bought a house in Pudsey which had a tennis court. It was quite a big affair and at the side of the court we were able to make a concrete pitch with some coconut matting. It was totally impossible to get Leonard out. There was no way I could have bowled Len Hutton out. Even if he lifted his head, he was still playing so bloody straight.

After the war, when I played in the Yorkshire side, we used to have one beer at the ground and then we used to go to the hotel and sit in the bar and just have a couple of drinks before dinner. We didn't drink much after dinner. We used to get all the boys together and just listen to people like Len. It was absolutely wonderful. The Australians were over in 1948, with Lindwall and Miller, and it was very interesting to listen and hear how to deal with these fast bowlers. Len was predominantly a forward player and he liked to be, more or less, on his front foot. He had this theory that he had got to force himself on to his back foot; to make sure he was leaning in the right direction and make sure he got back and across. It probably didn't do me all that much good because it taught me that there was so much more to batsmanship than a young lad coming into the side had realised.

He didn't say a lot, but when he spoke there was total silence. It was like God speaking. He didn't speak much to me, I was too young, but I do know that some tried to force him to speak. He was a very modest man. He was very helpful always, but he wouldn't suddenly say now come on and do this. He'd pick a fault out and say you might be better doing that. To get him just to talk cricket was absolute magic.

We had a 200 partnership against Kent in 1952. I remember that he didn't go in the night before and I went in first because he was captain. He didn't go in first because he didn't feel like it; because he'd been fielding all day, I presume. Fred Ridgway was bowling very quick then. Len came in and we got stuck in. We had trouble with Doug Wright, who was bowling so well it was unbelievable. He was so unlucky because I was just prodding forward to him. Strangely enough, I seemed to take more of Doug Wright than anybody else. Doug Wright was a superb bowler; he was unplayable more or less. It was a very good wicket and he was still bowling beautifully. Len helped me through everything, as he would do. He'd be about thirty-six and I'd be about twenty-six. There was never any problem batting with Len because he was such a nice man. There was no big-headedness about him.

I've not the faintest idea why they appointed me captain for the 1956 season in July 1955 instead of October. Len was having a lot of trouble in 1954 and 1955 with injuries. He developed back trouble and I think that virtually finished him off, because physically he wasn't all that strong. If you were playing for Yorkshire and got past 21 July that virtu-ally meant that you were going to be playing for two years. You'd have been notified before that date if you weren't going to be needed. There was always a lot of joking after 21 July: 'Well, we're all right now then,' sort of thing. It was almost an unwritten contract.

I've no idea, but Len may have said to the committee in July that he couldn't go on playing and they might have appointed me captain to avoid speculation. I've no idea. I can't remember anything about it. When I resigned from Yorkshire cricket my father said: 'Well, if you don't resign I'm going to sell the shop.' That virtually forced me out of it. That was done before 21 July. That was a magic date for Yorkshire cricket.

I will honestly say this: I don't think that Len Hutton ever wanted to captain any county side. I'm quite convinced of that. I think Len, having captained England, didn't want the worry and bother. There's not even one iota of thought that Len wanted to captain Yorkshire. The last thing I would say that Len ever wanted to do was to retire from Test cricket and go and captain his county; the last thing in the world. He certainly wasn't very fit and I don't think he felt he could stand all the problems and carry-on that a Yorkshire captain's going to have. The possibility of him ever doing it never even cropped up; Len never even considered it. I don't think Len, if he was offered it, would have taken it, quite frankly. He'd finished by that time because of ill-health. The poor lad was struggling in those days, no doubt about it.

Len Hutton, even against fast bowlers, once he'd got established at the crease, he'd pick his bat up more or less at gully. Consequently he was in a position to play any shot, whereas these days they pick it up in the way Brearley started, and they're in no position to play shots. Len was always in perfect position and I'd say he picked his bat up more or less at gully. When he played against Lindwall and Miller he didn't do that, not when they were bowling at their fastest; then his bat would go up almost straight back. But he did this against most of the medium pacers, and the fast bowlers when he'd tired them out.

I remember Len coming down to Worcestershire. He'd been playing in a Test match and he was coming to join us with the masseur, Bright Heyhirst. Len had a sleep on the train. In those days Yorkshire players weren't allowed to drive past Birmingham. He asked Bright, who was a well-known character, to wake him up at Worcester. Anyway Bright forgot to wake him up and they ended up going all the way to Bristol or somewhere like that. Poor old Len didn't turn up until about 3.30 am and he woke me up because we were sharing a room together. He was moaning and playing all hell about Bright not waking him up, having to go to bed at this time and playing cricket the next day. I believe he bagged a pair in that match, back in the early 1950s. He bagged a pair and two ducks flew over the ground on that occasion, just before, so they say.

During 1943 or 1944, I'd finished school and went into a company called Thomas Owen, run by a man called William Harrison. I'd been there a few months when Len joined me. I had to move out of my digs, so I moved into the Derby Hotel in Bury with him. We were both in the new Bury paper mills in Gigg Lane, where the football ground is. Len had come up to do virtually what I was doing, learning about the paper trade, and I used to show him round. We were in the top floor room of this hotel; you could almost call it an attic bedroom.

One night there was a Palais de Dance going on, the equivalent of a disco. I asked Len if he was coming. Len was already married to Dorothy and he said: 'No. I'm certainly not going messing about at that sort of thing, Bill.' It was a twin-bedded room and I said: 'Well you don't mind if I go?' He said: 'No.' I came back at about 11.30 or midnight. The hotel was so cold that – I've never seen anything like it – Len was lying in the first bed and he was so cold that he'd put the electric fire actually on the bed. The whole place could have gone up in flames. I woke him up and said: 'If that tipped up the whole place would have gone up.' He said: 'Well it was so bloody cold, Bill.'

Michael Rines

Born 1933. Michael Rines is a marketing consultant. He is included here as a representative of Hutton's world-wide gallery of fans. He got closer than most to his hero as a schoolboy in the late-1940s, when he worked as a dressing-room attendant for the Yorkshire team at the Scarborough Cricket Festival. He later played in a match with Hutton in a country house fixture.

He relied on timing and technique rather than power, but still hit the ball hard. Hutton pulls a ball from Rowan majestically over mid-wicket against South Africa in 1947.

I was born and brought up in Scarborough, within sound of the applause from the cricket ground. I was cricket mad, and Len Hutton was my idol. He was also my model – not just where batting style

was concerned, but in other ways, too. I brushed my hair like his, and I carried my left arm in the characteristic Hutton manner – slightly bent, a little pulled up and held slightly away from my side – a legacy of the unfortunate war-time fracture. I even learned to write his autograph – and I can do it still, without having to think about it.

At first, he was a distant idol, seen in the middle at matches on the Scarborough ground, and even more distantly at Headingley in Tests, where I was in constant fear of his getting out. Later, in my early teens, my friend Eric Dixon and I became dressing-room attendants in the four first-class matches a year played on the Scarborough ground, and we got to know the players as few other people could.

There was always one county championship match, and at the end of the season there were three Festival matches. Hutton usually played in all of them, and seemed to score runs almost at will on what was then a batsman's paradise. For instance, in 1949 he scored 483 runs in the three Festival matches, for an average of 80.5. I still have some of the score-cards, including one for Yorkshire v MCC in which Hutton scored 147 in the first innings (caught Wyatt, bowled Compton, which probably pleased the latter a lot more than it did Hutton). He scored 52 in the second innings and in the course of the match reached his 3,000 for the season.

Our job as dressing-room attendants was to clean the players' boots and pads, run their baths, fetch their (often copious) amounts of beer from the bar round the back of the pavilion, look after the autograph books and clean up the two dressing-rooms at the end of the day.

It was a cricket-mad teenager's dream-come-true, to serve our gods, hear their gossip, hear them talking about their techniques and about other players. And when they had all gone off to the pub or their hotels at the end of the day, we could try their caps on and play imaginary strokes with their bats – of which Len Hutton's was always the lightest.

I always chose to work in the home side's dressing-room, because that was where my hero was. My friend Eric did not mind, for he was less of a fan, his interest being in wicket-keeping. Besides, the Yorkshire dressing-room was not a happy place. Some of the players were really very unpleasant and uncouth.

The Scarborough club professional was our supervisor. He was a West Indian, Hughie Croskill – an amiable, gentle man who had played first-class cricket for his island and was playing professionally for Scarborough while he was qualifying for the Bar. One day I heard a Yorkshire player address him as 'Sambo' when he was asking him to do something for him.

There were others we did not like – strangely, they were usually those who were most popular with the crowds: Johnny Wardle, for instance, who was later thrown out of the team because of his behaviour. They were not all bad, of course. Vic Wilson, Willie Watson, Ted Lester, Norman Yardley and Billy Sutcliffe were always very kind to us. Hutton was, too, but the overall atmosphere was not pleasant.

Hutton always had the same place in the dressing-room – the left hand one at the back, where he would sit, quiet and rather detached from the others, with those amazing eyes, often looking slightly to the left and slightly upwards, focused far away. And if he was telling a story, in his so soft voice with its elided consonants (battin' and bowlin'), his left eyebrow would lift just a fraction and there'd be the merest trace of a confidential grin.

If he wanted us to do anything for him, he always asked politely and always remembered our names, in marked contrast with the rough demands of some of the others. On one occasion, in 1949, he asked us to clean his boots and pads especially well, because he was having his photograph taken for a booklet about himself, so rather than compete for the honour, we each did one boot and one pad. I still have a print of the photograph, signed by Hutton.

One treasured memory was of a visit to the dressing-room by Wilfred Rhodes (he was blind in his old age but still attended all first-class matches in Scarborough and could tell whether a shot was a good one by the sound of the bat on the ball). Hutton asked him something about Jack Hobbs. Rhodes demonstrated with his white stick how Hobbs used to manage to drive a ball pitched very wide on the off-side. Before advancing his left foot forward and to the right, he first moved his back foot across to the off. Hutton was fascinated.

Wilfred Rhodes played in W. G. Grace's last Test in 1899, yet bowled so cunningly to Hutton in the nets after the Second World War that he described his bowling as 'a God-given talent of arc and flight sparingly bestowed'. Rhodes went blind in old age but still followed cricket by the sound.

I was impressed that a player who was acknowledged as the finest stylist of his time and at the height of his powers should still be willing to learn. I don't know whether he ever tried the Hobbs technique, but I would not have been surprised. He never had the reputation of being a great experimenter, but in the lighter atmosphere of the Festival matches, he was willing to have a bit of fun. I do know that when someone reminded him of the way the massively built Clyde Walcott could hit a straight six off the back foot, the slightly built Hutton had a go in his next innings, and fell only slightly short.

Hutton was by no means a muscular man and was handicapped by his weakened and shortened left arm. He played with it strapped above his wrist with wide rolls of elastoplast which we boys were told not to throw away after use, because he used the pieces more than once – in the 1950s even the greatest players were not paid very much. Hutton was nevertheless a very powerful player. Few people appreciated this, because he never bludgeoned the ball. He relied on his exquisite technique and timing, but Freddie Trueman told me he was the hardest hitter of a ball in English cricket, and underlined the point with the story of a giant six on to the balcony at Bradford's Park Avenue ground.

A few years after my days in the dressing-room as a boot boy, I achieved a long-held ambition by playing in the same team as Hutton. This was just after he had retired from the first-class game with persistent back trouble. We were playing country house cricket for Sir William Worsley's XI (he was later President of the Yorkshire Club) on his private ground at Hovingham Hall near York. The opposition was The Arabs, Jim Swanton's touring team made up mostly of age-ing ex-public school cricketers, plus a sprinkling of retired first-class amateurs, such as Gubby Allen, and a few younger players to compensate for the creaking joints of the rest.

I treasure one memory in particular. In those days, cricket writers seemed to me to be divided into Hutton men and Compton men, and Swanton was quite definitely not a Hutton man. I think he had given Len a bit of stick in his columns over the years, and Len chose an opportunity to get some of his own back.

The rather portly Swanton stood at mid-off, not very far back, so that he could speak to his bowler. Behind him was the longest boundary on the ground. Hutton drove past him with a shot weighted precisely to stop just inches short of the line, so that Swanton had to puff all the way out there while the batsmen ran three. His chest-heaving return to his position and flushed countenance were greeted by a trace of a Hutton grin and a gentle lifting of that left eyebrow.

At another stage of the game Hutton, who had an unrivalled reputation as a player of spin bowling, was batting against a young Australian leg-breaker. He cannot have been concentrating, because he failed to spot a googly and, in his efforts to correct his shot, fell over very awkwardly. For a man supposedly crippled by a back problem, he was back on his feet and ready for the next ball with surprising alacrity.

That incident, and an astonishing slip catch he took when we fielded, have always made me think that perhaps the bad back was an excuse by a very tired man for getting out of the game. Perhaps if he could have restricted his playing to Test matches he would have carried on longer. I had the feeling that he was just worn out. He was always rather reserved, and the strain of opening the batting, captaining England on the field and coping with the social responsibilities off it must have been very wearing. And watching him play for Yorkshire in the later years of his career I never had the feeling his heart was in it. There was just too much cricket, and the atmosphere in the Yorkshire dressing-room cannot have made the prospect of carrying on playing for the team when he was too old for Tests very appealing.

It was many years after that before I saw Len Hutton again. I had become a journalist and was covering the CBI Conference in Brighton for the CBI's own magazine. I read through the list of delegates to find people who would be interesting to interview. I found 'Hutton, Sir Leonard', representing Fenner Belts.

I thought for a long time before setting out to find him. I really wanted to remember him as he had been when he was the greatest batsman in the world. I didn't want the god of my youth replaced by the reality of an elderly, perhaps physically broken, shell. In the end I couldn't resist the temptation to find him, and I set off through the crowded, confusing corridors and lounges of the conference centre, peering at faces and badges, wondering if I would recognise him, almost fearing the moment when I would.

What relief! He wasn't broken. He was still the Hutton I remembered. There were still those eyes looking to the distant left, the slightly arched left eyebrow, the broad broken nose, that trace of a grin, and the extra wrinkles merely accentuated the character of the face.

Bob Appleyard

Born 1924. Yorkshire: 1950–58. 9 Test matches: 1954–56. Bob Appleyard was one of the finest bowlers ever to play for Yorkshire. Bill Bowes put him in the same class as S. F. Barnes and W. J. O'Reilly. He bowled fast-medium in-swing with a subtle variety of pace, and off-breaks. In his first full season, 1951, at the age of 27, he was top of the national averages. Having contracted tuberculosis, he played only once in the next two seasons, but returned in 1954 and took 154 wickets at 14.42 each. He played in four Tests on Hutton's victorious tour of Australia in 1954/55.

Leonard's career was definitely in two parts. He'd achieved an awful lot before the war as a young man and also he was quite a fast scorer. He could be an aggressive batsman. He understood what cricket is all about: it's about winning and about winning time and if a batsman takes too long to score runs he is losing winning time, he's losing time to get the other side out. He could push the score along.

After the war he was still the same player, still the same great player, but certain shots he didn't play, like the hook shot, because of his arm. He stayed a weekend here in 1989. It was a lovely day and we sat outside and he talked about his arm; how it happened and how it influenced his career. The operation took about 11 months in all, not one operation, but three, and then he had recuperation. It's an awfully long time. I was in hospital for the same amount of time when I had TB, so I know what it's like. It was a chap called Broomhead who got his arm right in the end. He did say that after a long innings it ached a bit, but he never complained, he wasn't that type. He was a private individual.

He had a marvellous aptitude for seeing and reading the game, the batsman's faults and weaknesses. I remember a match at the Scarborough Festival in 1951 when Yorkshire were playing the MCC. Bill Edrich had got some runs and was going well prior to lunch. After lunch, as we were going on to the field, Leonard said: 'The fourth ball of the over bowl one fairly well up, outside Edrich's off stump', and he positioned himself at long-on. On the fourth ball I did exactly that and Bill lapped it over long-on and Len hardly had to move, it went straight down his throat. He'd read the situation. He knew Bill and he knew his temperament and he had an insight into the game better than anyone I've ever played with, which obviously was part of his greatness.

I've seen decent players like Frank Lowson, who was a very good player, and Willie Watson, jumping about with little time to play and Leonard waiting for the ball. That's when the greatness of a player shows: with the amount of time they have.

Leonard came into the Yorkshire side in an era when the new player, however old he was, especially the youngster, would sit in the corner and say nothing. They would listen and take it in. Anybody voicing opinions from a young age would certainly be put down. He grew up in that era and therefore he wouldn't come along that often and offer advice. Some people criticised him because of that. I don't see it, though: I think it was his upbringing to be seen and not heard. You spoke when you were spoken to.

I can remember a game when I was bowling and everything was going down the leg side; sometimes this happened. I asked Leonard to watch and see if I was doing something wrong. The next over he came down and said: 'You're pointing your left arm down the leg side.' He spotted it straightaway and was right of course, that's all it needed.

He was a very knowledgeable player. Len gave Tyson an awful lot of help on the tour to Australia in 1954–55. He was wild, had a long run, erratic, and as much as anybody Leonard sorted him out. He shortened his run and helped him. I don't remember any great individual aspects of that tour on Leonard's part. It was a team effort, but he was there controlling it all. He put everything into it. He had to work at the game. If you make comparisons, which you inevitably do, with people like Compton and Edrich, who played at the same time, Denis was a flamboyant player who had flair, he didn't have the same control over his game as Len. Leonard had all the shots but he had more control. There is a big difference between the one who plays with an awful lot of natural ability, such as Denis, and Len, who'd got natural ability but also applied it rather more responsibly. That's not to criticise Denis Compton because he was a great player as well. Everybody's different.

Leonard was a good player when he was fifteen. There was so much good cricket in his background that if he succeeded in that cricket he was going to go on to succeed. He was a good player and he learnt fast, watched others and adopted technique. He was a great mover. A lot of people would class him in the same mould as some of the ones I played football with: Arthur Milton, Willie Watson, Denis Compton. All good movers. I was playing golf in the winter of 1952, very early on. Len invited me to play up at Fulneck. We were just walking to the first tee down some shallow steps and Len was walking in front of me. I suddenly got this feeling that his feet weren't touching the ground.

When you think about his cricket, his feet were moving all the time. His first movement, as the bowler was in his delivery stride, was half pace forward, then it was either further forward or back. His balance and his footwork were superb, that's why he was so good against spinners. We tend to think of modern players as fellows who stand with the bat up in the air and then they lunge forwards or backwards or flash at the ball with a 3lb bat.

Len played when there were some very good quick bowlers about, pre-war and post-war, and also the best spinners we've seen almost in the history of the game. Certainly after the war there were some great players. Surrey had Lock and Laker. Every side had good spinners, both leg-spinners and googly bowlers. He played in an era when all the skills were demanded of a batsman.

There's plenty who can get hundreds, fewer who can get 200s and very few who have got 300. You need concentration, stamina and will to get 300. He told me that he never found it hard to concentrate. The problem was unwinding afterwards: 'I was concentrating, I couldn't stop concentrating', he said. He told me this story about the toothache: such was his concentration that toothache went away while he was batting and came back when he returned to the pavilion. I suspect part of it was natural but also he would work on it. You can work on concentration and it's just as important as any other aspect of batting. You can work at it, you can make it better.

I remember a brilliant innings at the Oval when the ball was turning and Lock, Laker and Bedser were bowling. He was just outstanding. He got 76 against good bowling in difficult conditions. That's when the test comes. He could play on difficult wickets better than anybody else, that's why he stands out in front of all others. He was the best on all wickets. His reactions were so fast, that's why he had time to play the shots. He had a special quality there. He was very exceptional. He was quite a good bowler too.

I've seen people who were good in their own way but nobody as complete on all pitches. If he wanted to score quickly he could. Leonard would have got runs in limited-overs cricket because he knew how to score. He might not be hitting sixes all the time, but he'd be getting ones and twos. Again, you see, that was the other great thing about him – he may not seem to be very active and yet after an hour you look at the scoreboard, and he'd probably got twenty or forty in the first hour by pushing these singles and twos to mid-wicket. He got a lot of runs in that area, not spectacular but from decent length balls that he couldn't hit for four. All the good players do that, if you watch them, in that mid-wicket area. There are ones and twos there for the good players.

I recollect one conversation we had here once when we spent hours talking. He was saying what a great influence Bill Bowes and Hedley Verity had on the Yorkshire side. He came from a very successful side in a very successful era of county cricket. I don't suppose it was a great change, playing in Test cricket, from county cricket. The overseas teams weren't as strong as they are now. George Hirst had a big influence on Leonard and so did Herbert Sutcliffe, of course, and Wilf Barber and Arthur Mitchell.

I just have a feeling that, had they not made Billy Sutcliffe the captain when Leonard was in Australia captaining England, he might have . . . He wanted to be Yorkshire captain. It was bad thinking on the part of the Yorkshire club at the time. He never played under Billy Sutcliffe. But at the same time he had this back, he was having trouble with his back. Whether he could have continued, I don't know. I don't think he played with Billy Sutcliffe, certainly not a season with him.

I don't know how he felt about being captain of England but not of Yorkshire. He would never divulge it. I think he would feel a bit miffed about it. He'd been a successful captain of England and that's far greater. Remember, though, that Yorkshire traditions were such that initially it would never have occurred to him, when he started before the war, that he would be the captain. When Norman Yardley was captain after the war, he wouldn't object to that because he had a high regard for Norman Yardley, that's how he'd been brought up. When Yardley retired it was a different ball game. Len was captain of England by this time. It seems a crazy decision not to have made him Yorkshire captain.

Of course, by the same token, when he started in the Yorkshire side he could never in his wildest dreams have visualised the situation where he would become President. The Yorkshire side still carried the tradition of Lord Hawke. Len would never have believed that a mere working lad, a joiner, could ever become Yorkshire's captain or President. None of the professionals of the time could have visualised that.

He was over the moon to be Yorkshire President. It meant more to him than the captaincy of England. It was just tragic that he wasn't there longer and that it came so late. But for the Boycott situation, when the club was divided, I am sure Leonard would have been invited to become President before. I suspect Leonard would have been the automatic choice after Norman Yardley. He'd been knighted and it would have been a natural progression.

He wanted to come back to Yorkshire. He said to me: 'You know, the people are not the same in the South.' He wasn't being derogatory. He'd got a great longing to come back. We were sitting outside, not so long ago, when he really opened up and it wasn't often he did, and he said that he'd been thinking about it. He'd been talking to Dorothy about it.

His sense of humour was very sharp, you had to know him, often, to understand what he was saying. He didn't have a lot to say, but nearly everything he said was meaningful. Again, that's because of his early upbringing – he was taught to say little. I knew him. If I hadn't known him, I'd have been puzzled by him, like a lot of other people. He had a marvellous sense of humour. What he said was very meaningful, make no mistake.

You rarely found Len in an ugly position at the crease. He was always in position and his timing was perfect. That's what I mainly remember. In the field we used to bowl twenty or thirty overs, that was our kind of ration. You'd be tired and you wanted to get your head down on a bench and have a bit of rest. But it was compulsive watching for me, however tired I felt after bowling, whatever the state of the game, when Len went out to bat. I had to watch. I always felt this was something special that you were not likely to see anywhere else. So that's the effect he had on me. Nobody else has ever had that effect on me, and as a bowler you probably appreciate it better or in a different way from the crowd.

The weakness of any batsman is the first ball. There was an incident when he and I were sitting in Melbourne, in the Windsor Hotel after dinner having coffee, and Denis Compton, Godfrey Evans and Bill Edrich came down the steps all dressed up. This was the night before the Test match. Len said: 'Look at these three, they're going out and the excuse will be that they've got to relax before a match.' Then he said: 'This is the time to be thinking about the match', and he was.

He was going through in his mind, time after time: who would be bowling? It would be Lindwall. The first ball. He knew that Lindwall worked on the fact that the first ball is the one most likely to get a wicket and that Lindwall went out and practised before a game started. The best ball has got to be the first ball. It is no good having a couple of overs of looseners and giving the batsman sight of the ball. Leonard knew this, you see, and that's what he was working on, where the field would be, what the pitch was going to be like. He was like a computer. Working at it well in advance, so that he was tuned in mentally and physically. I'll bet he used to play shots all through the night during a long innings.

J. R. Burnet

Born 1918. Yorkshire (Captain 1958–59): 1958–59. At the age of 39, Ronnie Burnet was made captain of Yorkshire without a previous first-class appearance. Appointed to sort out difficulties in the dressing-room, he had been captain of the second XI and played for Baildon in the Bradford League. He sacked Johnny Wardle in 1958, a cricketer for whom he said he had the 'highest possible regard'. In 1959 he led Yorkshire to the Championship, ending Surrey's run of seven years at the top. A useful middle-order batsman, Burnet went back to playing for Baildon, but remained a powerful figure in Yorkshire cricket.

I never played in the same Yorkshire side as Hutton but I watched Yorkshire from about 1928 onwards and I remember Hutton coming into the side. To get into that side in the first place took some doing because they won everything before them from the 1920s to the 1940s. Len came into the side in 1934 and everybody thought: 'Well, he's a young upstart, trying to get into this side.' He got 196 against Worcestershire fairly early on, which showed what he could do, and very soon he started opening with Herbert Sutcliffe.

The main thing that I remember about Len was that prior to 1938, when he got that 364 at the Oval, if he and Herbert had put on a hundred you could reckon that Herbert would score 60 and Len 40.

Hutton with Herbert Sutcliffe in 1937 – 'he led me through those early years of doubt and indecision'.

He was very meticulous, with a beautiful technique, but he wasn't a very fast-scoring batsman. After he got the confidence of beating Bradman's record, the role was completely reversed. Out of a hundred partnership between the two in 1939, you could reckon that Hutton got 70 to Herbert's 30. It changed round completely.

He tore attacks apart in 1939. I remember talking to him at Bill Bowes's funeral. We were reminiscing about Bill and about before the war and I said: 'You know, Len, I think you were at your absolute best in 1939, before you had that arm injury, after you scored that record.' He said: 'You know, I think you're right.' When I heard him speak at the anniversary dinner at Leeds in 1988, to celebrate his 364, he said: 'You know, I think I was at my best in 1939.' He just quoted the same words that I'd used. He really did tear attacks apart.

If you look at his record in 1939, before the war broke out, he scored 2,883 runs that season and he still had the rest of the match at Hove, six possible innings up at Scarborough in the Festival, and Champion County versus The Rest. So how many runs he would have scored that season I don't know, because he was scoring centuries every other innings. He was superb, superb.

He didn't dominate in the League during the war at all. I think he was finding his feet, finding out whether he could continue to play after his arm injury. His left arm did look very much thinner than his right. He did everything at his own speed. Two hours for 63 in League cricket is a nonsense really; if you're in the whole time you should be well into three figures. You could tie him down. I had an off-spinner called Sutcliffe, from Accrington, who tied him down completely. Len kept saying to me: 'Won't you take this fellow off', and I said: 'No, I'm enjoying this.'

At that time I didn't think he would come back into cricket, not county or Test cricket. But he did and I think it's a measure of his technique that he was able to. Before the war it was the left arm that was dominant, as it is in any good technique, but he adapted so well that he made the right arm the dominant arm and he was still fantastic. He could still take an attack apart after the war when he felt like it, there's no doubt about it. I've seen him play some fantastic innings. I remember once at Bradford we needed 109 to win in forty minutes or less. He got 79 in thirty minutes, but we just failed to get them.

His arm certainly stopped him being a hooker. He did everything before the war, but he adapted so well to his limitations that it was hardly noticeable. Had it not been for his arm, and the six seasons he missed in the war, how many centuries would he have got? The mind boggles. People say: 'Well, that's equalled Len Hutton's record.' It's absolute nonsense because Len would have been so far ahead of everybody else by then, nobody would have got near him.

Apart from Don Bradman, he was certainly the greatest batsman I've ever seen. Don was a one-off, different style altogether. Len's certainly the greatest English batsman I've ever seen. Had the war not started in 1939, I think that that is the time Len would have become a Bradman. In those six years I think he would have been superb. I never heard Len mention his injury; others did, but I never heard him.

I think it took him some time mentally to decide whether he would be able to play properly after the war. Having done so and altered his technique, he was a delight to watch. The ball never left the carpet, never left the turf at all, absolutely marvellous to watch.

One always thought, in the 1920s and early 1930s, of Holmes and Sutcliffe as a pair. Well, Holmes retired at the end of the 1933 season and then Herbert opened with Mitchell for a couple of years and then Len came in. Herbert had a tremendous influence on Len. I had the greatest admiration for Herbert Sutcliffe. Of all the cricketers I've watched, I'd have him fighting to save my life sooner than anybody else. Herbert had a tremendous opinion of Len and I think he guided him, both coming from Pudsey. I think he was definitely a sort of father-figure to Len.

In the match at the Oval in 1948 England were all out for 52 against Australia, and Len was the last man out for 30 – that indicates his technique on wickets that were impossible to play on. Park Avenue, Bradford, springs to mind when I think of some of the greatest innings that I saw him play. He seemed to like it. He was a very good player on a sticky wicket, as was Herbert, and I think he learned a lot of that from Herbert.

I'm not being critical of Len when I say that Yorkshire became less important to him after he got the captaincy of England. It became noticeable that he would play superbly up to a hundred, the ball never left the carpet, and once he'd got a hundred he would start skying it all over the ground. That fact obviously didn't go unnoticed with the powers that be in the county. I think with the England captaincy he got mentally tired rather than physically, although he did have a bad back at the time. I think he would have taken the Yorkshire job if it had been offered and then retired from the England one.

When it came to Norman Yardley announcing his retirement and giving up the captaincy, I was on the cricket committee as the second eleven captain. Both Norman Yardley and Sellers said that, although Hutton was captain of England: 'Well, we can't consider Len because he hasn't played for Yorkshire for two years' – that was the attitude. They did an unprecedented thing, which was to appoint Billy Sutcliffe as captain in July. Len obviously took good note of this because normally the captain's not picked until the first meeting in October, so that was virtually saying: 'Well, there's no way you're getting it.'

I attended a New Year's Eve ball at the Belle Vue Barracks in Bradford, with Eric Winston and his Orchestra, and Len and Dorothy were guests. Len said to me: 'I shall never play for Yorkshire again, you know.' I said: 'Don't be bloody ridiculous, of course you will, mark my words.' Nothing happened at all, we all went to the nets at Headingley in April, went to the indoor sheds, and Len was there every time. We went right through until one week before the season started and Len went to see a specialist, said he'd got a bad back and retired, and never did play. He had no intention of playing, I'm certain of it, but he waited until one week before the season started.

It was a tremendous insult really, the fact that you're captain of England and you don't get Yorkshire offered. He was absolutely shattered. If he'd got it, of course, neither Billy Sutcliffe or I would ever have been captain, that's for certain, and I think he would have played for another seven or eight years. I saw him play seven years after he'd finished playing county cricket and he was just as superb to watch. He only needed to go and have a couple of nets. I saw him play in one or two charity matches and he'd come in against first-class players, who were playing all the season, and tear them apart. This after he'd been retired for five, six or seven years.

Certainly I think he expected and wanted the Yorkshire captaincy, without a doubt, and he was very, very hurt when he didn't get it. Certain of it. Norman Yardley and Brian Sellers said: 'Well, he's not considering the side at all, he's just collecting hundreds.' Len certainly got on all right with Norman; whether he always got on with Brian Sellers I wouldn't really know. I don't think anybody ever really got on with Sellers.

To be fair, it was noticeable. You couldn't get away from the fact that before he got a hundred the ball never left the turf and once he'd got a hundred they were flying up in the air, all over the place until somebody caught it. And that often on occasions when, if he'd gone on to get 150, Yorkshire would have won. It just looked as if it didn't really matter what Yorkshire wanted at that time, it was just a question of: 'I've got a hundred, that's enough, I've done my share.' Yet he was virtually God to us at that time.

I don't think Norman spoke to him; I don't think Norman ever tried to stop anybody doing anything. Norman was a great tactical captain, but if you look at the side that we had from 1952 to 1958, when Surrey won those seven championships, I think Yorkshire should have won at least three of them. Norman was a marvellous judge of a pitch, marvellous tactical judge, but I don't think his handling of men was very good. He was too easy-going, he let them do as they liked. I think Len would have appreciated a more professional captain. I don't think Len ever suffered fools gladly.

I could never understand why, when Hutton was captain, Tom Graveney very rarely got into the Test side. I asked Len about this and he said: 'Haven't you ever noticed Ronnie, he's got a ruddy complexion. Never trust anybody with a ruddy complexion.' I told Tom this and he said: 'Well, I knew he had something against me but I didn't know what it was.' Anybody with a ruddy complexion was suspect in temperament, that's why Graveney didn't play much under Hutton. He got these little bees in his bonnet without a doubt. If your face didn't fit you hadn't a chance with Len, he'd got these little prejudices. That one about Tom always shattered me because I thought Tom was a fantastic player. It wasn't a question of applying himself, it was because he had a ruddy complexion.

Ramadhin and Valentine had a marvellous series in 1950. Nobody could read Ramadhin and he was bowling us out more or less how he pleased. Len at that time had a sports shop actually called 'Len Hutton', in Bridge Street, Bradford. I went into the shop one day and was talking to him. He said: 'I've found out how to play Ramadhin. I play him now purely as an off-spinner, I play just inside the line. If it's the wrong one and it goes away, all right it beats the bat and I look a fool but I don't get a touch. If it's his normal ball, which comes in, I'm all right, I'm on it. He'll never get me out.'

That was after the fourth Test and the next innings was at the Oval and he batted through for 202 not out. We had to follow on and there were about twenty minutes before close of play. Ridiculously, I thought, Freddie Brown sent Len in to open the innings again and he was out for 2 before the end of the day. I don't think Len would have told others his method of playing Ramadhin, I think he would have kept that to himself. He did keep a lot to himself.

Valentine got him out three times in that series, which was most unusual because he was an orthodox left-arm slow. I always thought Len played left-arm slow superbly and was not very good against off-spin. Hughie Tayfield used to tie him up. It was always shattering when he got out for a low score, one never expected it. When Lindwall yorked him for a duck in the Test match at Headingley, I think you could have heard a pin drop in the whole crowd.

I reckon one of the greatest innings of all time was in a Roses game at Leeds in 1939. Lancashire got 217, Yorkshire were 163, 50-odd behind on the first innings. On this sticky wicket they bowled Lancashire out for 92 and Yorkshire needed 147 to win. Hutton got 105 not out; the highest score apart from that was 13. We were 147 for 5. That wicket was virtually impossible to bat on.

We didn't see Hutton at all at Yorkshire for years after he retired. Not at all, nothing. He went to live in Kingston and was the London rep for Fenners. He very, very rarely came up after that. But I think it was absolutely marvellous that he became President in the end, that his career finished and he died as President. I think that was a lovely thing to happen.

Fred Trueman

Born 1931. Yorkshire and Derbyshire: 1949–69. 67 Test matches: 1952–65. A formidable character and a great fast bowler, Fred Trueman was nicknamed 'Fiery Fred' by Norman Yardley, his captain at Yorkshire. He was an excellent short-leg and a hard-hitting tailender. On his first tour, to the West Indies in 1953/54, he was involved in controversy which cost him several subsequent tours. He went on to have an outstanding career and in 1964 became the first bowler to take 300 Test wickets. He was unhappy in the Yorkshire dressing-room of the 1950s, but played for twenty years and took 2,304 wickets at an average of 18.29. Harold Wilson described him as 'the greatest living Yorkshireman'.

The first time I ever saw Len Hutton was at Bramall Lane in 1948. I was just a kid going to the nets. I first met him in 1949 when I played for Yorkshire against Lancashire in the traditional Roses game. He came into the dressing-room, he had a trilby on, and shook hands with me and said: 'Hello, how nice it is to meet you. Welcome into the side and I hope you have a good career. I've heard very good reports about you.'

The match was delayed because of rain. He batted in the afternoon and was not out overnight. The Sunday papers gave him some stick about being slow, but he came out on the Monday morning and I think the first ball, from a fellow called Dick Roberts, a slow left-arm bowler, he hit straight over the sight-screen and went on to score 201. I just sat there and watched him. In the second innings he went in a bit later on and finished with 91 not out.

That was my first game with him and you suddenly realised that you were on another planet. He's the greatest player I've ever seen, on all wickets, technically. He could play shots that nobody else could. He executed them with finesse. He was unbelievable. He would get inside and drive the ball down to third-man. I know it sounds silly, but he did. He would hit the ball from outside the off stump through mid-wicket.

One of the greatest performances I ever saw was against South Africa at Sheffield in 1951. 'Toey' Tayfield, that wonderful bowler, came over to replace Athol Rowan, and Leonard made 156. He hit Tayfield through the covers, so they brought a man round, and he got inside and hit him through the covers again and they brought another man round. It got to the last ball and there was only one man on the on-side. I said to Norman Yardley: 'Well, where do you think he's going to hit this?' 'Through mid-wicket, I suppose', and he did. That is what he was like.

Another time, I remember, he made a century in each innings against Sussex at Brighton. I sat there watching him and said to Norman Yardley: 'What a great player, a truly great player.' He took his pipe out of his mouth and said to me: 'You should have seen him before the war, when he wanted to bat.' So what he was like in the 1930s I don't know; I don't know whether I saw the great years of him or not. But my memories of him will be of this frail sort of man, wrists of steel, timing, his knowledge of the game. He was just tremendous.

Before the war he was a youngster, nineteen or twenty, an age when you want to do things. And, of course, as you get older, you probably don't want to do things. He'd be about thirty-four in 1951. His record is amazing. He squeezed everything into about thirteen full seasons, including his tours abroad. His record of 129 centuries is unbelievable. His average is head and shoulders above anybody else's. He carried the England batting side, and that included the great Denis Compton. Compton was a genius of course. Different player; different outlook to Len in every way. Leonard's performances in Australia after the war were unbelievable. Even the great Don Bradman, who I've talked to on many occasions about Leonard, said that his concentration was unsurpassed.

Physically he wasn't a strong man, and with the accident in the war, he was left with an arm two and a half inches shorter than the right arm. The left arm to a right-handed batsman is a guide and master. At the Oval in 1951 he put on another great performance against Surrey. I saw him holding his arm and said, 'Are you all right, Leonard?' He said: 'My arm aches a bit, Freddie.' He got a Harrow-sized bat, which is a schoolboy's bat, and he went out and scored 151 with it.

His biggest problem came against off-spinners, with the left arm being short. He played the greatest innings on a bad wicket I've ever seen, which was at the Oval, against Surrey. It was in 1953 and he made 76 in the second innings on a rain-affected wicket against two great spin bowlers, Lock and Laker. He came in and he sat there with perspiration dripping off him. I can see him now, smoking a cigarette, with a towel over his shoulders. The man was physically and mentally drained.

It was sheer artistry; concentration. It was the greatest innings I've ever seen on a wicket where the ball was lifting and turning. The only ball he lifted off the ground was a full-toss bowled to him by Tony Lock. He hit it about six inches above the ground on the on-side and Tony Lock, a brilliant fielder, flung himself across and caught a magnificent one-handed catch. I think he would have probably gone on and made a hundred. It would have been the greatest hundred that I'd ever seen. He was a master of his trade; the absolute ultimate master of his trade. He was just superb.

I had the distinction of clean bowling him in the Test trial at Bradford in 1950. Mind you, he had made 85 when I got him out.

He was my first captain in Test cricket in 1952, against India. No matter how well I was bowling, he would say: 'Okay Freddie, have a rest.' I'd say: 'I'm okay', but he'd insist: 'No, no. Have a rest.' I realised later in life what he was doing, of course. He wasn't burning me out; five or six overs, have a rest; four or five overs, have a rest. Bring me back for the new ball. Five or six overs with the second new ball, have a rest. This was a strategy. He didn't believe in killing his fast bowlers. He believed in pace bowlers – very much so. He said that pace bowling was the most difficult to play.

I feel sure that, although it didn't happen, he would have loved to have Tyson, Statham, myself and Trevor Bailey in Australia in 1954–55. I was told that Leonard didn't want me, but he always denied it. I was told by a couple of the selectors that I had equal votes with everybody else and it was left to the captain and he went for Peter Loader, which surprises me a bit, because I always thought Leonard was a great friend of mine. He would always have a word with me, shake hands with me and all that kind of business. I've heard him say on television, in interviews: 'Freddie always blamed me for not going to Australia, but I can assure you that it's not true, it wasn't me. I would have dearly loved him in Australia.' So I'm left with the question. But I can tell you that it upset me.

I remember cartwheeling somebody's stumps at Leeds and Leonard was acting captain, with Norman Yardley off the field. And he said to me: 'It's the greatest sight in the world, Freddie.' I said: 'What's that?' He said: 'To be able to stand at mid-off and watch an off stump go cartwheeling through the air on the third day of play.'

Playing at Trent Bridge in 1951, I'd bowled Notts out and taken a hat-trick. Len was putting his pads on and smoking a cigarette. 'Oh', he said, 'I think I'll make it 90 something.' I said: 'Well, you might as well get the other few runs and make it a hundred.' So he said: 'No, I mean my 97th hundred.' I just laughed, because he very rarely said anything like that. He never boasted about his great powers of being able to bat. At the close of play he was 100 not out. And on the Monday he said he'd try to beat Vic Wilson's highest score, which was 223 against Scotland at Scarborough, and he made 194 not out. The man was unbelievable.

We called him 'skipper'. He was the first appointed professional captain of England and he was the man for the job. He was quiet and authoritative, a fine captain. He knew the game backwards.

I was overawed by his presence. You know, a mere lad from down the villages at the bottom end of South Yorkshire, mixing with the

The Yorkshire four: Willie Watson, Fred Trueman, Johnny Wardle and Len Hutton on their way to the West Indies in 1953. It proved to be a tempestuous tour for Trueman, who was nearly sent home.

cream of the world; because he was probably, in the 1940s and early 1950s, the greatest player in the world. He was number one. And he carried the burden of captain and made hundreds, which sometimes makes me a bit sick today, when they say the captaincy affects their batting.

What people don't realise is that he was a very fine leg-spin bowler, besides being a wonderful slip fielder. In 1939 he got 44 wickets.

He loved to play snooker and billiards. I played with him on many occasions. The hotels we used to stay in, especially the railway hotels, nearly all had a snooker table. And so after dinner, coming back to the hotel, the boys would play snooker. He said to me one night in Cambridge as I sat in the hotel, only a kid of 18 or 19: 'What are you doing?' I said: 'Nothing', so he said: 'Do you fancy a game of snooker?' I said: 'Yeah', because I fancied myself as a snooker player. We walked somewhere he knew and went in and they said: 'Hello, Mr Hutton', and he said: 'This is Freddie Trueman, a young Yorkshire cricketer. I hope one day he'll play for England.' I shook hands and they said: 'Come in.' 'Can we have a game of snooker?' 'Oh, certainly.' It was a Gentlemen's Club. I played snooker with him until about 9.45 pm and walked back to the hotel with him. He might have had a half of beer or a whisky. I didn't drink in those days, very little anyway, and off to bed by about 10.30. I think I beat him, but he was a good player.

I'd worked out, even then as a kid, that if you bowled a bouncer at wonderful players like Harvey or Morris, with their pride they'd go for a hook shot. I felt that if I could bowl them the bouncer outside the off stump and it was quick enough, if they tried to hit me they'd have to fetch the ball, and there was a chance they couldn't keep it down. At the Oval in 1953 I fortunately got the ball in the right place and Neil Harvey went for the hook shot and hit the bottom of the bat. It went straight up in the air and Leonard caught it behind square leg, running backwards. It was a wicket we badly wanted and Peter May said to him: 'You look as though you've just had two weeks in Blackpool.' He was thrilled.

We stayed at the Great Western Hotel and I remember coming out and the news vendors had big placards with drawings of the Ashes urn. Written underneath was: 'They're ours!' That was a wonderful fillip. Anyway, we went to the Oval and won it, which was tremendous for Leonard. He was so successful as skipper. In 1952, we hammered India out of sight; in 1953, we won the Ashes back after twenty years; we went to the West Indies in 1953–54, which was a bad tour, but we came back from two-nil down to square the series; then we went to Australia in 1954–55 and retained the Ashes; he came back as captain against South Africa, but he took ill.

As far as I'm concerned, I think Leonard could have been a little more helpful to me on the West Indies tour than he was, but of course he had such important things to do. We got to Jamaica after Christmas and I remember being briefed in a hotel called The South Camp Road Hotel. I was only a kid; it was the first time I'd been abroad anywhere. We were briefed not to go out after dark, after 6.30, unless we were in a motor car because it wasn't the best place in the world for white people to be. I was a bit worried in my own way and it would have helped if we'd had a good senior professional. We had a weak manager as well, Charlie Palmer, nice man but weak character as far as I'm concerned. Leonard was taking on more and more on his own, from what I could see. I think he could have helped me more than he did.

I was immediately in trouble because I was very friendly with people like Frank Worrell and Everton Weekes – wonderful people, great players. We were instructed by the management not to fraternise with the opposition. Well, they were staying in the same hotel as us and I couldn't work it out. There was no way I wasn't going to speak to Frankie Worrell or Everton Weekes, Gerry Gomez or Jeffrey Stollmeyer.

We played in a two-day game and I could bowl a bit quick. The great George Headley came in to bat and the crowd were chanting 'King George, King George' and Leonard told me who he was. I'd never met him. I'd read about him and heard about him, of course. I let the bouncer go and hit his arm and the crowd went berserk. Leonard said: 'What have you done? What have you done? There'll be trouble here.' And they were clawing at the big wire fencing. The police were standing by to take me off the ground after I'd hit poor old George. He was the idol, a great player.

They picked him in the first Test match in 1954. Tony Lock bowled him, clean through him. George Headley was picking the bat up when he knocked all three stumps down, and he was a slow left-arm bowler. I remember poor old George's face and him saying: 'This isn't cricket Freddie', as he walked off with me. And I knew it too.

Then, of course, we had problems in Barbados, where Tony Lock was no-balled for throwing by Clyde Walcott's uncle, who was the umpire. I think there's a picture somewhere of Gary Sobers, clean bowled, leaving the ground and the umpire, Walcott, with his arm up at square-leg, signalling a no-ball, which of course was another burden on Leonard.

It was a bad tour, a terrible tour for me all round. I had a very stern disagreement with Leonard. Down in British Guiana somebody called the umpire a black bastard and it was reported that it was me but it wasn't. I took a hell of a rollicking from Leonard and Charlie Palmer and I was adamant that I hadn't said a word. In fact, I said: 'There's a boat in the bay; give me a ticket and I'll go home.' I was fed up by now, because nobody was helping me. Anyway, Leonard said: 'Don't be silly; you're going to stop here and you're going to bowl.' I said: 'Well, I didn't insult the umpire.' He said: 'The incident is forgotten.'

Well, I wouldn't let it rest and I saw the umpire the next morning and told him what had happened. He said: 'I never said it was you; I just said it was a Yorkshireman.' Tom Graveney, when we found out who it was, told the certain person that he thought it was an absolute disgrace that he should allow me to get the blame. I was practically in tears for something I hadn't done and he knew it. Leonard never apologised to me about it; if he had, I'd have been quite happy. I got blamed for things like that and came back with a bad reputation, really through no fault of my own.

There was great rivalry between Yorkshire and Middlesex, going back before the war to R. W. V. Robins and probably back to Lord Hawke's time. There was a power struggle. Norman Yardley, a Yorkshireman, was vice-captain in Australia under Wally Hammond. He came back, captained a poor England side against Australia in 1948, who hammered us out of sight. In 1949 they dropped Norman and made George Mann, of Middlesex, captain. In 1950, they brought Norman back against the West Indies, a tough assignment. He won the first Test, but lost the rubber because we weren't a good side.

Then in 1950 they asked George Mann to take the side to Australia, over Norman Yardley again. George Mann refused and I understand they came back to Yardley and he said: 'No, thank you, I don't want it.' That let in a fellow called Freddie Brown, whom we could have done without. Then they made Denis Compton vice-captain above Leonard. Denis Compton, great player that he was, didn't have a cricket brain; knew nothing about the game at all.

You'd play for Yorkshire against Middlesex and the back-biting, the jealousy, between Compton and Hutton, and Edrich and Wardle,

Brennan and Appleyard; it was awful as a kid to play. I kept out of it all the time. I wouldn't join in. It was only when lads like Peter Parfitt and Fred Titmus came along that it all came to an end.

Leonard was always well-mannered and proper. He'd drink with anybody if they paid. He would take a cigarette from somebody and later take one out of his pocket, put his packet back and smoke. Whether he knew he was doing it or not, I don't know. But I'll never forget those sparkling blue eyes and that immense talent.

He wasn't a great speaker because he was a shy, retiring sort of man. He always spoke very quietly; he had a dry sense of humour with a wry smile on his face. I can see him now, that smile on his face, those blue eyes.

I was with Leonard on the Saturday night at Lord's, the weekend before he died. I was chatting with him in the Committee Room. There was Hutton, Compton, Miller, Trueman, Sobers, Hall and Cowdrey. I had to go to London on the Wednesday morning and heard on the seven o'clock news that he'd been taken ill and I was a bit stunned. I rushed to the hospital during the night, but they didn't seem to think there was much hope. I went to London to open a printing factory and I came back, got the train to Hull to speak at a charity dinner, and as I was driving into the hotel grounds I heard on the six o'clock news that he'd died. So I knew I was never going to see him again. I was glad I'd had that couple of hours with him on that Saturday.

Leonard had trouble with the off-spinners because of his left arm but leg-spinners, he knew what they were bowling before they bowled it. A lot of the old players from the late 1930s and 1940s used to say: 'The only time you got Len Hutton out was when he wasn't ready.' He was so quick on his feet, like a ballet dancer.

Once, when I batted with him, we put on a hundred. I made 50, the first I'd ever made, and it was his inspiration, because he made it look so easy at the other end. The bat looked wider than the stumps. He said: 'Just keep playing forward. Stay here.' I said: 'Well, why are people getting out?' And he said: 'Playing bad shots; just stay here.' He'd gone in late; hadn't been feeling very well.

It was against Gloucestershire at Bristol. I stayed in with him and they took the new ball and he asked me: 'What are you like?' 'Well, if it swings, I'm struggling', I said. He said: 'Don't worry; I'll take it,' and he did. For eight or nine overs I never faced a ball; I might as well have sat in the stand. If he wanted to take a single off the last ball, you couldn't stop him.

Another great thing was that when you chased runs against the clock, he never went down the order, like some opening batsmen. He always went in first, and because he was such a great stroke player he possibly scored quicker than anybody else anyway. Once he got in he started to play shots, and you could see the field start to disperse into a defensive position because they knew what was coming. He could hit the ball anywhere.

He would have been a very fine captain of Yorkshire, but he would have had problems because the amateurs were running the game.

They still run the game. Leonard didn't have a great deal of time for many amateurs. I'm not talking about people like Peter May or Colin Cowdrey; he thought they were very fine players. A lot of the old amateurs, he didn't have time for them.

People always said that Norman Yardley would never give up the captaincy until Leonard retired, and I laughed at that because I never saw any problem between Leonard and Norman; always great friends as far as I could see. But when Leonard announced his retirement in 1955, ironically Norman announced his, so whether there was anything in it or not, I don't know. I kept out of it.

A lot of the old amateurs seemed to take a delight in trying to put down or ridicule the great professionals. Why, I don't know, but they did. But Leonard, he just went on and on. It must have been very difficult, being captain of England but not of Yorkshire. He seemed to carry it okay. We'd sit in the dressing-room and he'd be about 120 and then suddenly he'd start playing shots all round the ground and somebody would say: 'Get your gloves ready because it looks as though he's going to get out.' And he probably did.

There are conflicting stories about Leonard. He was in Australia and Denis Compton was captain of the side against New South Wales when they were piling on the runs. I don't know how true it is, but they say Denis went to Leonard and asked him what to do. Leonard said: 'Send a telegram for some more bowlers', and walked away. Because that's what he was like when he'd been overlooked by the authorities.

He used to tell me not to bowl every ball as fast as I could; to keep the quicker ball up my sleeve; pace myself. He used to say: 'Watch batsmen. See what they do.' He used to say: 'This fellow can't play a short delivery,' or 'We'll have an extra slip or gully because this fellow can't play the one going away from him.' He knew all those sort of things. You could ask him for a man to be put somewhere and he'd try it. If it didn't come off he'd say: 'We'll try it my way shall we?'

He was a typical Yorkshireman who didn't give much away. His conversation, 85 per cent of the time, was money. He was very money-conscious was Len; amazing. The old Yorkshire saying: look after your pennies and the pounds will look after themselves, he was well steeped in that. He wouldn't spend a penny if a halfpenny would do.

In the West Indies in 1953, I arranged for a representative of John Player to let the lads have some free cigarettes. He sent 200 cigarettes each and they all went to Len to share out. Some of the boys didn't smoke and said their room-mate could have theirs. I smoked a pipe and as I was sharing a room with Tony Lock, I said: 'If you want my 200 cigarettes, you can have them.' Len dished these cigarettes out to the smokers, and as far as I know he kept the rest for himself.

He'd come right up to you and say: 'How are you?' and whisper, 'You're saving a bob or two, aren't you?' He probably meant well when he said that; something for the future. In many ways he was a strange man, and in many ways a good man. He was of a rare religious group, Moravian. He was difficult to understand, but when you got underneath him there was a warmness there. He kept to himself basically, a reclusive sort of a man. A very quiet man. After he assumed the England captaincy it altered him a bit, in that he had to be seen doing the right thing all the time, which wasn't difficult for him.

Ray Illingworth always says that he went to see Leonard for advice on batting and he practically came out in tears because he took the mickey out of him. Colin Cowdrey says that when they were in Australia in 1954–55 he was batting and watching the master at the other end not missing a ball. Colin was playing and missing and he went to Len and said: 'What do you think I should do?' Leonard said: 'Go back behind t'office desk in London,' and walked down the wicket. I've heard those sort of things about him.

They try to compare Boycott with Leonard. Well, as far as I'm concerned, Leonard's at the top of St Paul's Cathedral and Boycott's down on the causeway somewhere, that was the difference between them. He couldn't light a candle to Leonard.

Leonard moved south when he retired and it always made us laugh because he said in an interview that Yorkshiremen think too much of their money which, coming from him, was a music hall joke. Leonard went south, 200 miles south, basically because it was warmer in winter and that helped him with his lumbago and arthritis. He always tried to get abroad in winter.

Sometimes we used to have a table in the dressing-room and when we were youngsters we'd lob the ball over the table, just to hit the edge of the table, and catch it, testing reactions. Once or twice in the early 1950s, when he was getting a bit older, Leonard would say: 'Do you mind being quiet, you lot?' The dressing-room, at times, was like a morgue. Nobody spoke or laughed.

I'm quite open about it, if I had my time again I'd go to another county. I remember a committee man saw me with a smile on my face and he said: 'What's the matter with you? You look happy.' I said: 'I've been chosen to play for England.' 'So what?' he said. 'If you play for Yorkshire you expect to play for England.' What it was like before the war, when the amateur had a stranglehold on the game, I don't know. Some of the amateurs were downright rude, bad-mannered people. I'm sure Leonard must have thought the same. He might not have said so, but I bet he thought it. He was the best of them all, a tremendous player.

Brian Close

Born 1931. Yorkshire (Captain 1963–70) and Somerset (Captain 1972–77): 1949–77. 22 Test matches: 1949–76 (Captain in 7 Tests 1966–67). Brian Close was a courageous all-rounder who batted left-handed and bowled right-arm seamers and off-spin. He often fielded dangerously near the bat. In his first season he did the double and became England's youngest Test player at the age of 18. He had an unhappy tour of Australia in 1950/51 and didn't get back into the England side until 1955. As a captain, he won six out of seven Tests and the Championship four times in eight years with Yorkshire. He would have led England more but for a controversy about slowing the over rate down in a county match against Warwickshire. He became an England selector, and manager and chairman of Yorkshire. He also played football for Leeds United, Arsenal and Bradford City.

I played five or six years with Leonard. I first played for Yorkshire in 1949. Leonard was obviously up on a pedestal to all would-be Yorkshire players and Yorkshire cricket followers. It didn't matter a damn about him not speaking much, it was just watching him. He was such a perfect player it just wasn't true. In the month of June 1949, he made 1,294 runs, a record number in a month, and I saw every single

Hutton with a youthful Brian Close on the 1950/51 tour to Australia – 'he gave me a rollicking when I was out. It was only three words. You can guess what they were.'

one of them. I was at the other end a few times. That month was probably the greatest exhibition of batting anybody could have given. He got three ducks running too.

He wasn't a conspicuous character. I suppose it was those pre-war years with a powerful Yorkshire side; it was a real tough side. He'd become powerful as he'd grown up, his class and ability had taken him right to the top, but he didn't force it on anyone at all, ever. You wouldn't get more than a couple of words out of him because he'd be concentrating on his own job. He'd just say the odd thing here and there. Whenever he got out, he never made a song and dance about it, he'd go and sit where he changed in the dressing-room, chin on his hands, resting on his elbows. You could see him working things out, thinking about the job. Obviously, as a junior, you didn't interfere; he was engrossed. His concentration was magnificent, not to mention his stroke-play.

Leonard was a responsible man. He felt he had to see that he did well at what he was best at, which was batting. In those days we had uncovered wickets, which was fair enough; you got more than your fair share of good wickets to play on. But to see him playing on a turning wicket was a dream. You couldn't help but learn from him, the way he put his feet and hands and positioned himself.

I've always been an outgoing person and I've never been frightened to say something. But I always found Leonard very difficult to talk to, even right at the end. It was as if he was trained not to express himself in some respects, always guarded, wondering whether somebody was going to jump on him. He hadn't a lot of conversation with anybody. Obviously he came out with some fairly profound remarks at times, when you did get him to converse; occasionally, when you were on tour with Yorkshire and you were in the hotel and you'd had a few drinks. If Leonard had had a few drinks, then he'd relax and talk and he was wonderful. He'd reminisce about his experiences and how bowlers bowled, that sort of thing.

Facing anybody really quick Len moved onto his back foot first; anybody other than that he moved onto his front foot and from there he judged it. He used to go forward to play back or back to play forward. Bowling that moved off the wicket he moved towards, his first movement, bowling that moved in the air he moved away from. That was the basis, the foundation. Everybody has an initial movement and he used to do this perceptibly, almost as the arm was coming over. If it moved off the wicket, like a spinner, his front foot would just go a little bit, that would be his movement and it would trigger off his reaction. Then, in the course of the next fraction of a second he'd discover whether it was up enough to play forward, or whether he had to go back to it.

Another thing, when the funny spinners were on, often wrist spinners, they gave the ball a bit of air and he moved forward to them mostly. He was waiting for them to drop it short so that he could come back on his back foot and either pull or cut, or square cut. Unless it was right up to him he wouldn't risk it under normal circumstances.

He had a beautiful pair of hands. He could literally hit it early or late. He'd just got natural ability. I've not seen anybody like him. The only one I would compare to him is Denis Compton, but they were totally opposite kinds of people. Even Viv Richards, you couldn't compare him with Leonard. Viv Richards was very powerful, great eye, strong lad. Leonard wasn't strong. Leonard, in some respects, was delicate.

Bill Bowes, from whom I learnt a lot about the game, used to say that Leonard was magnificent before the war. He did wonderfully well to come back. You don't know what he would have done if he hadn't had that injury, but the fact that he got all the runs that he did meant that you weren't aware of it.

He was always of a delicate nature and his voice was never powerful when he said things. The only thing he was ever sure of was cricket. He didn't mention football. The only time we met was in the cricket season, and April for practising, and the main topic for conversation within the Yorkshire side in those days was cricket.

Myself, I don't think he'd have made a good captain of Yorkshire.

Hutton with Bill Bowes, 'the thinking fast bowler', who tested the boy genius at the Headingley Winter Shed.

He knew a lot about the game but he wasn't expressive enough. He never got that chance really because it was still in the amateur regime. Norman Yardley at that time was an excellent captain. I think Leonard would have had difficulty in sorting out the rough characters. You got lads who were, well, very tough lads. They all respected him, though, and admired his perfection at batting.

Captaining England was a different kettle of fish. Test matches only happen every now and then. It's not day after day after day like it is in the county season, where you're living with people, and you've got to play with them, even though you might not get on with them or have the same way of thinking. In a Test match you all come together from different parts, and if you have any differences you put that behind your back for the cause of England. A lot of people in county cricket are established figures, and even if they have a row or whatever, they're not going to be dropped.

I felt that Len was a negative tactician. Len was one of the first top players to realise that batting could not only draw certain Test matches but could possibly win them, when they became five days. When they lasted three days, bowling won Test matches because you needed to bowl the other side out twice, but when they became five days batting became more important.

When he went to Australia in 1954–55, he lost the first Test because he played all fast bowlers and had no variety. If three bowlers can't do it, what the hell have you got the fourth for? If it's green, as he thought it was, three bowlers can do it. He won the Ashes after that because he brought the spinners back in; Appleyard and people like that. Len thought that Jim Laker was a bit soft. Len was very hard in his approach but he didn't give that impression because he didn't dominate. He expected that if you played for England you behaved as an England player should.

Freddie Trueman was left out of that tour of Australia. To my mind a mistake, but he left him out because he didn't think he could control him. Obviously Fred's more refined these days, but in those days he was a rough diamond. In leadership you pick the best team and it's then your job to make them all pull together and play.

On my tour to Australia in 1950–51 I was naive and young and a bit out of my depth. I thought: 'Bloody hell, this is a marvellous experience', which it was. I grew up on that trip because I suddenly realised that the old 'uns were putting their damnedest in. They wanted to play for England because they'd lost five years of their lives in the war. Most of them probably thought, Len included, that it was going to be their last trip to Australia. (As it turned out, Len went again.) They wanted to enjoy Australia. Don't forget, we were still on rationing in Britain at that time and suddenly we go out to Australia, land of plenty. Wherever an MCC side went, the red carpet was out and they wanted to enjoy that. They were prepared to play for England, but they didn't want to have a young upstart like me to keep their eye on.

When I got back to England I'd more or less been written off, even though I'd got two centuries in state matches and a dozen wickets, in the few games I played before I got my groin injury. I played in a Test with my groin bad. By the end of the match I could hardly walk, hardly pull my leg through. However, playing the game was the one thing I wanted to do.

In 1952 I rejoined the Yorkshire side. I'd say that I was a reasonably strong character, quite capable of holding my own against anybody at that time and so Len, who was terribly respected by me, was no more than my equal.

I used to enjoy batting with him tremendously. He used to try to pinch the bowling; he was a good counter. He'd play the first five balls and maybe get a couple of boundaries or something, and then, on the sixth ball, he'd push it where there was one. On one occasion, I remember, we were playing Nottingham at Park Avenue, Bradford, and I went out to join Len. He finished 149 not out. Nottinghamshire had Harold Butler, Arthur Jepson, Bruce Dooland and Ken Smales, the off-spinner; they weren't a bad side. Len was pinching the bowling and I finished with 62 not out in forty minutes. It rained for two days and we never bowled another ball in the match. I had another forty-four minutes to get the other 38 runs for the fastest century of the season, and Len was pinching the bowling.

I batted with him when he made 269 not out against Northants at Wellingborough in 1949. He ran me out that day. It was the sixth ball of the over, but he was going so well it was a dream. None of the Northants bowlers could bowl at him. Len didn't do it by hitting, he did it by pure stroke-play, beautiful positioning, lovely strokes, timing, great timing. He never did it by pure power.

I remember him at Old Trafford against Lancashire when he made 200 and literally, wherever they put the men, he hit it somewhere else; placed it. The left-arm bowler had two deep men in the covers, right on the boundary, and in those days we played on the full arena, not the cut-down job they have for the Test matches now. Anyway, Leonard would hit it late and it would go one side of the fielder, and then he'd hit it early and it would go the other side. Lancashire finished up with seven out of the nine fielders on the off-side trying to stop him hitting it through; he was a brilliant cover driver. And then he lapped them and swept them on the on-side.

He won matches as a batsman because he got his runs quickly. He didn't faff about. Obviously there were times when he had to work hard for runs, but generally he was such a master that he scored off good balls. That was the difference between him and Boycott. If you ever needed runs against the clock, Len never said to his skipper: 'Drop me down.' He went in and took charge, and he got cracking from the word go. He went in and did his share, and he won matches like that.

I played in only two Tests with him. One was in 1949 against New Zealand and the other that one in Australia, when I was all strapped up with a bad groin. I do remember getting out in that match. I was naive. Jack Iverson was bowling at Melbourne from the top end. He was a funny bowler, his regular ball was the googly but he bowled the odd leg-spinner in between. I'd discovered which it was in his hand.

Len gave me a rollicking when I was out. It was only three words and you can guess what they were. The skipper, Freddie Brown, said nothing. I was left in Coventry to go through my miseries. Iverson bowled me this one outside my leg stump, just before lunch, and unfortunately I went and swept it. I was young and inexperienced and the ball had come down on my leg stump. It never entered my head about lunch and I saw it as an opportunity to get off the mark. I went down on one knee and swept him. I got a top edge and Sam Loxton caught me just behind square and I was out for a duck. I'd gone in with four balls to go before lunch.

I could tell which way Iverson was making them turn. I had an ability to read the leg spinners, or the funny bowlers as they called them in those days, and part of that came from Len because he was a great reader of spin. Almost every side had a funny bowler, a wrist bowler, and of course Len had played against O'Reilly when Bill was the great bowler in Australia. You had to read them if you were going to attack them and play positive shots. I wouldn't say I spotted everything, but I spotted most of them. We were taught. You'd listen to Len talking about bowlers and that's how we were taught. When I became captain and a senior player, that's how I taught the youngsters. I taught Boycott how to play bowlers, what to watch out for and all that. The trouble was that he never passed it on to the people he led.

Len did more than his fair share in a team. He didn't nose into other people's business, but if he learnt something he was prepared to talk about it, and he was well worth listening to. You never argued with Len. To a large extent you accepted what he said because he didn't say much. The things he did come out with were great common sense, which sometimes you can deviate around to the point where you don't see the real point. Len would make the real point.

Len became a good captain of England because first of all he was a certainty as a player. He was a hard man in that he knew what was demanded within the top flight of the game. He had at his command the best players in the country and there were a hell of a lot of good bowlers then. All masters of their own arts. In the 1940s and early 1950s England was at a disadvantage in fast bowling, but we suddenly had three of the best in the world: Frank Tyson, Fred Trueman and Brian Statham, and Peter Loader to back them up. Len was lucky to have them as captain.

You never saw Leonard play bat and pad. He said to me: 'Brian, if you have to rely on playing with your bat and pad together, you can't be any good. Your arms aren't doing their job; you've not got the freedom to move your hands if they're tied up next to your pad.' We've got loads of them now. You don't know sometimes, when you watch them now, if we're in the football or cricket season; you don't know if they're trying to hit it or kick it. They play with their bat behind their pads. When I was captain, none of my players ever played bat and pad, otherwise they got a rollicking. That's the one way you will never improve yourself as a player. You should play in front of your pad and allow your hands to move properly. It's only poor players who need to play with their bat and pad together. You'd see Len pad off and not play, because you could in those days. And he was a good judge, obviously.

You could see when it spun. There were a lot of good spin bowlers. Len always played at where the ball was going to go and he adjusted his shot if it didn't. Nowadays they play at the line and adjust if it spins. That's why Len was a great player on a bad wicket and I was always a great player on an awkward wicket. I enjoyed it, but only because I learnt from Len. He told me to watch a bowler as he ran up and see where the ball was in his fingers. If you didn't know, you worked on the following principle. Whatever type of bowler, left arm or right arm, if he moves it one way it can get you out bowled, lbw or caught; but if it moves the other way, if you get yourself in the right place and your legs in the right place, backing you up, you can only be out caught. So what do you play for? You play for the one that can get you out three ways, until you sort him out.

I learnt this from watching him and the odd chat, when a group of you were having a drink at night time. He wouldn't do it readily though, because he was always guarded, which could have been because of his background. I don't think Len was particularly intellectual and so therefore he was a bit frightened of expressing himself. Don't forget, either, that Len played in an era when you had to watch your step as a professional.

He was a cunning captain in the field and wouldn't give anything away. He'd had to earn his own runs and whoever was on the other side had to earn them as well. He had great faith in bowlers who could bowl line and length, which isn't everything in cricket. I think that was where he was limited: sometimes you might not be too accurate on line and length, but you might bowl an unplayable ball, which gets you wickets.

In some respects I had an opposite view of the game from Len. I felt that you could make things happen if you were in charge. There's always some way of catching the batsman on the hop; changing the method of thinking. I don't think Len was adventurous enough, and I always felt that that was what the game was about. My attitude was not: 'If you can't win, you don't lose', but: 'You never ever learn to win, you never ever learn to do the things that win matches, unless you're prepared to lose.' But I couldn't have held him in greater esteem than I did. He was the greatest I've ever seen.

One of the answers he gave when asked if he'd have liked to play limited-overs cricket was: 'Well, I suppose I would. It would have given me an excuse for getting out.'

In the last years prior to his death, I used to meet him at Test matches and always enjoyed a natter with him. That was when Yorkshire was going through all the trouble, internal strife, and we know who caused that.

I can remember one occasion – Viscount Mountgarret had come as President. Sir Leonard's first remark used to be: 'How's things up at the Club, Brian? What's happening?' By this time there'd been the shake-up, and Boycott damned near controlled the place. I'd say: 'Well, things are changing. He's losing his power a little bit. Brian Walsh QC and Detective Inspector Sidney Fielding (who had been Boycott's spokesmen at the Special General Meeting and won the day) have changed sides, now that they've been close to Boycott and realised.' And Sir Leonard said to me: 'Brian, what chance have the public if he could fool a QC and a Detective Inspector?'

I remember Sir Leonard's 70th birthday at Lord's. Richard, his son, who'd played under me by this time, and Don Wilson, who was the coach at Lord's, had decided they'd give Sir Leonard a birthday party. Sir Leonard was pretty good at golf. You always think the grass is a bit greener on the other side of the road and I can remember him saying: 'Oh, I wish I could have played golf.' Anyway, as it turned out, they'd got Henry Cotton to this party. I knew Henry; he was a good cricketer when he was a youngster but then went into golf. He always followed cricket. Sir Leonard and Henry coming together was funny because Henry would have given almost his right arm to be Len Hutton and Len would have given his right arm to have been Henry Cotton.

Arnold Silvester

Born 1920. Arnold Silvester worked for 44 years for J. H. Fenner and Co. Ltd, the company which employed Hutton after his retirement from cricket. Based in Hull, the firm are power transmission engineers, manufacturing equipment for the coal-mining industry world-wide. From 1965 to 1980 Silvester was personal assistant to Dr Sidney Hainsworth, chairman and managing director of the company. Dr Hainsworth, who had known Herbert Sutcliffe since the First World War, employed Hutton to work on the public relations side of the business. Hutton also captained the S. B. Hainsworth XI against Yorkshire XIs to raise money for beneficiaries during the 1960s. From 1971–81 Silvester organised the Fenner Trophy competition at Scarborough which replaced the long-established Yorkshire match against the MCC. He is a member of the MCC and a Lord's Taverner.

Leonard started with Fenners in 1960. Mr Sidney Hainsworth, the managing director, had been a life-long cricket enthusiast and was Herbert Sutcliffe's best man. Cricket was a driving force in his external activities. Leonard at that time was playing stockbroker golf at Wentworth. He was resident at Wentworth and if a stockbroker wanted to bring clients down to play with Leonard that is what he was doing. We took him on in 1960 initially on the power transmission side; not an easy subject to get into, so he wasn't used a lot.

We decided to use him on the mining side and he set about learning enough about mining. He was instructed in the conveyor-belting product. He went round pits, NCB coal mines, getting to know about where belting was used. He was very well received down below and he learnt enough to be able to talk intelligently about belting and we used him internationally. He was appointed a non-executive director to the international company in about 1973. You couldn't have a knight just wandering about selling.

Fenners in the past had a very big export business worldwide. Then countries like India, Australia and South Africa started putting embargoes and tariffs on. You had a quota of imports, so the way to continue the business was to put a factory up to make some of the products and then you were allowed to import the others. The factories that went up were in South Africa, Australia, India, America, Germany and New Zealand. The three main ones were cricketing countries, so it was obvious sense to use Leonard in those countries to do a PR job.

If he went to South Africa, say, he would find out where the mine managers came from. Generally they came from this country, so when he went out there, and they had receptions and so on, he'd be able to talk to the manager about where he'd come from and what they were doing in the UK. He was well received and he had this big advantage in that they all liked to play golf. He knew the cricketers who liked to play golf, so he'd get them along too. In Australia he used to get Keith Miller along, for example, to play golf with him and some of the managers. Basically it was a PR job and he did a very good job.

A lot of my colleagues thought that he was an unnecessary overhead and never, early on, accepted that he could do a good job. But I would say he did a very good job and he opened a lot of doors that would never have been open before. Mr Hainsworth took him to a CBI dinner in London in the early days of his career. On the top table was Lord Robens, chairman of the NCB. Leonard's son was at Repton and Robens's son was also at Repton. They met at this dinner and Leonard introduced Mr Hainsworth to Robens, from which developed a relationship; not only a business relationship, they just clicked. And that stood the company in very good stead.

We used to import cotton from India and at one stage there was a lot of trouble in getting export permits in India to get the cotton off. There was a consignment on the docks in Bombay and we couldn't get it released. The buyer was going to see the Indian Trade Commissioner in London to see what he could do. I said to take Leonard with him. This chap rang Leonard to let him know and Leonard rang back an hour later to say that he'd cancelled the appointment and that they were going to see the High Commissioner instead. They went and Leonard was greeted effusively. Anyway, the buyer talked about the problem and Leonard just sat there. It was going all right and about halfway through Leonard said, 'Oh, High Commissioner, "Vinoo" Mankad. He played for India against England when I was in the side. I've kept in touch with him. Do you think it would do any good if I dropped him a line because he's on the Bombay Council, isn't he?' The buyer went on with his spiel and again Leonard interrupted and said: 'The Maharaja of Baroda. I knew him once. He's in government isn't he? Do you think it would do any good if I wrote him a note?' The consignment was released the next day. That is a silly story, but it illustrates what Leonard could do. It might have taken the buyer three or four visits to get to the High Commissioner himself.

At the other end of the scale is his relationship with people in the mines. He used to come up to the Fenner Trophy, which I organised at Scarborough. We had eleven years of it. He ultimately became President of Scarborough Cricket Club. At one time we were having a lot of trouble getting into a potash mine in North Yorkshire. The fellow who used to call there asked if Leonard could go with him. He went about a week before the Festival and they kitted him out and he went down the mine, met the manager and so on. When they came out, Leonard said to the bootman: 'I do like these boots, they're beautifully supple. They'd just do me for gardening, do you think I could have them?' The bloke said he thought he could manage that and Leonard asked him if he liked cricket. 'Oh yes,' he said. 'I go to the Scarborough Festival every year.' Leonard said: 'Are you going this year? Well when you go, if you go to the gateman there'll be two tickets for you.' The bootman, not to put too fine a point on it, is just the old stager dishing out the boots. He went, and sure enough there were two tickets for the bootman from Barlby potash mine. That swept through the place, and all our efforts to talk to managers and things like that paled into insignificance compared to the fact that Leonard had made a promise and kept it.

Over the years he went to Australia, South Africa, India, Germany, and a mining exhibition in America. A lot of people said: 'What the hell's the use of sending Leonard to America?' However, he was feted as though he was the world's number one celebrity; that was in 1978. They took him to the baseball and there he was with a baseball bat in his hands showing them what he'd do with a cricket bat. They thought the world of him and he did a good job. He never sold a thing but he opened the doors that enabled the technicians to get at the people who mattered. Mainly he went to the cricketing countries and coincided his trips with the time the cricket was on. He hated flying but he did it. I reckon it put a great deal of strain on him. He was interested in mining and he went down mines without any problem at all.

He was very diffident and you couldn't get him to talk much unless you were out of the circuit of people. He said to me once: 'You know Arnold, a lot of people think that I'm a bit slow and that I don't know how to answer things on television. I can tell you where that comes from. In 1954, when I went to Australia as captain of England, the whole of the Australian press was there to greet us, and throughout the whole tour they wanted to talk to the captain. The press are so adept at taking a little answer and multiplying it into a crisis that I always used to wait and think what I was going to say, and if it could be misconstrued. Because I had to concentrate on what I said on that tour, it stayed with me. So when I'm asked a question I think: Can they use what I'm going to say in the wrong way? That's why I hesitate.' He did seem to hesitate a lot of times on television.

He was a shrewd man, very shrewd indeed. He'd come up with some very shrewd technical comments at times. On his trips down the mines he'd spot something and then bring it out at the appropriate time. The Stock Exchange was one of his great interests.

At the Scarborough Festival we always used to have a dinner in The Cricketers' Room at The Grand. It had photos of cricketers all around the room. The first time I went to one of these dinners at the end of the Festival I was intrigued because I could see Richard's photo there but not Leonard's. I said to him: 'Are you in bad books here, because your photograph's not up here.' 'Oh no, Arnold,' he said. 'There are only photos of amateurs who've played in the Scarborough Festival in this room.' Richard, of course, was originally an amateur.

I remember he gave my son, David, one of Richard's bats. He knew that he'd had a lot of coaching and had been captain of the local school side here. He'd been to the nets at Yorkshire and was going to university. Leonard wrote David this five-page letter. Now, if you ever got a report out of Leonard of more than one page you were doing very well. The gist of this letter was: 'Now you've had your coaching and established yourself in your school side, forget about it all and just enjoy your cricket.' He didn't need to write. There were a lot of people who had just that sort of attention from him.

Leonard used to come and captain a side in benefit matches for the Yorkshire beneficiary. In the late 1960s he asked to be excused from doing it. He said: 'I'm on a hiding to nothing. I know people want to see me playing in these matches but I'm captaining Sidney's side against Yorkshire. The prime object of that Yorkshire side is to bowl Len Hutton out.' To hell with who else was playing. He said: 'You know, my eyesight's getting a bit dim Arnold, but they all expect me to score fifty. The fellow at the other end, the whole object of his day here is to get me out.' So he got to the stage where he didn't play, but he always used to come.

Hutton the salesman – at Fenners, the Hull-based mining equipment firm where he worked after his retirement from cricket.

PART FOUR

From the Other Side

Bill O'Reilly
Bill Brown
Ernie McCormick
Lindsay Hassett
Ian Johnson
Ray Lindwall
Keith Miller
Arthur Morris
Bill Johnston
Neil Harvey
Sonny Ramadhin
Colin McDonald
Alan Davidson

The Australians congratulate Hutton on beating Bradman's record at the Oval
in 1938. One of the two missing fielders is 'Tiger' O'Reilly, who said he could
think of '364 reasons' for not joining in the celebrations.

Bill O'Reilly

Born 1905. New South Wales (Captain 1940–46): 1927–46. 27 Test matches: 1931–46. In Bradman's opinion, W. J. 'Tiger' O'Reilly was the greatest bowler of his time. A medium-pace leg-break bowler who could have, Bradman wrote, 'a belligerent ferocity . . . almost like disturbing a hive of bees'. As well as his googly and top-spinner, O'Reilly, who was 6ft 3in tall, could make the ball bounce. He toured England twice, in 1934 and 1938, and topped the Australian bowling averages both times with more than 100 wickets. He devastated England's batting with Grimmett in 1934, Hutton's first year in county cricket, and Hutton spent the next four years preparing himself for O'Reilly's next visit. He went on to write about cricket for the Sydney Morning Herald.

What do I remember of his 364? I remember that I did 13 and a half hours hard yakker out there and bowled 85 overs. Nowadays they get big money for bowling ten and if they bowl over ten they're thrown out of the union. I have a very, very solid memory of that because for three days I was a cricketing labourer. It was a tremendous feat of concentration. Despite the 54 years that intervene, it is still a simple thing for me to recall that Gethsemane at the Oval when Hutton ground us into the dirt. I remember vividly that when he'd got 331, three less than Bradman's record, there were three maiden overs, and I bowled two of them. In one of my two, there was a no-ball and he didn't even drop his concentration and whack into that. I admired him for that.

I have another recollection that clings to my soul much more. After that Test, I was in London and met Hutton and we were both going to the Piccadilly Hotel, where the Australian team was stationed. So we walked up the street together and went into the hotel and I bought him a drink. And I said: 'There's one thing I can't work out about you Poms' – using the term with respect and reverence, as much as you might expect from someone with the name of O'Reilly. 'Oh', he said, 'what's that?' I said: 'It's why you won't have leg-spin. Why did Douglas Wright get crucified? Suppose you were in the nets at Bradford and a likely kid was sent to you as the best juvenile leg-spinner in the West Riding. What would you do?' Len said: 'I'd advise him to become an off-spinner.' I thought: 'God stone the crows. I ought to take that drink back.' You see, from the time we first saw Doug Wright we thought he was the best bowler in England. But the English said: 'Oh you fellows are only trying to hoodwink us.'

I have a high regard for Hutton, but I don't hold him as high as Hammond; Hammond could belt the hell out of you: overpitch, and you were gone. The first time we struck Hutton was at Trent Bridge in 1938. He got a hundred, and so did Compton. England made 658.

I think we drew. I thought of him as a stickeritaw (a word we used as boys when your marble hit another marble plumb in the middle and stood still – i.e. it was immovable). That's the way we regarded him when we first met him. He impressed me as a Sutcliffe, who had been a pain in the backside to us for years. Yorkshiremen: this team now without a Yorkshireman is like a hearse without a driver, don't you reckon? The selectors dropped Hutton in 1948 after the Lord's Test when he made a few air swipes at Lindwall. There were three selectors, all county players from south of the Trent; Clay was one of them – the only one from the north was Yardley and he was a sort of office boy. But Hutton made the hell of a good comeback. That shows you how selectors sometimes haven't a bloody idea of what's going on.

He was a very quiet bloke. I would say he was never guilty of sledging, which they tell me started about fifteen years ago. He was a quiet man in the field. Two of his finest digs: one was in Brisbane in 1950 when he got 62 not out on a sticky wicket, and one in Sydney when he only made about 37 in 24 minutes in the second Test of 1946–47 and reminded me of Hammond; that was the best I ever saw of him, and the only fault was that there wasn't enough of it.

He was a bit slow to shout, a bit tight-fisted, but that's Yorkshire, isn't it? You almost had to say to him: 'Hey, it's your turn, mate!' But I found him a good bloke, and I reckon that's the greatest compliment an Australian can pay a Pom, because it means he's accepted fully.

Bill Brown

Born 1912. New South Wales and Queensland: 1932–50. 22 Test matches: 1934–48 (Captain in 1 Test 1945/46). Born in Toowoomba, Brown was the first Queenslander to captain Australia. Son of a farmer, he was a classical right-handed opening batsman who scored 105 in his first Test at Lord's in 1934 and 206 not out in his second in 1938. He was 21 when he first toured England, selected ahead of Jack Fingleton, and opened with both Woodfull and Ponsford.

I'm not going to make any comparisons, but there's no doubt that he was a great, great batsman. It was his wonderful balance that impressed me. I thought that fifth Test innings in 1948, when he got 30 out of 52, was an absolutely splendid innings. I fielded all through his 364 at the Oval, and that was a tremendous effort both of technique and concentration. Later on he developed more strokes; I don't in the least want to sound condescending.

He was a very calm, very cool player, and one of the things that struck me when he came out to Australia after the war was that despite his injury it didn't interfere with his batting. He had an easy, confident stance, the hallmark of a really good player: a classic stance. He didn't stand with his bat in the air, and nor did Bradman; no one did in those days – perhaps we were all wrong.

At the Oval, he came out with the same expression every morning as if to say: 'I'm here for the day', and he was. For sheer concentration and determination I have not seen anything to surpass that innings, though I've seen better batting. I'm not denigrating him; only saying that in 1938 he didn't have the same fluency that he developed later in life. I fielded mainly on the fine leg side of short leg to Bill O'Reilly, which wasn't too bad when Len was batting, as he wasn't a great sweeper; but with Denis Compton it was a pretty dangerous position, and we didn't have the equipment they wear these days. Old Bill, he didn't care what happened to you; as Neville Cardus wrote, he ran to the wicket preceded by waves of hostility.

Ernie McCormick

Born 1906. Victoria: 1929–38. 12 Test matches: 1935–38. Ernie McCormick, well known for his jokes, bowled very fast off a run-up of 31 paces. He ran to the wicket with his long arms stiff at his sides. In the first Test of 1938 Hutton played him on to the wicket in his second over, but the ball came to rest against the centre stump without removing a bail. Hutton and Barnett went on to score 219 for the first wicket. In seven Tests against England he dismissed nine opening batsmen. He batted left-handed and bowled right-handed.

He was a magnificent player. Typical Yorkshireman. Great fighter. His technique was correct; nothing like the ex-captain of England in the present team. A marvellous player. Hammond was more flowing, more attractive to watch. Hutton and Leyland, they were real workmen; Eddie Paynter was another one. They were all very hard to get out. Hutton was very hard to get out and a very nice bloke. He didn't like the real quickies, but I don't know who does. In 1938 I bowled him a ball and he played back; the ball hit his pads, dropped between his pads and the wicket, hit the wicket, bounced back again on to his pads, and didn't move a bail. I didn't say: 'Oh dear, oh dear', though I might have said something that meant the same. With Sutcliffe, in 1934, exactly the same thing happened.

I was out of the Oval Test in 1938 with an injury, so that was like winning the lottery. It was even terrible to watch. Tiger (O'Reilly) bowled him a full toss and he pushed it back; it was cruel to see a great bowler like Tiger with no skin left on his fingers. I struck another wicket like that in Africa, and suggested they lay a wreath on it.

Did I ever bowl bouncers at Hutton? Oh yes, yes. But he saw the ball very early; I didn't bowl to hit him, just to get him on to his back foot. I got him out once; I think he went to hook it and Bill Brown caught it. That might be why he never hooked again.

Lindsay Hassett

Born 1913. Victoria (Captain 1946–53): 1933–53. 43 Test matches: 1938–53. (Captain 24 times 1949/50–53) A short, slightly built right-handed attacking batsman, reliable in times of trouble. A technically astute captain, he had the difficult job of carrying on where Bradman had left off. Of the 24 Tests in which he was captain, he won 14 and was unlucky to be in charge when the Ashes were lost, after twenty years, to Hutton in 1953. His impish sense of humour won him great popularity. After his retirement he became a broadcaster with the ABC.

Our attack against Hutton varied a terrific amount. When he made his record score in 1938, the Oval wicket was very unresponsive and we had a very weak opening attack; McCormick was injured.

His concentration was wonderful. People say he was slow; but he made his runs in 13 hours 17 minutes, so if the bloke at the other end had scored at the same rate . . . In 1948 in England we had Lindwall and Miller, Bill Johnston, Ian Johnson, Toshack, Ring and McCool. Lindwall and Miller were at their top. It really was a very fine attack; and Len I think headed the English averages. Later on, in 1950–51, and 1953, our attack had gone off; Lindwall and Miller were still very good, but a little past their peak. So our attack was a little below a really good Test attack. But he was a great player, no doubt about it.

I reckon I learned to bat more side-on from watching Len; I remember telling some of our players that, and they did the same and felt they had improved. He was a very good striker of the ball, with nice strokes, great application, good temperament, and enormous powers of concentration: a very great technician. I think Ray Lindwall worried him, with his pace, and swinging the ball. He bowled Len a few times. Also Ian Johnson. He got him when Len was not coming out to the flighted ball, playing a bit from the crease, and Ian got him between bat and pad, though that was rather rare. He was not a great hooker and was out a couple of times from a ball at shoulder height. But he was seldom incommoded by bouncers. He could get singles. He had all those defensive strokes and hit the ball at the right pace. I don't think he did a lot about dodging particular bowlers.

He was a good, solid captain. He didn't make any tactical mistakes that I can recall. But it's not so much the captain makes the team as the team makes the captain. In Test cricket, there's no room for being spectacular; and in any team, with a reasonably experienced side, there are three or four who could do the same job, you know.

One thing sticks in our minds. Was it at Leeds in 1953? He slowed down the over rate, almost beyond the bounds of sportsmanship. The fast bowlers would follow through almost to the wicket-keeper. Then they wouldn't start to walk back at once, and only then walk back slowly, a slow walk back. That did annoy quite a few of us. It's always easier to bat when the deliveries are coming at a normal rate

Lindsay Hassett, captain of the Australian team which lost the series to Hutton in 1953, waves to the Oval crowd: 'He was a great player, no doubt about it'.

than it is having a hit and then waiting a few minutes for the next ball. But there was nothing you could criticise about his batting; he didn't hook, but then hooking is a mixed blessing.

I won all five tosses against him in 1953. He was a Yorkshireman, and Yorkshiremen are always supposed to be a bit tight-fisted. In the fifth Test he produced a crown piece, and I won the toss again; Len picked up the coin and heaved it out into the crowd. I said: 'That couldn't have been yours.' He said: 'No, I borrowed it.'

Ian Johnson

Born 1918. Victoria (Captain 1953–56): 1935–56. 45 Test matches: 1945–56 (Captain in 17 Tests 1954/55–56). Ian Johnson was a rare Australian right-arm off-spinner who flighted the ball well and a dour middle-order batsman. He toured England in 1948, taking Hutton's wicket 4 times, and 1956, but was too slow to make use of the conditions. He led Australia against England in 1954/55 and in 1956 but lost both times. He was an excellent slip fielder and in 1957 he became the secretary of the Melbourne Cricket Club, a post he held for 25 years.

The first time I saw Hutton was when he came out in 1946–47 with Hammond. He was my first wicket in a Test match. I remember it clearly. It was in Sydney. The ball turned back and he glanced it and Tallon caught it; he was a bit unlucky. Then of course I played against him in 1948, and in 1950–51, and in 1954–55 I captained the side. I like to think we were pretty good friends, though he was a hard person to know; he was really quite intense, concentrated on the game a hundred per cent.

I'll give you an example. That first Test in Brisbane in 1954. The previous week, England had played Queensland and the wicket had looked good and turned out to be pretty lively. Came the Test. Len and I went out to toss and the wicket looked pretty good. Len didn't say a word, rubbing and poking and prodding the pitch, and walking slowly up and down it three times. Subsequently, it was obvious he was thinking that it looked good but was going to be lively again. Finally we tossed and Hutton won. Still he didn't say a word. We walked off and he still hadn't said a word except 'heads' and we were almost at the gate when he said: 'You can bat, Ian.' I said: 'Thanks, Len.' He made a mistake and we made 601 and won after England had to bat on a wet wicket. But the point was that afterwards Len was terribly depressed, really down in the dumps, so much so that I said: 'Come off it, there's no need to despair; it's only a game.' He said: 'You don't understand. Back there in England, it's cold and wet and miserable, and the least we could have done was something to cheer them up.' That was how seriously he took it.

As a captain he was strictly orthodox; he took no chances of any kind whatever. I liked him very much. In 1956, we played a match at the Duke of Norfolk's ground at Arundel; a social match – he had retired. It was the custom in those games to give people a full toss to get off the mark, and Ray Lindwall bowled him a full toss at half-pace on the leg-stump. Len played it very defensively. Ray bowled him three full tosses in a row, and Len played them all defensively; but he did get out for a duck. I said afterwards: 'What the hell are you up to? We feed you full tosses and you won't hit them.' He replied: 'Never trust you buggers.'

He was absolutely superb; the best opening batsman I've ever seen. The only other one who comes close would be Arthur Morris. If he had a weakness it would only be when he was going for a cover drive; but his cover drive was absolutely superb. I've never seen a lovelier. To make it look really good, the bat has to leave the body; and with Len that was the only time it did.

I got him out a few times between bat and pad. I would hold one back a bit. In our early meetings I got him out half a dozen times bowled or stumped. But he worked it out, and from then on he wouldn't use a cover drive to me. He would play me easily, but it allowed me to bowl him a lot of maidens.

I remember after the Test in 1948 at Leeds. We won at twenty past six and had to catch a train to Derby at seven, which didn't leave much time to celebrate. We were all feeling pretty high. The train stopped at a station outside Leeds, and a little lad was wandering along the platform with an autograph book. Tallon, not normally given to gestures, called out to him: 'Come on laddie; we'll autograph your book for you.' 'Who be thee?' asked the boy. 'We're the Australians!' said Tallon. 'I don't want thee. I'm looking for Len Hutton.'

He started the slow over rates. In 1948, when there was a new ball every 55 overs – every 40 in Australia – we averaged 118 deliveries

With Ian Johnson, the Australian skipper, in 1956 – 'the best opening batsman I've ever seen'.

an hour. In 1953, with Hassett as captain, we averaged 110 an hour. In 1954–55, we averaged 112 an hour. Len slowed it down to 90 an hour against our 112; that was absurdly slow. The first time he did it, it was said that it was to spell the fast bowlers. I don't believe it. I think it was to break the concentration of the batsmen. We used to reckon that 60 runs an hour was even time; so that if there were 120 deliveries an hour, that meant a run every two balls. But if the rate is slowed to 90, it's quite obvious that if you score at the same rate you're only going to make about 40.

This is the greatest problem in cricket today, and I'm afraid Len started it. With spin, you can bowl 150 to 160 an hour. I worked out that in 1921 in England, Gregory and Macdonald, the Australian pace bowlers, bowled 61 per cent of all balls delivered in the Test series. The average rate was 120 an hour. Benaud was the first Australian captain to slow it down, and he did so in retaliation. In 1958–59, he slowed it down to 100 an hour; the fast bowlers bowled the same proportion of deliveries as they did in 1921, so the rate went down from 120 an hour in 1921 to 100 in 1958–59. So you lose 120 balls a day, say 600 balls in a five-day Test, which is a full day's play lost. At Len's rate, you lose one and half day's play. So I say very sadly, Len was the one who started it.

Len was a fairly shy character; reserved. He was in many respects not unlike Don Bradman. Bradman rarely offered advice, but he'd bend over backwards to help if asked.

I remember at one time there was a lot of talk about Don's grip; how he held the bat in such and such a particular manner. Len and I were having dinner with the Don and talking about cricket and Len said: 'My grip is the same as yours.' Don Bradman said: 'Nonsense.' Len said to young John Bradman: 'Go and get a bat.' John got a bat, and Len said: 'Now put it down with the handle towards you between your feet.' John did so. Then Len said: 'Now just pick it up normally.' John did. Then Len said to Bradman: 'That's your grip.' Bradman said: 'My God, it is too.' He thought he held the bat in some special way, with his left hand around the bat more anti-clockwise than most. It was thought that that was what allowed him with his pull shot to hit the ball into the ground. He thought it a peculiarity only he had. There was quite a lot of talk about it.

Len was unimaginative as a captain, but very sound; he rarely took an initiative and he rarely made a mistake. He wasn't so much a slow thinker as a cautious thinker; before he tried anything, he wanted to make sure that he'd really thought about it. He made very very few mistakes. The way he walked up and down at Brisbane showed that he didn't want to do it, to put us in, but the way the pitch had played the previous week preyed on him. He thought he could use his fast attack. The fact that he took so long to decide indicates his reluctance.

Ray Lindwall

Born 1921. New South Wales and Queensland (Captain 1955–60): 1945–60. 61 Test matches: 1945–60. (Captain once in 1956). Hutton thought Lindwall 'undoubtedly the greatest bowler of my time', adding that his fast yorker on leg stump was the most dangerous ball he faced. The prospect of Hutton facing Lindwall at his best was widely relished as a battle between two great tacticians. J. M. Kilburn wrote: 'Lindwall's bowling had the beauty of power under smooth control.' He left New South Wales in 1954/55 to captain Queensland. He scored two 100s in Tests and retired to run a flower shop in Brisbane.

I didn't have any different plan of attack for Len than for any other opening batsman; I just bowled. If he had a weakness, I would try and attack it, and if he didn't, I'd try and keep the runs down. If Len had a little weakness it was to the ball outside off stump; when he drove, his bat was a little bit away from his body; but his footwork was so good that if the cover drive was his weakness it was also his strength as well.

My yorker didn't worry him. He would move forward and get it on the full. His judgement of length was so good. I bounced a few at him from time to time, but he wouldn't play a shot; he didn't like bouncers but he didn't get out to them. I don't think I ever hit him. He was very good at getting out of the way.

I regarded him as a very good friend, and his only fault was that he was a little bit suspicious off the field. He wouldn't have a drink with us. We used to ask Compton and Edrich to have a drink and they would, but Len didn't like it or approve of it; he had a funny idea that we were trying to get them out – off the field. In fact, the only reason we asked them was they were such nice fellows. After he retired, I bumped into him outside the Australia Hotel in Sydney, and he said: 'I've known you for ten years and you haven't bought me a drink.' So I took him into the hotel and we were there for an hour, a lovely time, having a chat; came out, he went off, and I suddenly thought: 'He still hasn't bought *me* one!'

Bradman was the best I've ever seen, but Hutton must have been very close, the next best. Was I trying to get him caught down the leg side by Don Tallon at the Oval in 1948? I couldn't say I was – no, I can't say it. That was a very good catch. Just one of those things. You would be very lucky if you were trying to get Len out leg glancing and did so, because it was a perfect shot of his. His footwork was so good; the only thing, as I say, was that when he drove his bat was a foot away from his legs, but it scarcely mattered because if he saw the ball moving he could pull his bat out of the way. He was nearly perfect, and no one is perfect; even Bradman wasn't perfect. Hutton was relaxed; he knew what was going on.

Hutton was a very good captain. He beat us in 1953, and again in 1954–55, so you couldn't say he wasn't, could you? He knew cricket backwards. I don't know that you can really blame him for putting us in in Brisbane. We'd cleaned them up on the same wicket in a state match the week before and I suppose he thought the Test wicket would behave in the same way. But the atmosphere was not there; it was hot, but not overcast. Tyson was quick in Brisbane, but when he shortened his run he got more accurate, that's all.

Len wouldn't play the hook shot. I don't think he ever hooked while I was bowling. Someone who hooks bouncers is likely to get caught behind square leg because the ball is bound to go in the air; so I didn't bowl many bouncers at Len. My mate at the other end, Keith, he used to do that.

Len used to get away from the strike.

Everything he said had something behind it.

Keith Miller

Born 1919. Victoria, New South Wales (Captain 1949–56) and Nottinghamshire: 1937–59. 55 Test matches: 1945–56. One of the greatest all-rounders the game has known, Keith Miller was a natural. A wartime pilot in Britain, he played in the Victory Tests and from then on was an integral part of the Australian side. His casual manner belied an ability to change the course of a game with his right-arm fast bowling or his classical batting or inspirational catching close to the wicket. In Tests he scored 2,958 runs, including 7 100s, and took 170 wickets. Hutton thought him the most unpredictable cricketer he played against and the man he would most want in his side.

I won't call him Hutton, because he was Len to me. So Lindwall says he didn't bounce them at Len; well you get a bit respectful as you grow older. He gave him a few. I gave him plenty. Len didn't hook. Now Compton and Edrich, those two could hook and if you bounced them you might get a bit of a hammering, four four four, that type of thing. To me, hooking is the most exacting shot of all, because you've got to be spot on; I don't know how they can expect to do it at all now with the weight of the bats they use. I picked one up and said to Compton: 'God, Denis, how would you get on with one of these? You wouldn't get time to lift it.' I used to bounce a few at Len, thinking he might defend himself and get caught by a man sitting round the corner.

Len hardly spoke and Denis never stopped talking. Both were great players. Len was a copybook batsman; the finest. He and Boycott were academics who batted according to the book. And I'll tell you another thing. Len Hutton and Geoffrey Boycott were two of the best-dressed, on and off the field. Now some of them dress anyhow. Hutton and Boycott were the real purists of cricket.

I tried harder against Hutton and Compton because they were more of a challenge, those two. I thought they were the great players. Compo played shots Hutton wouldn't dream of; he'd play two completely different shots off exactly the same type of ball. I'd known Denis when he was in the army. We'd played in some match in Calcutta when there was a students' riot; Compo was on 90-odd and the leader of the riot came up to him and said: 'Mr Compton, you are batting very well but you must stop.' Compo said to me: 'Isn't he the fellow who was our host last night at dinner?' So Denis and I started saying: 'Salaam sahib' to one another and when I went out to bat I'd look for him and he'd have his hand to his forehead, salaaming.

Len never said a word. I would say, if Washbrook got fifty: 'Well done, Cyril,' and Len occasionally would say it, but otherwise you never got a word out of him. He was so bloody intent on the cricket;

his whole dedication was to the game. I've never known anyone else so dedicated. I might get fifty or a hundred but Len would never say anything.

At Old Trafford I was bowling to Compton and the weather was terrible as usual and we came off half-way through the over. The dressing-rooms were adjacent. Len didn't talk on the field; his idea

was to play it like a war. Godfrey, Denis and Bill were the other way. In the break, Denis came over and asked me to make up a poker four, so I'm in the English dressing-room with the fellow I'd just been bowling bumpers at and Len is frowning at the back of the room. Then the umpires are going out and out we go, me snatching up the money, and next thing, finishing the over to Denis. I'm trying to knock his head off. Len gets really annoyed, Denis said – cricket was his whole life.

Hutton, just retired, greets Keith Miller at Tilbury in 1956 – 'Miller's the one I'd always have in my side'.

After he retired I met him at a golf tournament. 'Oh, good to see you, Len.' He said: 'Can I buy you a drink?' so I thought: 'By Christ, this is bloody great' and said: 'By all means, Len.' So we go into the bar and Len says what do you want, and I say: 'I'd like a Scotch.' 'Large or small? ' So I say: 'Large, thanks very much, Len.' And Len says to the barman: 'I'll put that on the firm's account.' So I didn't catch him.

He was a dour, dour man. A lot of captains, like Bradman, set the other side an impossible task when they declare; on the other hand, Richie Benaud would give them a bit to go for. Over here in Australia the other day the Australians gave England 470. Now that's not captaincy. Hutton would do that kind of thing because he didn't want to lose; but if he declared earlier, and then if we had a go, we might lose a few wickets and he might win. But he made it so impossible you didn't have a go. Bradman was much the same.

Len didn't praise much. You might say that Frankie Worrell was a fine player, and Len would just say: 'Aye. Aye.' The year before Len died there was some occasion at the Guildhall and I was sitting between Illingworth and Hutton; Everton Weekes was opposite, and he was one of the greats in my book. Len and I were talking, when he nudged me and nodded over towards Weekes and said: 'Aye, now he was great.' That was one of the few times I heard him say anything like that.

He was in one of the worst decisions I've ever seen when I was playing. There was this fellow Iverson, who in New Guinea in the war had learned to flick a ping pong ball with his middle finger and thumb and he tried it with a cricket ball, and got into the Test side when he was 35 or 36. He was very accurate, got some lift, and was very hard to play. It's the Melbourne test in 1950–51 and I'm fielding at short mid-on, within handshaking distance of Hutton. Iverson bowled and Len came right forward and took his bat out of the way and the ball hit him on the kneepad and dollied up. Tallon grabbed it and Iverson, who knew nothing at all about cricket, appealed and George Cooper, the only Test he umpired in, gave him out. Len stood there and I could see the blood draining out of his face. I said: 'Oh Len, no. Len, no. Can't be.' There's a photo of it: here am I, hands on hips. If he'd snicked it, I'd be knocking Tallon over to get to it. Len never said a word. I never heard him complain. I never heard Don complain. Compo didn't complain. These great players didn't complain. These fellows today get their middle stumps knocked out of the ground and stand there.

He was a funny fellow. I knew him from the wartime, and Dorothy. He'd be talking, aye aye, and then he'd call you over and you'd think he was going to tell you a bit of a secret, and he'd mumble away and there'd be no story at all. I'd known Gubby (Allen) since the war too, and if you've known someone in the war you can confide in them. Gubby told me how Len rang him up. Len was captain of England and Gubby was El Supremo, and Len asked if he could see him, so Gubby put off a few things to meet him. Afterwards Gubby told me: 'I'm buggered if I know what he wanted to see me about; he just said aye, aye, and there was nothing there.'

Hutton's 37 at Sydney in 1946 was one of the greatest little bits of batting I've seen. I got him out just on lunch-time when his hand lost control and his bat fell on to the stumps. As I walked out, someone said it was bad luck, and I said: 'Bad luck for you, but bloody good luck for me.' A fellow called Freer was playing and I was in the slips and he had Hutton plumb lbw but he was given not out. I think Len thought it must be his lucky day and said to himself: 'I will now play some shots.' I never realised he could play like that. It was a pleasure to watch. That was one of the little gems of my whole career.

He was my first Test wicket. The first Test in Brisbane in 1946. Bradman was out for 28, caught Ikin bowled Voce, but given not out and then went on to make 187. W. R. Hammond said to him: 'That's a nice way to start the bloody Test' and we made over 600. Then there was a deluge for two successive days, the ground was like a lake, England batted late in the day and I knocked Len over for 7 – his first innings against Australia after his 364.

I would bowl him any bloody thing. But I bowled as I did because I was a batsman. I'll tell you something interesting. In the first game of the tour against Worcestershire in 1948 Bradman put me in at the end of the innings, ninth, saying: 'You've already played in English conditions', and I got 50 not out. In 1953 against Worcestershire I got 220 not out. The second match of the tour was always against Leicestershire. Against Leicestershire in 1948 I made 202 not out and in 1953 I was run out for 42. In 1956 I got 281 not out. So in the first two opening matches on three tours I had an average of 795. That's why I say I was a batsman. What I used to do, bowling to Hutton, was to say, right, the conditions are such and such, now if I was batting what would I not like now? Then I'd try and bowl it. That's the way I bowled to Hutton, and to Compton; they made me think more. It was like chess, bowling to those two. With others, I'd just run up and bowl.

Arthur Morris

Born 1922. New South Wales (Captain 1947–55): 1940–55. 46 Test matches: 1946–55 (Captain in 2 Tests). Arthur Morris ranks with the great Australian left-handers Hill, Darling, Ransford, Harvey and Lawry, and opened the batting for Australia 77 times. He scored 100 in each innings of his first-class debut against Queensland in 1940 and scored 696 runs, average 87, in Tests against England in 1948. He stood in as captain for Lindsay Hassett in 1951/52 against the West Indies and for Ian Johnson in 1954/55 against England. Alec Bedser got him out 18 times in Tests. In 1963 he made a brief comeback to first-class cricket.

I first played against Len Hutton in 1946. He was a great player, with the ability to get singles when he wanted them. I suppose, by 1946, his arm injury must have affected him to a degree, but I just accepted him as the great player that he was. He got his singles by placing, able to get them away from time to time, often between square-leg and mid-on – sometimes to get out of the way of the quicks. He used to get out of the firing line and watch with wry amusement Washbrook batting at the other end.

Cyril liked to hook. Hutton would sit back and watch without saying a word, but thinking: 'Good on you, Cyril!' He very rarely hooked; if he did, it had to be a very short one. He was able to play back and forward; not like some of the English boys on this current tour, who play forward all the time, committing suicide to my way of thinking; I think that's overcoaching. He'd go back and get behind the ball when it was necessary. He had great footwork; and that's the most important thing because if a batsman's feet are in the right place his bat will usually be in the right place too. He was a good on-side player. He was also a master of the one-liner. In 1946 once, when the balls were flying, he called me over. I said: 'Yes, Len?' He said: 'Cyril can't get ones.'

Was he a good captain? Captains are captains. There are probably half-a-dozen players on the field who are capable of captaining the side. A captain is as good as his team. If he wins, he's a good captain. Border in 1981 was a lousy captain. Later he was the greatest captain who ever lived. I'm very cynical about captains. A great captain is probably a great captain off the field, rather than on. Len had no problems off the field that I knew of. He was always well-dressed, on and off the field. You wouldn't see him in stubbies and thongs, like some of them nowadays. He was always the gentleman and it was always a pleasure to see him, over there or here.

Bill Johnston

Born 1922. Victoria: 1945–55. 40 Test matches: 1947–55. Tall, left-arm medium-fast bowler who took 160 wickets for Australia, providing powerful support for Lindwall and Miller. On the 1948 tour of England he took 102 wickets, including 27 in Tests. He took more than 20 wickets in a series on four occasions. Of his batting it was once written: 'He played with limbs seemingly independent of each other, aiming his bat at the ball with arms and legs flying and, on contact, prancing down the pitch in bounding good spirits. Occasionally he would connect.'

I first saw Len in 1946 batting out here in Australia. I was in my second season for Victoria, a struggling fast bowler. I had begun as a slow bowler, but Victoria was short of fast bowlers and they endeavoured to turn me into one. My first introduction to top-class cricket was England v Victoria. In my first over for Victoria I got Washbrook for a duck – an inswinger that rose a bit and followed him in and hit him on the glove. Hutton was playing a few shots and making a few runs and in my second over Miller, who was playing for Victoria then, was at square leg, and I bowled one – I was very inexperienced – too short and Hutton went to hook, mistimed, and it spilled just out of Miller's hands; I thought if he'd moved a little earlier and a little faster he could have caught it. I was immature. So I tried it again and this time it went into the grandstand.

The next time I saw him was in 1948; I always thought he was one of the best batsmen I ever bowled to. He was probably the most correct, too; he had a tremendous defence, yet unlike a lot of opening batsmen with a good defence he could also score runs quickly without making too much of a fuss. In the fifth Test in 1953 he was going along well with 82 and I was bowling spinners; I didn't spin it much but I bowled an arm ball and it just sneaked between his bat and pad, which was quite surprising.

He was a quiet fellow. I remember him in the 1950s as captain, the first professional captain. In Brisbane in 1954 we were staying in the same hotel as the Englishmen, the old Lennons, which they've pulled down, and Lindsay Hassett and I were a little late in coming in to dinner; Hutton was on his own and had just finished eating, but we went over and he asked us to sit down. Besides being shy, he was really quite sensitive. He showed a little bit of concern and asked Lindsay and myself how he was getting on with his captaincy; we had the conviction that he was anxious to know whether he could improve. There wasn't as much aggression between the teams then as there seems to be nowadays.

He and Arthur Morris were the greatest opening batsmen of my time. In that series of 1954–55 Len was captain when Victoria played MCC at the Melbourne Cricket Ground. My wife was expecting our first child, David, who later played for South Australia. There was a story in the papers about how a system of signals had been arranged to tell me, if I was on the field, whether it was a boy or a girl, which was quite untrue but made a good story and Len read it and took some interest. Anyway, when Victoria was batting and I wasn't needed, I went to the hospital and we had a son, the day the match finished. Len gave me a five-shilling piece, a crown, to give to the baby. I treasured it and gave it to my son when he was old enough, and he treasured it too. Then in recent years he was sharing a unit in Adelaide with his brother and they had a robbery and it was stolen. Of course, it was of no monetary value. But we both treasured it.

Neil Harvey

Born 1928. Victoria (Captain 1956–57) and New South Wales: 1946–62. 79 Test matches: 1947–63 (Captain in 1 Test, 1961). Neil Harvey was one of the greatest left-handed batsmen. In post-war Australian cricket he was second only to Bradman. He had an adventurous outlook and liked to advance down the wicket. He was often a class apart on bad wickets and scored Test 100s in 15 different cities. He was an excellent fielder at cover. He was disappointed not to be made the Australian captain after Ian Johnson retired in 1957 and played his only Test as captain at Lord's in 1961. Later an Australian selector.

I didn't see a Test until I played in one. I first struck Hutton in 1948 and I always classed him as the best English batsman I ever saw: him and May and Compton. He had a marvellous technique. You have to remember that he played on uncovered wickets when you had to have a very good technique; he had a soft bottom hand and the ability to read the ball off the pitch.

Iverson, in 1950–51 out here, completely mesmerised all the English batsmen, except Hutton. If he had gone to England, he would have cleaned up. Hutton is generally recognised as a player of pace bowlers but he also scored a lot of runs against a lot of spin bowlers. I've often seen him get down the wicket to slow bowlers, and make runs on bad, sticky wickets – you don't get wickets like that now. I don't know whether his short left arm helped him or hindered him. He was a tremendous player.

I didn't speak to Hutton much. I was 12 years younger, and kept myself to myself; I tried to sit in a corner and learn things. Fortunately, I was invited to Leeds for the fiftieth anniversary of his world record: Lindwall and me. That was a lovely evening.

He showed he was a good captain in 1954–55. We won the first Test so easily, and England fought back. That takes a bit of good leadership. You've got to have fellows who want to play for you. If they're not going to play for you, you're not going to be a good captain. Len had them wanting to play for him. And he led from the front; if you're able to do that, you're fifty per cent of the way there. He had the will and he had the attack and he wanted to win, and that's exactly what he did in 1954.

He had some great battles against Lindwall and Miller, and two better fast bowlers couldn't be imagined. It was an education to field at cover and watch them, and Hutton batting against them. There are a lot of players around now who think they know the lot; a couple of them in the present Australian team. In 1948, I was the only person who saw every single match of the tour. I was so keen to learn; and I was by seven years the youngest member of the party. Hassett, Bradman, Miller, Lindwall – it was worth listening to fellows like that. But that sort of thing doesn't seem to happen now.

The final Test at the Oval in 1948 was my second Test match. Hutton made 30 out of 52. I was fielding at fine leg, down in front of the old members' stand. Lindwall was bowling to Hutton, who played a perfect leg glance. I raced round the boundary to cut it off, and looked up and there was Mr Tallon almost at square leg; he had it in his left hand. Tallon was a very neat wicket-keeper, though he was over six foot. When he stumped anyone, he only took off one bail. Hutton was the only person who looked like scoring runs that day.

Lindwall and Miller tried often to hit him, but I think I don't recall them doing so. I've seen him duck a few times. Keith would mix up his pace, change his mind half-way back to his run, take eight paces and bowl; it might be a wrong 'un and it might be a bouncer. But Len had such wonderful technique and footwork and he picked up the line and length early. I get annoyed with some of these fellows now, with their arm pads and helmets. They make me laugh, too, because all the equipment has got to affect their mobility. Len didn't

Hutton hits out in Australia in 1954 – 'When he let go', said Trueman, 'you suddenly realised you were on another planet'.

have any of that, and there haven't been two faster or better bowlers than Lindwall and Miller.

Sonny Ramadhin

Born 1929. Trinidad and Lancashire: 1949–65. 43 Test matches: 1950–61. Virtually unknown in his own country, Sonny Ramadhin, with his 'spin twin' Valentine, bowled the West Indians to victory in England in 1950. His strong wrist delivered the ball quicker than the average spinner and batsmen found it impossible to tell which way the ball was spinning. He continued to be successful in Test cricket for 10 years, although in 1957 May and Cowdrey penetrated his mystery with a partnership of 411 in the first Test at Edgbaston. In that match he bowled a record 129 overs. He played in the Lancashire League from the early 1950s, for Lancashire in 1964–65, and for Lincolnshire from 1968–70. He also ran a pub in Oldham for many years.

Len Hutton played me off the pitch. He played for the off-spinner and then if it turned the other way his bat was a mile from it. He was a great batsman and I think I only got him out once or twice. I remember he went sweeping me once, he got a top edge and Frank Worrell took the catch.

He always played forward and he liked to get on the front foot, not only against me but against a lot of bowlers. I had an orthodox field for him – leg-slip, mid-off and so on. He always played with his bat in front of his pads, and although he may have used his pads he never kicked the ball. That was something which killed slow bowling. They didn't know how to play me, so they started using their pads. He played with his bat and pad very close, so if he missed, for instance an off-spinner, and it turned a bit too much, his pads were there. But he wasn't kicking the ball, with his bat behind his pad, he never played like that. He always played me along the ground.

His cover drive impressed me the most; yes, a beautiful cover drive. He'd come right out, lean forward and stroke it away. He'd do that to any bowler. He never moved down to the ball, he played it off the wicket, left foot thrust forward. He never danced down. I can remember that he did it once against Valentine and he was stumped, at Lord's in 1950. But he never went down the wicket and I never thought I'd get him stumped.

Hutton played me off the pitch and others tried to as well. It was the only way they could play me, but Hutton was so correct that he didn't seem to have much trouble. I used to bowl him more leg spinners because he played forward a lot, hoping that he'd get a little nick to the slips or something like that. I bowled him more leg'ers than off'ers and normally I bowled more off'ers. I'd normally bowl about two leg-spinners an over to make the batsman look, you know, sometimes one, but to him I bowled about three.

Sometimes we bowled all day to Hutton, but he didn't take many chances. He was cautious, but he'd pick the bad balls or the half-volleys and stroke them away. His scoring shots were mostly off the front foot. He didn't get much room for cutting. He got a lot of runs like that, singles mainly, not many fours. Hutton had a lot of patience. He never bothered if he missed, played and missed, played and missed. He kept his cool and carried on.

I remember he got 202 at the Oval in 1950, on a wet one, a wet turner as well. It was wet but he got a double century. We couldn't shift him. He could bat on anything, slow wickets, turners, fast wickets; never bothered. That was the thing, he played and missed. He must have missed a load of times but it never touched the bat, or the edges, so if he made a bad fault or a bad stroke, or anything like that, he didn't get a touch. He was a marvellous player.

Hutton used to play me with a dead bat, used to kill the ball right down by his feet. He never liked to play defensive and stroke it away. When he was playing forward defensively he'd play with a dead bat, like Trevor Bailey – he used to play with a long forward dead bat. He was another hard chap to shift. Bowl a bit shorter and they'd go on the back foot and have plenty of time to see it. Hutton didn't go back so often, only when you bowled a bad one or a full toss and he wanted to hit it away.

I remember Len asking me to bowl at him in the nets at Lord's after the Test match there in 1950. I said that he'd have to give me £30 but I wouldn't have done it anyway. He didn't take me on. We didn't talk a lot. We didn't mix. I don't think he was one for mixing a lot with other people. He was always on his own, it seemed to me. He was a bit of a loner and you never saw him after the match for a drink or anything like that. I thought it was terrible the way he stopped the England players fraternising with us when they came out to the West Indies in 1953–54. He was a hard captain, a very shrewd man, very hard. Didn't give anything.

Colin McDonald

Born 1928. Victoria (Captain 1958–62): 1947–62. 47 Test matches: 1951–61. Colin McDonald was a resilient and courageous right-handed opening batsman. He toured England three times but didn't get into the Test side on his first visit in 1953 because Hassett went in with Morris. In 1956 at Manchester, when Jim Laker took 19 wickets, he battled hard and was top scorer in both innings with 32 and 89. He became captain of Victoria in 1958, taking over from Neil Harvey. After retiring from cricket in 1963, he became Executive Director of the Lawn Tennis Association of Australia.

Any person who could bat at all would recognise him as a great batsman. I was an opener and obviously he was one of the people I was extremely interested in. One of the things I liked was his classical stance; I am completely unimpressed with the way some of the English hold their bats up in the air these days; Gooch is successful with it, but I don't know of many others.

Hutton's stance enabled him to take the bat straight back. I never talked to him much: it was just: 'Gidday Len', 'Gidday Col.' He played and missed more rarely than most. Not very often. Usually he got the ball in the meat of the bat.

One thing about him that was noticeable was that he played forward all the time. His theory was that if you go forward it cuts down the amount of deviation after the ball hits the wicket. If a ball is coming at 100 mph the mind hasn't time to correct for deviation. That was his reason for going forward. On English pitches, that's probably very sound: they are softer and the ball deviates more. But I don't necessarily believe it's the right method in Australia or the West Indies, where the ball doesn't deviate as much. It tends to limit your opportunity to get out of the road of the ball. If you play forward and it's short, you're a case for hospital.

He was a magnificent driver of the ball, which is probably another reason he went forward. He wasn't a natural hooker or cutter. He could do anything, of course, it was just that he did some things better than others.

His stance was important. Because it was side-on, he didn't get the body in the road of the bat. One of the things I notice about Australian players now is that they tend to get front-on. When they pick up the bat it goes back to point. Front-on players tend to get caught in the slips. Hutton was side-on.

I had a bad tour in 1953 and coming home on the ship Hassett said: 'How about playing a bit more side on?' It had never occurred to me. I became a much better player. Hutton was always side-on; you can do a lot of things you can't do if you're chest-on. You can duck much quicker. If you're side-on and moving to the pitch, you've got more time to react; you can walk towards point instead of making an ungainly stumble towards square-leg. That was the sort of stuff he did automatically.

If I was going to be extra-critical about Hutton, it would be about the over-rate. The fourth Test in Adelaide in 1955 was my first against England: they bowled eight-ball overs in those days, and England bowled 51 overs in a whole day. I batted most of that day and we Australians were criticised for being slow. In fact, off 51 overs, we made 203 runs, and that was against Tyson, Statham, and Bailey – very good, accurate bowlers. But it was quite definitely Hutton's policy to bowl as few overs as possible. Australian journalists, the non-cricketers, hated what they thought was slow scoring; a lot of it was to do with Len Hutton, but we poor batsmen got the abuse. A fast bowler would field at fine leg, fair enough, but then come on to bowl from the other end, which would give him a 130–140 yard walk. That was policy. As a person, Hutton was trying to win for England, but I don't think he served the game well in that area.

As a batsman there was a little bit of Boycott about him. He would point out that he was a professional; and occupying the crease was pretty important, particularly to a Yorkshire professional. He was more concerned with doing what he was paid to do than to entertain, and he took the view that he was paid to bat. With all his great ability, I think he was a little negative.

His wartime injury must have reduced his capacity, particularly to cut – not so much his driving.

We were the people to beat; I take that as a compliment. When Laker took those 19 wickets at Old Trafford in 1956, I got 32, and 89 out of 205. I had a good match. For the 89 I batted three or four days, because of injury and rain. We had no way of winning, and when I did get out Hutton said it was the first time he had ever wished an Australian batsman to make a hundred. We were the mortal enemy; so for that remark I commend him.

His relations with us were proper. Hutton wasn't loved by the opponents. Compton got on with everyone; but Hutton was not the hail-fellow-well-met kind. Everyone respected him, but he wasn't anyone's particular friend. One thing Australians are quite clear about. People tend to link Hutton and Bradman, which is not fair to either. Bradman was God; then there were a lot of other good players.

Alan Davidson

Born 1929. New South Wales: 1949–63. 44 Test matches: 1953–63. Alan Davidson was a dangerous left-handed all-rounder. Originally a spin bowler similar to Tony Lock, he became a fast bowler, swinging the new ball and cutting it both ways off the pitch. Tall and strong, he could hit the ball hard and he fielded well. He toured England in 1953, 1956 and 1961 as well as going on tours to India, Pakistan and South Africa. In 1960/61 against the West Indies he was the best bowler on either side; in the tied Test at Brisbane he became the first player to complete the match double of 100 runs and 10 wickets in a Test. He went on to become President of the New South Wales Cricket Association.

I think Hutton was a freak! His technique was the finest I've ever had the opportunity to bowl to, and I learned quite a bit from him: the way he went on to the back foot first, shifting his weight, and then was still able to go forward. His technique should have been recorded on film as one of the finest there has ever been. Lindwall could bowl a yorker at will, but Hutton would just move out an extra couple of feet or if it swung away would drop his hands and let the ball pass. I never saw him hurry; great players never hurry.

He was my first wicket in Test cricket in 1953; he was caught in the gully by Benaud. He went for a cover drive and didn't quite get to the ball. It was just a bit shorter than he expected; he was a tremendous top hand player, which gave him his control, but the ball had a little bit more angle coming from a left-hand bowler.

He and his wife were such a nice couple. We had a son while we were playing at Headingley in 1953 on the first morning of a Test: the day Hutton was bowled by Lindwall for 0. After that we went to Scarborough, and Lady Hutton by then had made us a pram shawl.

He liked the fact that he'd beaten Australia; he came out here several times after he retired, and used to get a twinkle in his eye when he talked about it. Let's face it, he was fairly successful! He was not showing off; he just had a sense of achievement.

As a captain he was a bit dour; he could become very negative. In 1954–55 he had the quicks bowling eight-ball overs, and he slowed it down, setting an example that is copied very well today. The fewer balls you bowl, the fewer runs they can score. If the other side is getting on with it, only one side can really win. In fact, the other side is forced to try to score faster than they normally would. In that series he really harnessed his forces: Tyson, Statham, Bailey, Appleyard. He worked to a plan. Even when England had injuries Graveney came into the side and made a hundred.

I was never coached a day in my life; a country boy. I used to practise by myself in front of a mirror, learning cover drives from that famous photograph of Hammond driving, with Oldfield crouched behind the stumps. I would bat in front of the mirror, with the book open on a chair; in effect, the mirror turned me into a right-hander. That meant I was playing basically a front-foot shot, and so I was in trouble against real pace, playing a bit early. Then I watched Len playing Lindwall and Miller and he had so much time. I realised it was so much easier if you went back first; his first movement was back, then forward.

I never really bounced them at him. If you did, he looked at you. Once he read the length, and realised the height, he was either in a position to get out of the way or to drop his hands and let the ball through. So the bowler wastes his energy. Cricket is a game of endurance. A day's play lasts six hours; the more tired the bowlers get, the more opportunities there are for the batsmen late in the day. I don't remember him being hit. He was so perfectly side-on so there wasn't much chance. If Lindwall and Miller tried to intimidate him and failed, there wasn't much use my trying. He would only have had a thigh pad, a bit of sponge rubber; not fibre glass, like they have today.

He was a marvellous cutter. He knew exactly where his stumps were. No one in the last England side knew whether Reid was pitching on or outside the off-stump. Len always knew. He had the ability to select the right ball to cut and was always over the top of the ball; I can never remember seeing him caught off his cut.

PART FIVE

Life With My Father
Richard Hutton

Hutton on Bradman

IN MEMORIAM:
Sheppard on Hutton

Hutton's Career Record
compiled by Geoffrey Copinger

Richard, aged three, takes a net as his father leaves for Australia in 1946. He was away for nearly six months. He said in later life: 'there has always been a certain eccentricity about my father.'

Life With My Father

Richard Hutton

Born 1942. Cambridge University and Yorkshire: 1962–74. 5 Test matches: 1971. Sir Leonard Hutton's son Richard, born in Pudsey, was a tall (6ft 4½in) and strong all-rounder. In each of his three years at Cambridge (1962–64) he got a blue. For Yorkshire he scored 1,000 runs in two seasons and in his last Test, against India, he shared in a seventh-wicket partnership of 103 with Alan Knott. He retired from cricket to become a chartered accountant and is the editorial director of The Cricketer *magazine.*

During my childhood I discovered most about my father through the back page of the daily newspaper; quietly leaving my bed in the early morning, I waited patiently by the letter box for its arrival. I learned to read by picking out my father's name and his score from the score-sheet. Often they were in the headlines, which made it easier. Eventually I moved on to the match reports, and thence to taking cricket books to bed. By then I was devouring every written word about my father; he had become greater than God. To be sure of seeing him when I wanted to I had to go to the cricket ground. For hours I would sit enthralled as I compiled his score in my own scorebook, anguishing over every ball in the fear that the apparent frailty of his play, which I failed to recognise as artistry, would let him down. How little I knew, and I wonder if he had any idea of the torture I suffered.

At the age of ten I disgraced myself, my mother and my school in public on that awful day at Headingley when Lindwall bowled him out second ball. It was made worse by the fact that, as far as my young eye could judge, there was an easy single off the first ball. Before too long, however, I was bathing in the reflected glory of the Ashes victory and then the successful defence in Australia.

After his retirement there seemed to be little left to follow. Instead, the nature of his influence shifted, and my adolescence met the hand of paternal discipline, as if the returning hero felt the need to make up for lost time.

During my school holidays, aware of my desire to play cricket, he arranged for me to play for Bradford Second XI in the Bradford League. In the following summer I graduated into the first team as an opening bat and in my first match scored a 50, so qualifying for the traditional collection. Returning home with my pockets over-flowing with coppers, threepenny bits and sixpences, all donated by a generous crowd, my great joy was in no way lessened by my father's expression of horror that his son, and a schoolboy at that, had actually received money for playing cricket.

The next match was an away game at East Bierley, and at lunchtime it was still not decided whether my father would drive me to the ground. Pointing out that I could get on just as well without parental support, I got the bus into Bradford and caught the trolley out to East Bierley, arriving in time for what I thought was a 2.30 pm start. In fact the starting time was 2 pm and as the match had already begun and Bradford were batting, I was put down at number six as a punishment for arriving late. In the meantime and unknown to me, my father had decided to go to the match and, in the comfort of his motorcar, had arrived before me to find that Bradford were 0 for 1 (last man 0). Seeing that I was not at the crease and assuming that mine was the wicket to fall, he went straight home without showing himself to anyone.

Eventually when my turn to bat came, I was fortunate enough to make another 50. The collection was even more overwhelming than the week before and, since the after-match activities held no interest for me then, I hurried home in total ecstasy to display my proud winnings for the second week in succession. Opening the kitchen door I was confronted by my father, who posed the clever question: 'So, where's the collection this time, then?' Seeing my moment, I emptied my pockets, and hundreds of coins cascaded across the kitchen floor, rolling to rest in every nook and cranny. The superior grin facing me altered its shape to open-mouthed amazement and remained so as if set to stone until he found the wit to say that it is quicker to travel by car than by bus!

If this was one of the best moments of my life, probably the worst also involved my father through his own exquisite sense of timing. By 1968 I was just about holding a Yorkshire place when I had an appalling day at Lord's in a match against Middlesex, which was also John Murray's benefit game. To put the varied careers of my father and myself into perspective, I suppose I could say that my bad days were as numerous as his good days, and my good ones about as infrequent as his bad. On this dreadful day I could find neither length nor line, and Murray himself, as befitted the occasion, took full advantage and was on his way to a large score. As I trudged off to my field position, after one particular over in which he savaged me for several boundaries, including a six, I heard the public address system being put into operation. 'This is Sir Leonard Hutton speaking,' it said. I was suddenly panic-stricken with the appalling thought that I was about to receive a public admonishment for improper bowling. A snigger went round the ground, and I stood breathless as I prepared for the worst. What followed was an appeal on behalf of John Murray's benefit fund, which hardly relieved me – but the Yorkshire captain did.

There has always been a certain eccentricity about my father; particularly one can never be sure of the response he might make to certain situations. I was abroad at the time when I telephoned him to announce my intention of getting married. There was a deafening silence as though the shock had killed him. Eventually, in his woe-ridden manner, he informed me that only on that very day the Government had been forced to take over British Leyland and the rates were doubling. Nevertheless, I said, I was still going to get married.

With Sir Don Bradman in 1953 – the legendary Australian described Hutton
as 'one of the great craftsmen of all time'.

Hutton On Bradman

Sir Leonard Hutton's tribute to Sir Donald Bradman on his eightieth birthday in 1988 first appeared in The Observer. *It coincided with the fiftieth anniversary of the match in which Hutton broke Bradman's world record 334 for a Test innings.*

To hear that Sir Donald Bradman is 80 years old is not that surprising. He seems to have been part of my life for so long that I would be surprised only to learn that he was really 180, or perhaps 16.

The Don is rather more than a normal human being. He first registered with me when I was eleven or twelve. The huge scores by Bradman and Ponsford made an enormous impact on me, particularly Don's 452 not out against Queensland in 1929–30. Whatever Ponsford did, Bradman would go one better, and quickly.

I counted the days to his arrival in England in 1930. He began with 236 and by September he was close to 3,000 runs. It was early in July of that year that the Australians came to Bradford and, a few days after my fourteenth birthday, I was there to see my idol.

I suppose I should have had more faith in Yorkshire, for they allowed the great man only a single before winning an lbw appeal. I went home to Pudsey feeling very dejected.

Soon afterwards came the third Test at Headingley. England had won at Trent Bridge, Australia at Lord's, Bradman scoring a century in each match. I was a very early spectator at Leeds, my first Test match. (The next time I saw a Test match, it was as a player.)

Australia won the toss and soon lost Archie Jackson to Tate. Bradman made his way to the wicket very slowly on that sunny morning: by lunch he had passed 100, by tea 200 and at the close he was 309 not out. This was batsmanship of a class never seen before: a ruthless, systematic destruction of an England attack that included Larwood, Tate, Geary, Tyldesley and Hammond.

I had been told that Bradman was unorthodox and that his bat was not always straight. On that occasion and on the many times I saw him play afterwards I never saw any part of his cricket that could not be emulated by a schoolboy.

Bradman was a little below medium height, perhaps the ideal height for a batsman. His head was always in line and any movement to the straight ball of good length would be forward or back, never across. No batsman, certainly none between 1928 and 1940, saw the ball earlier or moved more quickly to meet it.

All these images flooded the mind of a schoolboy batsman who was transfixed by Bradman's manipulation of the field: if third man was moved square, he would cut between slips and gully. If third man moved fine, he would cut square.

He obviously memorised the position of every fielder and detested directing the ball towards one. I was fascinated to see how he aimed for maximum reward for each stroke and how well placed he always was to achieve that.

Even when he made an error in that astonishing innings at Leeds, he was quick enough to profit. He charged at one of Tyldesley's slow leg-breaks, slipped when well out of his crease and, just as Duckworth was waiting to collect the ball to effect the stumping, Bradman somehow got his bat to the ball as he fell, cut it down to third man and, instead of being out, got away with a single.

With Bradman 309 not out, I went back to Pudsey feeling sorry for England. There was enough daylight left to find a few friends and to improvise, 19 days after my fourteenth birthday, a game of cricket in which I tried to play shots long into the dusk after seeing the greatest innings ever played in England. Eight years on, Don was the first to congratulate me on reaching 335 and he was most generous in his praise of my performance.

How good was Bradman? One likes to have one's own opinions vindicated and I was fortunate enough to be able to put that very question to Wilfred Rhodes who, of course, thought a little while before he replied: 'I bowled against all the best from 1900 to 1930 – Hobbs, Trumper, Grace and Ranji among them and many, many more – but Bradman was the greatest.'

As a judge of players Rhodes was almost infallible and he never gave an opinion lightly. Wilfred passed on many tips for playing in Australia and it was out there that I had another insight into Bradman's formidable expertise. Much of his boyhood development came from batting on concrete covered with matting where he must have learned to use his feet like, well, Fred Astaire.

Bradman then went on to play on the Bulli Creek soil pitches prevalent in Australian cricket before the war, which were just as hard as concrete. England batsmen grow up on much slower surfaces and are always at a disadvantage.

Bradman had another incentive: he had a deep love of cricket that ensured he not only played as long as his physical fitness permitted, but committed him to serving the game as Australia's leading administrator for many years.

He was not the easiest man to converse with, for he held very strong opinions and could have been described in Yorkshire as a man who liked the sound of his own voice. That is a little unkind, for Bradman spoke much good sense and more influential people in cricket should have listened to him, certainly over the post-war years, especially in Australia.

During the 1954–55 tour I was given an evening of excellent hospitality at his home in Adelaide and it was there that I realised there was much more to him than his cricket. His quick mind embraced many topics and I left convinced that Bradman would have been famous, in England and Australia, whatever career he had followed.

I was lucky to play in three Test series against Bradman. At Adelaide in 1947 he was dismissed by the best ball I have ever seen from Alec Bedser. It moved into him through the air, Don shaped to play it down the leg side, but on bouncing the ball became a fast leg-break that struck his middle and off stumps. A lesser batsman might not have lost his wicket to such a delivery, for he would not have spotted the movement through the air quickly enough.

If Bradman's concentration when batting was 150 per cent, he missed nothing as captain. He was quick and merciless in his estimation of a batsman's weaknesses and Australia's young bowlers in 1946 and 1948 owed much to their captain's briefings.

As an opponent I learned much from him by watching him bat, lead the side and, in his earlier days, as a fielder. In 1930 his throw was so swift and accurate from any position that he must have been close to the world's best.

We in cricket ought to be grateful that he has given us so much of his life, his time and affection. To Australian cricketers he will always be the shining light, the model to emulate. No cricketer played the game harder and no man gave the game more untarnished fame and distinction. Don Bradman is a genius who showed the world how cricket could be played and on his happy birthday let us thank and salute him.

Sir Leonard and Lady Dorothy in 1988
– 'both Bradman and Hutton were lucky in their wives'.

The Sir Leonard Hutton memorial gates at Pudsey St Lawrence cricket ground, opened by Lady Hutton in 1991. Hutton once said: 'Many of the most blissful hours of my life were spent with Pudsey St Lawrence'.

In Memoriam: Sheppard On Hutton

This address by the Right Reverend David Sheppard, Bishop of Liverpool, was given at the memorial service for Sir Leonard Hutton at York Minster on 19 November, 1990.

Born 1929. Cambridge University (Captain 1952) and Sussex (Captain 1953): 1947–62. 22 Test matches: 1950–62/63 (Captain in 2 Tests 1954). David Sheppard was a stylish right-handed batsman with great concentration and a memorable square cut. In 1952, when he was Cambridge University captain, he came top of the national averages. In 1954 he captained England twice against Pakistan because Hutton was ill and there was speculation that he would take the side to Australia in 1954/55. He was ordained in 1955 and became the first priest to play in Test cricket when he scored his first 100 against Australia at Old Trafford in 1956. He became the Bishop of Liverpool in 1975.

This is a great Yorkshire occasion, a great cricket occasion, and at its heart a very personal occasion. We give thanks for the life of Sir Len Hutton, honoured as only the second professional English cricketer to be knighted after Sir Jack Hobbs. For many of us he was the greatest batsman of his generation. He captained England when we won the Ashes back from Australia in 1953 after that gap of 20 years; he led the England team back from 2–0 down in the West Indies to draw the series in 1953–54, and he led the 1954–55 team to win the Ashes again in Australia. That's the public person. We remember today a man who was sometimes a very private person. We express our deep sympathy to Lady Dorothy at her loss after their long and close partnership. Len was a loyal and loving husband, and others of you in the family will have your memories of father and grandfather.

Many who never met Len Hutton feel they had a personal involvement with him; that's one of the bewitching properties of cricket. We switched on the radio at six o'clock in the morning, full of apprehension that England would be struggling; we went to a Test match with our hopes pinned anxiously on a vulnerable figure who might today heroically keep Lindwall and Miller at bay, and we held our breath for him. Len never seemed a robust player, but there was a toughness and concentration which won through on every kind of wicket, like the determination which saw him through those two bone-grafting operations on his wrist in 1941, and his timing and technique meant that he would often stand perfectly still after a cover drive, knowing that no fielder was going to stop it.

The Yorkshire team of the 1930s provided a very tough school for a sensitive young man, who didn't easily join in or appreciate the banter. He told me Hedley Verity's quiet friendship meant much to him then. When he came to playing for England, he told me he liked batting with Wally Hammond. 'He never said anything to me,' he said, 'and I never said anything to him.'

I had sat on the grass at the Oval in 1938 and watched him proceed from 160 to 300 on the second day of that famous innings, and it was the fulfilment of unbelievable dreams when I went in first for England with him. After about an hour of silence at the wicket he made overtures for a conversation in the middle of the pitch. 'Are you all right?' he asked, eyes open wide, eyebrows lifted. That was all the conversation. The England team of 1954–55 gave him a silver salver with their signatures engraved all round the edge, and in the middle they had put the words: 'Are you all right?'

Colin Cowdrey has described the way Len warmed to him as he realised that Colin really meant business in wanting to learn the game. The master didn't have a lot of time for players who didn't work at their game or who kept on making the same mistakes, but when eventually he realised that you were genuinely keen to learn, the door to Len Hutton's wisdom was open and, Colin went on, 'he would take on a new personality and expand with enormous confidence, and with the trick of the actor arresting his audience he would peddle his expertise, not so much as a schoolmaster, more a university don. As I know, once he decided to take you under his wing, he was a firm encourager. In my first match in Australia, against Western Australia on a very fast pitch at Perth, I was out for 5 after battling it out for 50 minutes. Len greeted me with: "Well played." I looked rather sharply at him. "I mean it," he said, "you've made it easy for the others." A whimsical humour developed; he loved to expound improbable theories. I stayed with them in their Pudsey home; over breakfast he expounded the belief that no one with a pink and white complexion has ever been any good in big sport. Dorothy objected: "But I've got a pink and white complexion." "I know," he said, "but you're not meant to be a Test cricketer. You're a very good cook. We're not all meant to be Test cricketers."'

After retiring from first-class cricket, there was golf, greatly enjoyed until seven years ago. There was travelling the world for the Fenner organisation, Len insisting in later years that Dorothy should go with him. He had a strong sense of duty, and despite frail health he took on the demanding office of President of Yorkshire County Cricket Club. The grandchildren gave him great pleasure, and it's an engaging thought of Len bowling at the boys in the garden.

Dorothy has shared with me this week a letter from the Archbishop of Canterbury, Robert Runcie. It echoes the experience of a number of those who met Len in his mellow years, and Archbishop Robert had many conversations with him. He wrote this: 'When you have idolised anyone in youth, it's sometimes a disappointment to meet them in later life. Of nobody was this less true than Len. Someone so modest, so free from cant or pretentiousness, was an inspiration. He seemed to me to have the highest standards for character as he did for the game of which he was such a master. Of course he was the first to admit that he was a sinner like the rest of us, but aiming for the best and knowing his faults and being such a natural delight as a human being. I will never forget my last conversation with Len at the India Test at Lord's, just five days before his death. It was as if we had always known each other, and we talked of Coombe Hill and the golf course I know so well. He was so brave in those last few days, and his eyes shone brightly at good cricket and good companionship.'

I introduced Len to Professor Norman Sykes in Cambridge. Norman Sykes was a passionate follower of Yorkshire cricket. He was the Dixie Professor of Ecclesiastical History and there was one window in his college, Emmanuel College chapel, which was left plain; Norman Sykes always believed Len Hutton should be put into that window in the chapel.

Len was always proud that he was born and brought up as a Moravian in Fulneck. Most people know nothing about the Moravian church; Norman Sykes was probably the greatest authority on the Moravians in the country, so he would ask Len to dinner every time he came to Cambridge, and they would sit and admire each other. That childhood upbringing and faith remained important to Len Hutton. It tended to mean more to him as he grew older. He went to great lengths to buy a picture of the Moravian chapel in Fulneck which hangs on the drawing-room wall, and it's appropriate that the faith of his childhood should have a mention in his memorial service as we come with that mixture of thankfulness and sadness.

The Moravian brethren, or the Moravian church, came into being under the protection of Count Zinzendorf in Moravia nearly 300 years ago. The church continues in Britain, Europe, North America and South America. Perhaps the greatest influence which the Moravians had on Britain was through the changed life of John Wesley. Going as a missionary to America, he travelled with a group of Moravians. He was touched by the depth of their faith, ready to do the most menial tasks, never complaining, obviously trusting deeply in God when the ship was in great danger in a storm. In a few years' time, John Wesley returned to England aged 34 a very unsuccessful missionary. In London he met another Moravian missionary en route for America. A series of conversations followed, until the day in a meeting house in Aldersgate Street in London, when John Wesley said his heart was strangely warmed.

It is said that had he died in his 35th year, he would have been an unremembered man, capable, hard-working, but pedantic, legalistic, irascible, unloved and well-nigh unlovable. His heart was strangely warmed when the penny dropped and he grasped that his standing with God depended not on his earnest sincerity and hard work, but on the undeserved love of God. From then on he was confident that nothing could separate him from the love of God in Christ, and John Wesley became the man through whom God touched the lives of more people in Britain than perhaps any other preacher has ever done. That heart of the Moravian church's faith, in which Len Hutton grew up, stops our approach to death from being full only of fear or grief. It is in that confidence that we can speak of death as a gateway, and that we can today remember the life of our friend, Len Hutton, with great thankfulness.

Hutton's Career Record

Compiled by
Geoffrey Copinger

*Signifies not out

Batting (All first-class Matches)

	Season	Inns	Not out	Runs	100s	50s	Highest inns	Average	Catches
	1934	28	2	863	1	5	196	33·19	8
	1935	23	3	577	1	1	131	28·85	6
Yorkshire in Jamaica	1936	5	2	123	0	1	59	41·00	0
	1936	49	6	1282	1	8	163	29·81	26
	1937	58	7	2888	10	12	271*	56·62	26
	1938	37	6	1874	6	5	364	60·45	12
MCC in South Africa	1938–39	19	1	1168	5	4	202	64·88	7
	1939	52	6	2883	12	8	280*	62·67	38
	1945	16	0	782	2	4	188	48·87	3
	1946	38	6	1552	4	7	183*	48·50	13
MCC in Australia	1946–47	21	3	1267	3	8	151*	70·38	5
	1947	44	4	2585	11	7	270*	64·62	23
MCC in West Indies	1947–48	10	1	578	2	3	138	64·22	6
	1948	48	7	2654	10	13	176*	64·73	23
MCC in South Africa	1948–49	21	1	1477	5	7	174	73·85	8
	1949	56	6	3429	12	17	269*	68·58	40
	1950	40	3	2128	6	11	202*	55·99	24
MCC in Australia and NZ	1950–51	25	4	1382	5	7	156*	65·80	18
	1951	47	8	2145	7	9	194*	55·00	33
	1952	45	3	2567	11	12	189	61·11	31
	1953	44	5	2458	8	10	241	63·02	15
MCC in West Indies	1953–54	12	2	780	2	4	205	78·00	3
	1954	28	2	912	2	4	163	35·07	7
MCC in Australia and NZ	1954–55	25	2	1059	2	6	145*	46·05	7
	1955	19	1	537	1	4	194	29·83	5
	TOTALS	810	91	39950	129	177	364	55·56	387

Aggregates

	Inns	Not out	Runs	100s	50s	Highest inns	Average
In England	672	75	32116	105	137	364	53·79
In Australia	63	9	3425	10	18	156*	63·42
In West Indies	27	5	1481	4	8	205	67·31
In South Africa	40	2	2645	10	11	202	69·60
In New Zealand	8	0	283	0	3	69	35·37
TOTALS	810	91	39950	129	177	364	55·56

For MCC Touring Teams (Excluding Tests)

	Inns	Not out	Runs	100s	50s	Highest inns	Average
In Australia	35	4	2255	8	11	151*	72·74
In South Africa	25	2	1803	8	7	202	78·39
In West Indies	10	2	510	2	2	138	63·75
In New Zealand	2	0	102	0	1	69	51·00
TOTALS	72	8	4670	18	21	202	72·96

Test Matches

Season		Inns	Not out	Runs	100s	50s	Highest inns	Average
1937	(v. New Zealand)	5	0	127	1	0	100	25·40
1938	(v. Australia)	4	0	473	2	0	364	118·25
1938–39	(v. S. Africa)	6	0	265	0	2	92	44·16
1939	(v. West Indies)	6	1	480	2	1	196	96·00
1946	(v. India)	5	1	123	0	1	67	30·75
1946–47	(v. Australia)	9	1	417	1	2	122*	52·12
1947	(v. S. Africa)	10	2	344	1	1	100	43·00
1947–48	(v. West Indies)	4	0	171	0	2	60	42·75
1948	(v. Australia)	8	0	342	0	4	81	42·75
1948–49	(v. S. Africa)	9	0	577	2	2	158	64·11
1949	(v. New Zealand)	6	0	469	2	2	206	78·16
1950	(v. West Indies)	6	1	333	1	0	202*	66·60
1950–51	(v. Australia)	10	4	533	1	4	156*	88·83
1950–51	(v. New Zealand)	3	0	114	0	1	57	38·00
1951	(v. S. Africa)	9	2	378	1	2	100	54·00
1952	(v. India)	6	1	399	2	1	150	79·80
1953	(v. Australia)	9	1	443	1	3	145	55·37
1953–54	(v. West Indies)	8	1	677	2	3	205	96·71
1954	(v. Pakistan)	3	0	19	0	0	14	6·33
1954–55	(v. Australia)	9	0	220	0	1	80	24·44
1954–55	(v. New Zealand)	3	0	67	0	1	53	22·33
TOTALS		138	15	6971	19	33	364	56·67

Test Match Aggregates

	Tests	Inns	Not out	Runs	100s	50s	Highest inns	Average
Australia	27	49	6	2428	5	14	364	56·46
South Africa	19	34	4	1564	4	7	158	52·13
New Zealand	11	17	0	777	3	4	206	51·51
West Indies	13	24	3	1661	5	6	205	79·09
India	7	11	2	522	2	2	150	58·00
Pakistan	2	3	0	19	0	0	14	6·33
TOTALS	79	138	15	6971	19	33	364	56·67

Test Match Hundreds (19)

v. Australia (5)	364	at the Oval, 1938
	156*	at Adelaide, 1950–51
	145	at Lord's, 1953
	122*	at Sydney, 1946–47
	100	at Nottingham, 1938
v. South Africa (4)	158	at Johannesburg, 1948–49 (Second Test)
	123	at Johannesburg, 1948–49 (Fourth Test)
	100	at Leeds, 1947
	100	at Leeds, 1951
v. West Indies (5)	205	at Kingston, 1953–54
	202*	at the Oval, 1950
	196	at Lord's, 1939
	169	at Georgetown, 1953–54
	165*	at the Oval, 1939
v. New Zealand (3)	206	at the Oval, 1949
	101	at Leeds, 1949
	100	at Manchester, 1937
v. India (2)	150	at Lord's, 1952
	104	at Manchester, 1952

County Championship Matches

	Inns	Not out	Runs	100s	50s	Highest inns	Average
1934	25	1	801	1	4	196	33·37
1935	19	3	411	1	0	131	25·68
1936	43	6	1108	1	6	163	29·94
1937	36	5	1728	5	7	271	55·74
1938	17	3	631	1	3	107	45·07
1939	40	4	2167	9	6	280*	60·19
1946	26	4	1112	3	5	171	50·54
1947	23	1	1551	6	4	270*	70·50
1948	22	5	1565	8	4	176*	92·05
1949	38	5	2098	6	11	269*	63·57
1950	21	2	1125	4	4	156	59·21
1951	26	5	1222	5	4	194*	58·19
1952	26	1	1482	7	6	189	59·28
1953	21	1	1149	4	4	178	57·45
1954	19	2	676	1	4	149*	39·76
1955	18	0	535	1	4	194	29·72
TOTALS	420	48	19361	63	76	280*	52·04

Mode of Dismissal

Bowled	207
Caught	372
LBW	94
Run out	21
Stumped	19
Hit wicket	5
Obstructing the field	1
TOTALS	719

Bowling

	Overs	Maidens	Runs	Wickets	Average
1934	103	17	379	11	34·45
1935	22.1	5	79	2	39·50
1935–36	7	0	45	1	45·00
1936	173.3	44	479	21	22·81
1937	315	56	1025	28	36·60
1938	227.1	51	576	20	28·80
1938–39	24	1	108	2	54·00
1939	220.7	38	822	44	18·68
1945	35	0	167	5	33·40
1946	58	11	173	9	19·22
1946–47	18	1	116	2	58·00
1947	109	18	344	12	28·83
1947–48	5	1	20	0	—
1948	26	5	102	0	—
1948–49	1	0	7	0	—
1949	102	29	286	7	40·86
1950	28	5	90	2	45·00
1950–51	3.6	0	11	1	11·00
1951	11	1	44	4	11·00
1952	10	1	43	1	43·00
1953	31	8	129	0	—
1953–54	6	0	43	0	—
1954–55	00.6	0	2	1	2·00
TOTALS	1293.5	292	5090	173	29·42

and 243.3 eight-ball overs

These figures exclude one first-class game in 1957 in the Old Trafford Centenary match (MCC *v.* Lancashire, scoring 76 and 25), and two in 1960 – 0 for Colonel L. C. Steven's XI *v.* Cambridge University at Eastbourne; and 89 for MCC *v.* Ireland at Dublin.

Perchance to dream: Hutton takes a nap on the boat to Australia for the 1950/51 tour, where he was 'undisputed as the greatest batsman in the world'.